SOUNDS AND
SWEET AIRS

SOUNDS AND SWEET AIRS

*The Forgotten Women
of Classical Music*

ANNA BEER

ONEWORLD

A Oneworld Book

First published in North America, Great Britain and
Australia by Oneworld Publications, 2016

ISBN 978-1-78074-856-6
eISBN 978-1-78074-857-3

Cover illustration *Élisabeth Jacquet de La Guerre* (c. 1704) by François de Troy.
Our sincere thanks to the owner of the portrait for allowing its reproduction.

Typeset by Hewer Text UK Ltd, Edinburgh
Printed and bound by Clays Ltd, St Ives plc

Oneworld Publications
10 Bloomsbury Street
London WC1B 3SR
England

Stay up to date with the latest books,
special offers, and exclusive content from
Oneworld with our monthly newsletter

Sign up on our website
www.oneworld-publications.com

For Roger

A chantar m'er de so qu'ien non volria
I must sing about it, whether I want to or not.

La Comtessa del Dia, c. 1175

CONTENTS

LIST OF ILLUSTRATIONS

Francesca Caccini
Title page of *Il Primo Libro delle Musiche 1618* (Wikimedia Commons)

Barbara Strozzi
Portrait by Bernardo Strozzi, c. 1630–40 (Gemaeldegalerie Alte Meister, Dresden, Germany © Staatliche Kunstsammlungen Dresden; Bridgeman Images)

Élisabeth Jacquet de la Guerre
Portrait by François de Troy (private collection)

Marianna Martines
Portrait by Anton von Maron (DEA/A. DAGLI ORI; Getty Images)

Fanny Hensel
Portrait by Wilhelm Hensel (© Pictorial Press Ltd; Alamy)

Clara Schumann
Portrait – *Clara Wieck im ihrem 21. Lebensjahr* – by Johann H. Schramm, 1840 (Robert-Schumann-Haus Zwickau)

Lili Boulanger
Photograph, 1913 (Bibliothèque Nationale de France)

Elizabeth Maconchy
Photograph, 1941 (Nicola LeFanu)

Venice, 1568

Maddalena Casulana, the first woman to publish her own music, challenges the 'foolish error of men' who believe that they are the sole masters of the 'high intellectual gifts' necessary for composition. She suggests that those gifts might 'be equally common' among women.

The Convent of San Vito, Ferrara, 1594

A man hearing the nuns sing their sublime music is overwhelmed. He writes that the nuns are 'not human, bodily creatures, but were truly angelic spirits'. He listens in a culture in which, whether heard as angels, sirens, saints or sorceresses, whether deemed *super*natural or *un*natural, women's exceptional ability goes against nature.

Berlin, 1850

Reviewers respond to the publication of works by Fanny Hensel, the elder sister of the celebrated composer Felix Mendelssohn. They are sure that, because she is a woman, the music lacks 'a commanding individual idea', an 'inner aspect', the 'powerful feeling drawn from deep conviction'. They are sure that music will always betray the sex of its composer.

NOTES FROM THE SILENCE

This book is a celebration of the achievements of a handful of women over four centuries of Western European history. Neither angels nor sorceresses, merely formidably talented human beings, these female composers demonstrate, again and again, their 'high intellectual gifts'; they express, again and again, 'powerful feeling drawn from deep conviction'. They created their music in societies that made certain places off-limits for a woman, from the opera house to the university, from the conductor's podium to the music publisher – societies where certain jobs, whether in cathedral, court or conservatoire, were ones for which they could not even apply.

But it is the cultures of belief within which they lived that made their task all the harder. From seventeenth-century Florence to twentieth-century London, women creating music triggered some profound and enduring fears. The Book of Samuel states that 'listening to a woman's voice is sexual enticement', and that was enough to silence women, in church and synagogue, if not beyond. It is a fairly straightforward step from the Book of Samuel to the recommendation made by an early Christian Father that nuns should sing their prayers, but make no sound, 'so that their lips move, but the ears of others do not hear'. These prohibitions upon woman's expression may have taken less draconian forms as the years passed, but the fear underlying them, of the sexualized threat of the creative woman, remained. This is why each composer in this book composed her music in the shadow of the courtesan, her sexual life scrutinized, her virtue questioned, simply because of her trade.

Every female composer knew that her work would always be understood in terms of her sex, or, rather, what her society believed her sex was capable of achieving. When, in 1919, a violin sonata by British-born American Rebecca Clarke won an important prize, questions were asked. Had the work actually been submitted by the male composers Ernest Bloch or Maurice Ravel under a pseudonym? How could a woman have created such a formally rigorous yet powerful work? Rebecca Clarke could and did do just that in 1919, but her career was not to be sustained. Clarke was not the first, nor would she be the last, woman to give up composing, worn down by her society's ability to silence her, succumbing to her own self-doubts. Because women, just as much as men, believed the stories we tell ourselves about genius, so often an exclusive men-only club. Clara Wieck, soon to be married to (the tortured genius) Robert Schumann, wrote: 'I once thought that I possessed creative talent, but I have given up this idea; a woman must not desire to compose – not one has been able to do it, and why should I expect to?' The world-renowned teacher of composition, Nadia Boulanger, knew what she had to sacrifice in order to pursue her successful career in music: 'Artists think only of their art, and they consider it is totally incompatible with the joys of family life. From the day a woman wants to play her one true role – that of mother and wife – it is impossible for her to be an artist as well.'

How to exorcize the ghost of Clara's despair? How to challenge Nadia's definition of the 'impossible'? The pioneering efforts of feminist musicologists offer one response to Clara Schumann. These scholars were, and remain, determined to show that women were 'able to do it' (the *International Encyclopedia of Women*

Composers alone has more than six thousand entries) and it is both revelatory and humbling to read of the experiences of some of the early feminist researchers. Back in 1979, Professor Marcia Citron, seeking to find out more about Fanny Hensel's music, first started work in the Mendelssohn Archiv at the Stattsbibliothek Preussischer Kulturbesitz (West Berlin). There was no library catalogue of Hensel holdings. Instead, the director Rudolf Elvers informed scholars as to what they were, or were not, allowed to see. Professor Citron battled on, often desperately copying out scores by hand in the justified fear that she would not be allowed to see the same manuscript again on her next visit. She was therefore surprised, in 1986, when the director, Rudolf Elvers, said that there had been no 'qualified musicologists' interested in the Hensel manuscripts. He was, in his own words, 'waiting for the right man to come along', and, in the meantime, expressed his irritation with 'all these piano-playing girls who are just in love with Fanny'. Elvers's verdict on Hensel? 'She was nothing. She was just a wife.'

Marcia Citron, and her fellow recuperative scholars, believed that their work would not only reveal hidden music, but inspire women of today to claim their place as equals in the world of composition, and encourage orchestras to put female composers on their programmes. They, along with many other commentators, are bemused that neither of these things has quite happened. It 'is difficult to understand the hesitancy to explore and promote music composed by women that persists today', write the editors of a major study of women composers, whilst the music writer Fiona Maddocks admits that 'it seems baffling, if not shocking, that even now we still use the two words *woman* and *composer* together as a collective noun, whereas it has long been out of date to refer to Barbara Hepworth or Tracey Emin as *women artists*'.

Perhaps the ghost of Clara's despair will not be laid to rest by yet another recuperative scholarly exercise. Perhaps it is not enough simply to, in the words of one scholar, 'rewrite music history on the principle of *add women and stir*', although those women do need to be added to the mix. As the composer Rhian Samuel, born in 1944, remarks: 'I have always been aware of women composers . . . Not that they were considered normal; they were considered absolute freaks, but they did exist.' It is not only that we need to think again about what constitutes 'greatness'. Above all, we need to find new ways of telling stories about creative, powerful women.

Take, for example, Kassia, probably the earliest female composer for whom there is surviving music. Her hymn to Mary Magdalene, written in the mid-800s, is still sung in Greek Orthodox churches in the early hours of Holy Wednesday. Kassia's music, written on the seventh hill of Constantinople, the Xerolophos, in a now vanished Byzantine world, has therefore lived on, astonishingly, for twelve centuries. But, if Kassia is remembered at all, she is not remembered for breaking new ground, nor for her concise, syllabic settings of text, or her groundbreaking use of musical motifs 'to symbolize and mirror the words' (word painting *avant la lettre*). No: the story goes that her beauty and wisdom led to her being offered, amongst others, as a wife to the Byzantine Emperor Theophilus. The wise and cautious emperor questioned his prospective brides before he saw them, in order not to be blinded by their appearance. Kassia's witty responses, however, apparently humbled, perhaps humiliated, the mighty Theophilus, who therefore rejected her. The convent swiftly followed, from where Kassia was said to have written her penitential hymn on Mary Magdalene because *she* felt shamed by her desire for the emperor.

These kinds of stories provide the pegs upon which to hang the woman's life, whether the nun taken from the world, the sacrificial wife or the courtesan composer. Love, marriage, motherhood and (proper and improper) sex: these can all be lovely things, but they are not the only things to define the lives of the women in this book, and they certainly do not define their compositions. A quick glance at pre-Romantic ideas about marriage and mother-hood acts as a reminder that love had very little to do with the former, whilst, for centuries, carrying and bearing a child was simply something one tried to survive, rather than the event that defined one as a woman. Love (and loved children) exist along-side rape and prostitution, madness, despair, illness and loneli-ness in death.

Then again, the romanticization and sexualization of women's lives at least offers an alternative to catalogues of injustice and despair. Take the composer Johanna Kinkel. Born in Bonn in July 1810, she was mentored by Felix Mendelssohn, taught by some of the great figures in German music, praised by Robert Schumann for her songs, and walked out of an abusive first marriage. Kinkel responded to the life imprisonment of her politically radical second husband by fleeing with him and their four children to England, where she earned her living teaching music and writing, holding the family together both financially and emotionally while her husband continued on his revolutionary path, now in America. Once in England, she did not compose again. Before she died, Kinkel wrote a novel, with a struggling, desperate composer for a hero: the fact that the hero is a man does little to conceal the work's status as misery memoir. A visiting friend noted that she 'accepted her lot, but not without serious dejection'. Her health was deterio-rating, 'conditions of nervousness' began to appear, the news from America 'did not suffice to cheer the darkened soul of the lonely woman'. Kinkel's life ended on the pavement below her home in St John's Wood, north-west London. She fell, or threw herself, from an upper window. The composer's posthumous life is just as dispir-iting. An enemy, one Karl Marx (also exiled in London), viewed her as an 'old harridan' and was disgusted that her husband, his political opponent, received sympathy merely because his wife had 'broken her neck'. Mr Kinkel, for his part, never realized his plan to publish his wife's compositions.

It would have been all too easy to find a bookful of Kinkels, to represent every female composer's life as a futile struggle against impossible odds. Instead, I want to celebrate the achievements of the eight composers here – Francesca Caccini, Barbara Strozzi, Élisabeth Jacquet de la Guerre, Marianna Martines, Fanny Hensel, Clara Schumann, Lili Boulanger and Elizabeth 'Betty' Maconchy – to show how they overcame the obstacles in their path, to glory in the songs and sonatas that they did write, rather than grieve for the operas and symphonies that they could not. In doing so, I am working within what has been described as a narrative of 'overcoming', exemplified in music history by Beethoven, the composer who decided to grab fate by the throat and – instead of killing himself over the loss of his hearing – continued to compose. In recent years, scholars of disability have shown that these kinds of narratives, in which a person such as Beethoven overcomes his impairment, work primarily to reassure the able-bodied in their anxieties about experiencing similar fates, whilst at the same time diminishing the lived experience of the person who has the disability. Here, if each woman in this book is seen to overcome the obstacles in her path and still make her music, not only are those obstacles and struggles minimized but we might well be comforted and reassured to the point of complacency.

An image of Kinkel's broken body on a pavement in St John's Wood is one way to challenge complacency, but a less stark, but perhaps more profound, way of understanding what it was, what it is, to be a woman and composer is to explore the often complex experiences of individuals. Looking across the Atlantic, for example, at first sight the beliefs that informed and controlled the lives of women in Europe transferred effortlessly into the New World, proving powerful enough to ensure that, a generation after Kinkel, the virtuoso composer Amy Beach, able to hold a tune at the age of one and to pick out melodies on the piano by the age of two, would receive only the scantiest of educations in composition; would be married at eighteen and then have her public performances limited to one recital a year, for charity of course. A closer look at Beach's career suggests, however, a constant give and take between the social forces and cultural beliefs that were designed to stop a woman in her tracks and those that enabled her to move forward as a composer. Sometimes, paradoxically, a single belief – about 'women's intuition', for example – could work both ways, to stifle and to inspire. On the one hand, the teenage Amy was denied lessons in composition because her husband believed that instruction would spoil his wife's 'natural' ability: 'unspoken, but obvious, is Dr Beach's assumption that his wife's musical competency is intuitive; a gift, not a learned skill; received, not achieved', as the scholar A.F. Block explains. Beach, as a woman, is ill-equipped by biology or temperament to benefit from intellectually rigorous training, a new quasi-scientific take on the old idea of talented women as gifted angels, not professional human beings. On the other hand, precisely because her society valued her 'instinctual' ability, Beach was permitted, indeed encouraged, by her family and social circle to compose music, to publish that music and to have her music performed (by others). Her special gift needed to be used, not wasted, and Beach promptly broke new ground for women by writing large-scale orchestral works, such as her *Gaelic Symphony* premiered in 1896. A member of the extremely privileged artistic and social New England set in which Beach moved was fulsome in his praise:

> I always feel a thrill of pride myself whenever I hear a fine new work by any one of us, and as such you will have to be counted in, whether you will or not – one of the boys.

7

Her prize may have been to be 'one of the boys'; she may only have had the opportunity to compose because she was 'one of us'; she may not have been permitted to engage in a professional career as a pianist; and her hard work and professionalism might have been overlooked – but Beach, like all the women in this book, had found her own unique way to be a woman and composer. She was not yet thirty.

As the following chapters will show, again and again, individual women evaded, confronted and ignored the ideologies and practices that sought to exclude them from the world of composition. Again and again, a woman made her choice, took her chances, whether in the private, female sphere, or the public, male world. Many did this despite subscribing to their society's beliefs as to what they were capable of as a woman, how they should live as a woman, and, crucially, what they could (and could not) compose as a woman. Perhaps the overcoming of their own mind-forged manacles is where their true courage lies.

Often they worked in communities where to be a woman and a composer was a part of ordinary life – the Medici court in Italy, the city of Venice, a salon in Berlin, the court of the Sun King in France – for in these communities, virtuoso female musicians were expected to write music to display their own virtuosity, whether as a servant of the Church (and thus to the ultimate glory of God) or a servant to a prince (and thus to the ultimate glory of the patron) or a precocious daughter (and thus to the ultimate glory of the family). They wrote their music in cultures where performance and composition were inextricably linked, virtuoso performers and composers who cut their teeth on, and made their name by, writing works that only they would, sometimes only they *could*, perform. Others worked quietly but effectively to create environments in which they, and their successors, would find it just that bit easier to be both composer and woman.

Above all, these composers were pragmatic. They did not seek out, or seek to create, a female tradition, nor did they wait for a female teacher or mentor. They invariably worked with, and within, a male-dominated musical culture. They countered, over and over again, the attacks on their reputations. They wrote what they could, when they could. If they were permitted to only write sacred music, then sacred music it was. If only lieder, then lieder by the dozen. If it is, and remains, against the odds to be a woman composer, then the ways in which individual women have beaten those odds bears telling.

Working in landscapes of belief that would silence the vast majority of women, these eight composers each found a way to express their exceptional talent, often within an exceptional community. Brought together, their stories provide a complex and inspirational picture of artistic endeavour and achievement across the centuries, which deserves to be, but is not currently, part of our cultural heritage. We are the poorer for it.

'She worked such stunning effects in the minds of her listeners that she changed them from what they had been' Cristofano Bronzini

Chapter One

CACCINI

It is carnival time in Florence, and the Medici court is celebrating a great military victory against the Ottoman Turk achieved by their honoured guest, Crown-Prince Wladislaw Sigismund Vasa of Poland. No matter that the Battle of Khotyn, four years earlier, had been in reality a shambolic, bloody stalemate in which Wladislaw had played little active part. A lavish, spectacular entertainment is needed, one that not only demonstrates the triumph of goodness over evil, but the immense wealth and power of the Medici family, rulers of the grand duchy of Tuscany. The story chosen will tell of a wicked sorceress, Alcina, who seduces a knight, Ruggiero, entraping him on her island in order to take her pleasure. Worse still, he, and a host of other previous victims, seem to enjoy the experience. Fortunately, however, a 'good' witch, Melissa, triumphs over Alcina, and liberates Ruggiero and his fellows. Part opera, part ballet, no expense is spared in the production, which will end with an extraordinary *balletto a cavallo* (dancing horses) that the audience watches from the balconies and terraces of the Villa Poggio Imperiale, a ruinously expensive symbol of Medici power, linked to the city of Florence below by a tree-lined avenue.

The date is 3 February 1625, and the entertainment is *La liberazione di Ruggiero dall'isola d'Alcina* (The Liberation of Roger from the Island of Alcina). The composer is thirty-six-year-old Francesca Caccini, working at the height of her career. Many forces and

11

factors have contributed towards this remarkable moment: Caccini was, for example, lucky to be the daughter of two exceptional musicians; she was fortunate to have been born in Florence, the creative centre of the Medici world. But these propitious circumstances of breeding and location are as nothing when set against the simple fact that Francesca Caccini is a woman. Every note on every score that Caccini writes offers a challenge to the dominant values of the world beyond Villa Poggio Imperiale. *La liberazione* is a hard-won triumph.

As a young girl, Francesca had been set on her path to this remarkable February day in the hills above Florence by Giulio, her ambitious, talented father. Her mother, Lucia di Filippo Gagnolandi, died when Francesca was only five, leaving her daughter with little except the inheritance of a beautiful singing voice, and leaving her husband with three children under the age of six, and a son, Pompeo, aged fourteen, from an earlier liaison. Giulio's second marriage to an impoverished eighteen-year-old singer, Margherita di Agostino della Scala, known as '*Bargialli*', did nothing to shore up his finances, but did introduce another talented singer to the Caccini stable. Growing up as the daughter of Giulio Caccini would prove to be a mixed blessing. On the one hand, he was the second most highly paid composer and musician on the staff of the Medici household, and renowned as the author of by far the most influential singing manual of the seventeenth century, *Le nuove musiche*, published in 1601, and then translated and imitated throughout Europe.* On the other hand, Giulio was proud to the point of self-destructiveness (house arrest followed his refusal to acknowledge a social superior

---

* As late as 1694, John Playford's English translation of Caccini's work told his readers that they could approximate the sound of the *trillo* by shaking the finger upon the throat, and also that it could be done by imitating the 'breaking of a sound in the throat which men use when they lure their hawks'.

in the street); profligate financially and sexually (a love of gambling made it hard to support his, at a guess, ten children by three women); and sought to dominate his immediate family, sometimes, it seems, simply for the sake of it, as when he withheld the dowry of Francesca's younger sister, Settimia. Pompeo, Giulio's eldest son, even apparently allowed himself to be charged with the rape of his intended wife, Ginevra, so that the courts would require him to marry the young woman, since it was the only way to circumvent his father's opposition to the union. As for Settimia, Giulio eventually paid the dowry in 1611 when her new husband's family abducted her and held her for ransom in the city of Lucca. This particular crisis precipitated the final break-up of the Caccini family as a performing group, but until that point, and for many years, Giulio's women had been used to showcase his exceptional talents as a composer and a teacher. Living or dead, they served to display his ability, as he explained to his readers: 'How excellently the tremolo and the trill were learned by my late wife [Lucia] ... may be adjudged by those who heard her sing during her life, as also I leave to the judgment of those who can now hear in the present wife [Margherita] how exquisitely they are done by her.'

It was Francesca's exceptional musical talent, however, that offered Giulio his greatest opportunity. For years, his ego and drive had ensured his success as a composer, performer and teacher in the competitive and changing musical world of the early seventeenth century. He knew only too well that singers required higher and higher levels of ability, since he himself was creating the new music that was making new demands on performers. As one anxious father noted, 'there are so many musical compositions and the level of diffi-culty has reached the most difficult possible', thus his daughter needed to be able to handle 'with ease any song, no matter how weird or hard'. Now there was Francesca. Her voice, they said, spun 'a finely focused thread of sound'. Not only that, but she had the musical intelligence to use that voice creatively, adding 'dissonances' that seemed to 'offend' but, paradoxically, like a lover mixing disdain with kindness, opened the way to a 'more delightful path to harmonic sweetness'.

Giulio's response to Francesca's raw talent was to educate his daughter as if she did not belong to the artisan class into which he and she had been born. She studied Latin, rhetoric, poetics, geometry, astrology, philosophy, contemporary languages, 'humanistic studies' and even a little Greek. Crucially, she also learned composition, primarily to enhance her performances, since it was expected that singers should be able to improvise and, on occasion, perform their own song settings. Francesca's progress was rapid. Just turned thirteen, on 9 October 1600 she was ready to appear in one of her father's works, *Il rapimento di Cefalo* (The Abduction of Cephalus), alongside three, maybe four, other performing members of her family. It was the young Francesca's first introduction to court spectacle: her stage, the Uffizi Palace in Florence; the occasion, the celebrations attending the proxy wedding of Henry IV of France and Marie de' Medici; the audience, three thousand gentlemen and eight hundred ladies; the work, an opera lasting five hours; the cost, sixty thousand scudi, around three hundred years of salary for Francesca's father.

Il rapimento provided a further lesson for the young Francesca, one in the politics of the music industry. Her father's opera had been intended to be the primary spectacle of the Florentine 1600 winter season, but it was overshadowed by a work that had been performed just three days earlier at the Medici's Pitti Palace: Jacobo Peri's *Euridice*. Peri's work has entered the music history books as the earliest opera for which complete music has survived, but, on the day, Peri quite simply judged his audience better than had Caccini. He not only gave the tragic story of Orpheus and Eurydice a happy ending, fitting for the happy occasion of Henry and Marie's nuptials, but used to great effect a striking new technique, continuous recitatives between the set choral numbers.

Four years on, and Francesca's breakthrough came when, in the summer of 1604, and the young singer approaching her fifteenth birthday, Henry IV and Marie de' Medici, the royal couple for whom Giulio had written *Il rapimento*, asked the rulers of Tuscany if they could 'borrow for several months' Giulio's ensemble 'and his daughters'. And so it came to pass that Giulio, his second wife, two daughters, a son, a boy singing pupil, two carriages, six mules and 450 scudi (more than twice his annual salary) left the grand duchy on the last day of September 1604. They journeyed through the northern regions of a politically fractured land, for it would be more than 250 years until the first precarious unification of the Italian peninsula under one king. They stopped at Modena to sing for the ruling Este family; at Milan (controlled by the Spanish Habsburgs) because Francesca contracted malaria; then at Turin, where they performed for the Duke and Duchess of Savoy, and Francesca and her sister Settimia received gifts of jewellery. After just over two months of travelling, the Caccini family and entourage arrived in Paris on 6 December 1604 where they stayed with the resident Florentine ambassador – the happy recipients of kitchen privileges, firewood and wine. Giulio presented the time as the high point of his career, with visits from aristocrats, money available to 'dress my women in French fashion' and regular opportunities to perform for the French sovereigns.

The reality was slightly different, at least at first. Giulio's arrogance made him few friends at the French court, and the monarchs themselves quarrelled over which of them would pay for the musicians. Everything changed, however, when Francesca sang. Henry IV declared her to be the best singer in France. It was reported that Queen Marie was so keen to secure Francesca for her own court that she was even willing to provide 'the other', Settimia, Francesca's sister, with a dowry 'enough that she could marry'. (The convention of the time was to provide both a job and a husband to women musicians.)

Yet no deal was done. Giulio gave the impression that the Grand-Duke of Tuscany himself had refused Caccini permission to accept the job for Francesca from Marie de' Medici, but in fact he had his own agenda, writing that he had 'invested' much 'labour' in Francesca, and he did not want to lose his controlling interest, even to a French queen. Marie, in turn, gradually lost interest and the moment passed. Nevertheless, although Giulio was unwilling to admit it, a subtle shift in the balance of power between father and daughter occurred in Paris in the early months of 1605. He was now as much the father of 'La Cecchina' (little Francesca) as she was the daughter of the great Giulio Caccini.*

Francesca's social and musical education continued apace. She knew about the precarious nature of a musician's life from her own parents' history. Her mother, Lucia, had been fired from her job as a musician only a year after Francesca's birth, collateral damage from the arrival of the new duke, Ferdinando I, who wanted to purge his predecessor's luxuries, or at least be seen to do so. Francesco I had been something of a text-book Medici villain, known to history as debauched and cruel if also scholarly and introverted, so it is unsurprising that Ferdinando wanted to make a break with the past. Did Francesca also know that, six months after Lucia's death, her father lost his job in highly suggestive circumstances? A courtesan, known as 'La Gambarella', was having singing lessons with Giulio. Rumours began. La Gambarella's lover, who was bank-rolling the lessons, had Giulio fired. The case did

---

* This chapter draws heavily throughout on Suzanne Cusick's groundbreaking academic study, *Francesca Caccini at the Medici Court: Music and the Circulation of Power* (University of Chicago Press, 2009), which notes for example this shift in the balance of power.

not help Giulio to recruit young female singers to his studio in Florence, and for a time his career stuttered horribly. One Duke Vincenzo, for example, wanted his protégée, Caterina Martinelli, to gain more experience, but not in Caccini's house, the duke writing that Giulio 'insisted on trying to make me understand that she would be safe, but I closed his mouth with a single word'. Martinelli went elsewhere.

The return journey to Tuscany provided a chance for Francesca to test out the effectiveness of her social, political and musical education. Whilst the rest of the Caccini family returned to Florence, Francesca, still only sixteen, remained for six months at the Este court in Modena, where she taught Giulia d'Este, only one year her junior, to 'sing in the French style'. There, Caccini applied all the lessons she had learned about how to survive (or not) the vagaries of high politics and sexual intrigue, and gained yet more insight into the workings of the elite families for whom she might one day work. The Este family did not want her to return to Florence.

Then came the carnival season of 1607. The Medici family, led by the Grand-Duchess, Christine de Lorraine, were at the time based in Pisa, and were planning a court spectacle. It needed to be impressive, but also cheap (perhaps costumes could be reused, suggests Christine) and to allow dancing amongst the cast and the guests. Christine turned to Michelangelo Buonarroti, great-nephew of *the* Michelangelo, who designed and scripted what would be the major entertainment for the carnival that year: a *barriera*, a dance representative of a battle. It was Michelangelo who chose Francesca Caccini, not yet twenty, to write the music. With the 'advice and consent of her father' Francesca seized the opportunity, not only producing her scores efficiently but creating 'very beautiful' music, in Michelangelo's words.

We will never be able to judge for ourselves if Michelangelo was right, because, as with so many of Caccini's works, the music has not survived. According to her contemporaries, however, *La stiava* (The Slavegirl) was more than beautiful; it was *'una musica stupenda'*. The performance began with a sinfonia 'for many instruments' during which the cast entered, and ended with a five-voice chorus to which both the cast and audience danced, as per the command of the work's patron, Christine de Lorraine. Francesca embraced the new Florentine *stile recitativo* (now simply known as recitative), which had been championed by her own father, who, in the preface to his *Le nuove musiche*, praised its ability to make the singer 'speak in music' by employing a certain *sprezzatura di canto*. *Sprezzatura*, the hallmark of Renaissance sophistication, involved, in the words of its champion, the writer Castiglione, 'a certain nonchalance, so as to conceal all art and make whatever one does or says appear to be without effort and almost without any thought about it'. To sing with *sprezzatura* one had to have the skill to make the performance effortless and natural. Father and daughter, both experts in precisely this skill, asserted the new style in direct competition with the music being composed by Venice's musical avant-garde, led by that city's star composer Monteverdi, but also in competition with their own colleagues in Florence, composers such as Jacobo Peri, who had set out his own groundbreaking take on this middle ground between speech and song in his notes to his opera *Euridice*.

Not only Caccini's compositional talent, but her sheer professionalism, was on display in *La stiava*. She was not expected to travel to Pisa for the performance but she did everything she could to ensure the work was a success from her base in Florence, insisting not only that the parts were 'sung many times' under her own supervision, but writing them 'in a way that they can be revised there', at Pisa, during the final rehearsals. The pressure she was working under is visible when a last-minute addition to the text arrived, for which she had to produce music. She dashed off the necessary bars and sent it to Pisa, her half-brother Pompeo as courier, that very same evening.

La stiava was Caccini's breakthrough work as a composer and it provided her with vital insights into the politics of music at the Medici court, insights that would shape her future career. Christine de Lorraine, the most powerful person in the court, had insisted not only that Michelangelo change his original plot, but then that he transform the motivations of its male heroes. Faced with a Persian slave woman who, predictably, given the genre, is revealed actually to be the King of Persia's daughter captured by pirates en route to her planned marriage with the King of India, the knights fight for the honour of taking the princess to her proper consort now they know she is 'twice a queen'. Christine de Lorraine intervened to insist that the knights should be inspired to fight not by the slave's beauty but by her 'nobility, or novelty, or other evident merits'. As musicologist Suzanne Cusick writes, although 'presented amid many of the usual Florentine trappings of spectacle – music, brilliantly coloured costumes, mock battles, and solo and ensemble song – one overarching theme of the plot was the transformation of a woman from an object of desire, competition and exchange to a sovereign subject, a transformation wrought by her own self-defining voice'.

Christine de Lorraine's intervention was only to be expected in a world in which artists of all kinds knew that they had to tailor their work to the tastes of the particular individual, the patron, who had commissioned the work and upon whom they were dependent for their livelihood. The patron's power, whether political or religious, permitted him or her to tell an artist, composer or writer exactly what to do in their next work, and then, of course, to change his or her mind half-way through rehearsals.

Christine de Lorraine had come to wield power only recently.

She had been married to Grand-Duke Ferdinando in 1589, and spent the best part of two decades in the provinces, physically safe but politically marginalized. Now, Ferdinando was a very ill man, and Grand-Duchess Christine was beginning to flex her muscles. Her husband's death the following year, and the succession of the couple's son, Cosimo II, did not halt Christine's emergence from the shadows, because Grand-Duke Cosimo's health was bad at the best of times and he was confined to his bed for months at a time. Although without an official title, Christine remained the de facto leader of the Medici state.

In 1607, therefore, Francesca Caccini was in the right place, at the right time: a woman composer for what was becoming a woman's court. It was Christine de Lorraine who counted, and it was Christine de Lorraine who, on 15 November 1607, appointed Francesca Caccini as *la musica* to the Grand-Duke of Tuscany. She would be paid ten scudi per month for which she would sing, both as a solo virtuosa, whether improvising or *sopra'l libro* (by the book), and in ensembles, whether in church, chamber or theatrical settings. She would also play the lute, theorbo, harpsichord, guitar, harp 'and every sort of stringed instrument'. Although only twenty, she was hired to evaluate the performances of others and, crucially, to compose new music and prepare its performance in a wide variety of settings, in Florence and beyond. Musicologists Carter and Goldthwaite have recently revealed, in remarkable detail, just how dynamic, economically and artistically, Medici music-making was. To take just one carnival season, 1610–11, the first to be celebrated during Grand-Duke Cosimo II's reign because the court had been in mourning the previous year for the death of Ferdinando I: this season was to be filled with jousts, *sbarre*, comedies, a *balletto* (by Ottavio Rinuccini), a pastoral (by Michelangelo Buonarroti the younger), and a revival of Rinuccini's *Dafne*. In the *balletto*, performed at court on the last Monday of carnival (14 February),

Jacobo Peri sang the part of Neptune 'in his customary manner and to great applause', and was also charged with setting to music, in his 'most noble' recitative style, the remainder of the text, except for a few verses that were to be set to music by the same women who sang them: Vittoria Archilei, Settimia Caccini and Francesca Caccini, who sang two, and therefore presumably composed two.

Francesca Caccini truly deserved her title of *la musica*. Day in, day out, she produced new work to order, and to timescales that would horrify most twenty-first-century composers. A suggested timetable for those wishing to put on an early modern opera these days starts at least nine months before the opening night. To secure a famous singer takes even longer, and that nine-month figure does not include, of course, the writing of the opera itself. What takes months and years now, took Caccini days or weeks. Her most important collaborator was the man who had recommended her in 1607, and remained a loyal friend and supporter, Michelangelo Buonarroti. (The history books may have paid little attention to this Michelangelo, precisely because of his giant of a great-uncle, but ironically, it was the great-nephew's efforts, begun precisely at this time, to create the Casa Buonarroti museum/gallery in Florence that did much, and still does much, to ensure *the* Michelangelo's iconic status.) Michelangelo would send his poetry to Caccini as soon as the ink was dry on the page; she would set his words to music and then complete the process by teaching the new material to her singers. Caccini urged Buonarroti to stay ahead of the game, suggesting that he 'should start thinking about some little comedy for eleven actors, for that's how many we are . . . even though we don't have a sure decision, I have enough in hand to want to give you a warning, so you won't be caught off guard'. In addition to court entertainments, Caccini was expected to write for the church year, becoming by the end of the decade the most important composer for Holy Week in Florence. Again and again, she created moments of spiritual wonder, bringing touches of spectacle to familiar ceremonies, as when on 19 April 1618 the congregation heard the voices of her unseen female singers as if by magic because Caccini had placed the performers in the hidden network of corridors that linked, and still link today, the palaces and churches of the Medici.

At other times, Caccini was commissioned to write music that would not merely celebrate Medici God-given power, but serve to protect it. When Christine de Lorraine feared both for her son's life and for the Tuscan state, the one threatened by severe illness, the other by catastrophically bad weather, she was inspired by a divine vision to hold a forty-hour vigil in the Medici church of San Lorenzo. Heaven, purgatory and hell would be depicted in the church; every parish and confraternity would be rewarded if they processed to San Lorenzo; Christine's daughter-in-law, Maria Magdalena, and her young family would walk through the streets among their people, one small prince carrying a cross, followed by his brothers, and then his mother, accompanied by women on foot. It was a remarkably choreographed display of piety and humility, and it was Francesca Caccini who was required to create the music. The composer chose to have voices appearing from four directions, with two groups of men inside the church, and two groups of women in the hidden passageways.

These major, public events were rarer than those in which Caccini performed her own music in private or semi-private settings at the heart of this female court, whether a reception held by Maria Magdalena in her bedroom for the *gentildonne* of Florence to celebrate a successful childbirth, or singing at the bedside of the sickly Cosimo II. The irony is that the private, exclusive nature of her work, such a mark of her success in her own time, is just one of the reasons that Caccini's achievements have not been acknowledged in traditional music histories.

Caccini was gaining in confidence with each passing year, and working well with the equally energetic and pragmatic Michelangelo. When it came to massive court spectacles, however, Caccini was often merely a small cog in a very big machine involving poets, composers, singers, instrumentalists, painters and architects, as well as seamstresses, carpenters and masons. Once the poet's idea had been accepted, the superintendent of buildings acted as designer and producer, providing machines for the staging with the help of the court architect, whilst the court wardrobe master provided costumes. The superintendent of music then distributed the work and chose the singers, and the major-domo had to make sure that those who wrote or copied the music and the spoken parts were paid, in order that the parts were circulated in good time for rehearsal and performance.

In this profoundly collaborative working culture, it was only too easy for a woman's name to slip off the list of credits, as it were. Only now are music scholars uncovering Caccini's involvement in significant compositions, such as Marco da Gagliano's five-act, continuously sung and hugely expensive opera, Sant'Orsola, for which the scenery alone cost six thousand scudi. Caccini, now earning twenty scudi a month and, as such, one of the best-paid court servants, contributed music (primarily composed for 'her' singers) for both the 1624 and 1625 performances. The opera presented something of a production challenge, since it told the story of 'the martyrdom of Saint Ursula with the eleven thousand virgins her companions'. Gagliano/Caccini ended up with a chorus of eleven virgins. When the work was revived the next year, one of the virgins was found to be pregnant, leading to a rapid recasting.

For all the collaboration, each and every production relied

fundamentally on one person and one person only: the work's patron. In Caccini's case, two women were all-important to the continuance of her career as a composer. One, of course, was Christine de Lorraine, through whom Caccini had gained the position of *la musica*. The other was Christine's daughter-in-law, Arch-Duchess Maria Magdalena of Austria. She became principal regent in February 1621, on the death of her husband, Cosimo II, holding power on behalf of her son, Ferdinando II, then only eleven years old.

The robust, energetic Maria Magdalena was, if anything, even more involved with the productions she commissioned than her mother-in-law. Her letters show a woman who knew her music, knew her singers and knew how to command. Nowhere is Caccini's dependent status more visible than in the casual way in which her ability to produce compositions on demand is taken for granted by her Medici employer: 'Moreover, we command that you immediately let Maria [a singer] know that we have chosen the part of Urania for her, being satisfied that *La Cecchina* [Caccini's nickname] will compose for her an appropriate aria for the words that have been changed.' This is not to diminish Caccini's achievement. The great figures of her time were equally dependent upon their patrons, for good and bad. One year, Galileo Galilei might be offering his discovery of the 'Medicean stars' (four moons of Jupiter) to Grand-Duke Cosimo II and receiving a generous financial package in return. Another year, the Medicis would do nothing to prevent Galileo's silencing by the Inquisition, nor his death in 1642 under a *damnatio memoriae*.

The Medici family owned Caccini and her music. A letter dated 18 December 1614, written by the composer to her collaborator Michelangelo, complains that 'the women', Christine and Maria Magdalena, have heard the rehearsals for a performance, but that the Grand-Duke had not yet turned up, even 'though we wait from day to day to be thus commanded; indeed, one evening we were gathered waiting to do so until three hours after dark'. On another occasion, when a nobleman, Virginio Orsini, made a request that Caccini be 'detailed to his household in Rome', the Medici family simply refused. As Suzanne Cusick explains, just as 'fathers exchanged daughters to create and sustain relationships between their families, so princely households exchanged performances and artistic workers'.

In this patriarchal world, Caccini had her victories. The principal court poet Andrea Salvadori, a good-looking womanizer, was renowned for 'accommodating the parts and the music to favour the one who was in his heart', or in other words, seducing young singers who would then get preferential treatment. Salvadori did not count on Caccini's response, as recounted by a contemporary writer, Cavalcante (trans. Suzanne Cusick):

> Francesca Caccini, a woman as fierce and restless as she was capable in singing and acting, could not abide this behaviour, and began to expose and talk about him, first in passing and behind his back, and then openly and to his face, revealing his intentions, and designs, and the origins of his favouritism.

Caccini's whistle-blowing led to Salvadori being 'disdained', at least for a time, by the Medici women, and more importantly his supply of singer-victims dried up. Salvadori, unsurprisingly, vented his anger in the gloriously titled poem *Donne musiche parlano dall'Inferno* (Women Musicians Speak from Hell), which was probably performed at court in early 1621. Caccini, equally unsurprisingly, was furious, and 'it took a lot of effort to quiet her'.

In the short term, the two were forced to make peace, but Caccini waited for her moment. Six years later, Salvadori wrote a piece for the celebration of a noble marriage, over which he took great trouble:

> It had already been set to music, the [stage] machines sketched and the parts assigned when Francesca took her best revenge, like a man who waits for the worst place and time. Finding herself one day with the Most Serene bride, she sang the part that was to have been hers, and praised the verses and the workmanship of it, adding 'Serenissima, everything will go well, and I like it. I have only one remaining doubt.' 'What is that?' prompted the princess.

Caccini had her opening. She went on to suggest, delicately, that the plot *could* be construed as horribly offensive. Admittedly, this was a stretch, revolving around the idea that the male hero could be seen to be emasculated by the storyline, but, stretch or no, the princess insisted that the entertainment be changed and Salvadori was commanded to produce another comedy within eight days. He in turn gained a petty revenge by creating the character of Discordia and casting Francesca in the role. But the narrator of this quarrel ends by writing: 'Exulting at this, she always said that the response was not equal to the blow.' Francesca Caccini knew she had won.

Midway between the two major Salvadori tussles, a different kind of crisis threatened Caccini's position. When an opera from the previous season was revived, one of Caccini's pupils, Maria Botti, was promoted to a larger part for the revival, and Caccini asked that one of her own siblings take Botti's original role. She was over-ruled on this, and then Botti started causing problems, proving incapable of learning her new part. Caccini was fired. Enraged, the composer claimed that Botti was singing badly on purpose, whilst Botti claimed to have been ill-treated by Caccini. One commentator anxiously (or gleefully, it is hard to tell) wrote that he was beginning 'to wonder if it will be possible for *la Cecchina* to survive, because I know these emotions, and those tongues, and . . . what they have said on other occasions'.

Caccini did survive. Time and again, she reveals herself to be a canny operator in this often vicious world, working to manage the unrealistic expectations and arbitrary demands of her patrons, not to mention the attacks from rival artists. She could be fiercely protective of her (often exhausted, often very young) singers, whilst always taking care to couch any resistance in terms of abject humility, or to soften her stance with humour. Above all, her professionalism shines through. Writing to Michelangelo, this time from Pisa, in February 1618, Caccini thanks her friend for sending over his poetry: 'now it remains for me to match it with my part, that is, in composing and singing it'. She hopes to find a time to sing it to 'their Highnesses' but can't give a firm promise, 'given the surprises that can happen'. She can report, happily, that 'His Highness' has called for her each day, and she has taken the opportunity to talk up Michelangelo's work when in his presence. Caccini concludes that she is hopeful of being able to write good news to him soon, 'because if the [Medici] ball bounces to my hand I won't let it get away'.

Caccini's ability to hang on to 'the Medici ball' over many years relied on her ability to understand, and manipulate to her own advantage, the gender politics of the Medici court, as she had done in dealing so successfully with Salvadori. The extent of her triumph is, however, hard to comprehend because, despite the painstaking work of scholars that has revealed so much about Caccini's life as a composer, the vast majority of her compositions are lost to us.

There is an exception, and it is a masterpiece: Caccini's *Il primo libro delle musiche* (The First Book of Music), which appeared from nowhere in 1618. To listen to the songs collected together by Caccini in this, the first and only volume of arias she published, is to enter a world of intense feeling, expressed in musically innovative ways: desire – including my favourite, 'Rendi alle mie speranze' (Give Me Back My Hopes); loss – 'Lasciatemi qui solo' (Leave Me Here Alone); and anguish – 'Ferma, Signore, arresta' (Stop, Sir, Stop). Other songs are, in the words of eminent musicologist and Caccini's biographer Suzanne Cusick, 'mysteriously compelling despite the absence of so-called expressive devices', with 'Maria, dolce Maria' (Maria, Sweet Maria) and 'Jesu corona virginum' (Jesu Thou the Virgin's Crown) communicating ecstasy and tranquillity rather than agony by means of 'melodies so well organized and harmonies so modern as to render the deceptively simple songs unforgettable'.

At the core of the collection are Caccini's arias, brilliant compositions constructed from the harmonic building blocks that were the starting point for every composer in her time. Her favourite building block is the romanesca, consisting of two phrases, the first of anticipation, the second of resolution, all based around fourths in the bass part. A composer could follow the pattern to the letter (or rather, to the note), but the great composers/performers tend to push constantly, brilliantly and inventively against the framework. It has been argued that the romanesca was as elastic as the twentieth-century blues, in its flexibility and its encouragement of the creation, always from conventional or recognizable materials, of sound structures as never heard before. This is precisely Caccini's achievement.

Il primo libro delle musiche is remarkable in other ways too. It is a book of music written by a woman for women, offering examples of every genre that a female solo singer needed to master, revealing the 'myriad tricks of a musica's trade and much more'. These tricks include playing confidently with gender, often in suggestive ways.

'*Ardo infelice*', a breathless, desire-filled lament, is gender-neutral, in the same way that many of Shakespeare's most well-known sonnets conceal the gender of both the speaker and the beloved, allowing room for all sorts of combinations of desire. Meanwhile, '*Io mi distruggo*' is a duet so 'textually and musically explicit in its performances of longing, union, and fantastically ornamented singing as to leave little doubt that it is as much a lesson in sexuality as in vocality'. As Suzanne Cusick astutely observes, one of the tricks that Caccini is teaching her female musician reader is how to sing *about* desire without acknowledging any knowledge *of* desire.

Caccini was playing with fire with these kind of gender games. Indeed, her friend Michelangelo Buonarroti the younger would almost get burnt some four years later when he entered similar terrain, the year he published an edition of his famous great-uncle's poetry. To more recent commentators, the edition is 'one of the grossest misdeeds that an editor had ever committed', because Michelangelo not only modernized much of the language, but changed the gender of the works' pronouns to conceal their homo-erotic content. But Caccini's friend had good reason to make those changes. A hundred years before the edition of 1623, the artist Michelangelo had expressed love and desire for men and women in his poetry. Now, in the full glare of the Counter-Reformation and its Inquisition, such expressions were inadmissible. For three months at the end of 1622, the censors scrutinized the poems before, at last, letting them pass. That '*alcuna indecenza*' (nothing indecent) appeared may not, therefore, have been an expression of Michelangelo the younger's prudishness, but a reflection of the social and political reality of his time.

As for Caccini, there is absolutely no indication that her *Il primo libro* fell foul of the censors in any way. Why, then, was there not a second book? At the time, it was noted that the composer was keen to publish more, but 'was forbidden to do so' by both the Medici doctors and the Medici Serene Highnesses, 'for the sake of preserving her person, as she had been gravely ill'. Perhaps, but behind these words lies the reality that Caccini was only and ever a servant of the Medici and that any publication needed to be about them, and for them, rather than for Caccini herself. Until recently, Florence's rulers had suppressed composers' names in any and all documents, whilst showing little interest in print, at least when it came to music. Francesca Caccini's breakthrough work, *La stiava*, for example, had not been printed but instead was circulated in manuscript form, providing a vital representation of Christine de Lorraine's power at a difficult time of political transition. In this context, it seems all the more remarkable that *Il primo libro* appeared at all, a precious, momentary glimpse of Caccini's ability as a composer. The work made clear, to a world beyond the Medici palaces of Tuscany, that the baton had indeed been passed from Giulio to Francesca Caccini and it is pleasing to think that Giulio recognized and even honoured his daughter's achievement, for, when he died in the winter following the publication of *Il primo libro*, he left Francesca a magnificent hand-painted keyboard instrument, a symbolic tool of her trade.

Giulio's death did nothing to interrupt the rise of his daughter. In the winter of 1623–24, in an attempt to pour oil on troubled waters (the Medici and the papacy were constantly at political odds), Caccini was to sent to Cardinal Carlo de' Medici's Roman household as a gift to the Florentine Maffeo Barberini, whose election as Pope Urban VIII was being celebrated in Rome throughout that winter. Seven years earlier, on her first stint in Rome, Caccini had been very much the support act to Jacopo Peri. Now she was the star performer, playing for cardinals and music lovers, at *veglie* (artistic meetings) for Rome's elite women, for private visitors, just before or after a meal, often for several hours, alone or with the singer Adriana Basile, herself a gift from the Duke of Mantua, moving between the great Renaissance and baroque venues of Rome, including of course the magnificent Villa Medici, created by Carlo de' Medici's father during the days of his own cardinalate. At last, on the final Sunday in January 1624, Caccini was called to perform for the pope in his private apartments and for one day Florence and the papacy were reconciled by Caccini's music.

The tensions did not take long to resurface, because the Medici family needed papal support to annul a marriage arrangement for one of Cosimo II and Maria Magdalena's daughters, Margherita. She had been promised to the Prince of Parma, but now it was hoped that Margherita could be married to her mother's Habsburg nephew, Crown Prince Wladislaw of Poland, who would be visiting Florence during the carnival early in 1625. A four-month season of state entertainments was being planned, all part of Maria Magdalena's ongoing attempts to align Tuscany more closely with the Habsburgs, and thus to distance the Medici family from their traditional loyalty to France. This also illustrates the underlying power struggle for the entire Italian peninsula (and beyond) that was being waged between the established superpower of Habsburg Spain and a resurgent France.

It is in this context of dynastic power politics that Maria Magdalena commissioned the work that is most frequently associated with Caccini, by now a thirty-six-year-old veteran of court spectacles. The proposed entertainment would be performed in a space that Maria Magdalena 'had infused with an almost defiant affirmation of womanly power', the newly restored Villa Poggio Imperiale, in its commanding position above Florence, over a mile south of the Pitti Palace and its Boboli Gardens, through the Porta Romana, well beyond the city walls. Even today, taking a bus to the city gate, then walking up an immense tree-lined avenue, one gets a sense of why Poggio Imperiale was an ideal venue for Maria Magdalena d'Austria to display her power – as a regent, as a woman, as the ruler of Tuscany. She had the power to bring anyone who was anyone out of Florence, up to *her* palace, through *her* avenue of trees, into *her* domain, to see *her* entertainment, with music composed by *her* composer, Francesca Caccini.

The villa had, however, a disturbing female Medici ghost. Two generations earlier, in the building then known as the Villa Baroncelli, Isabella Medici-Orsini had been strangled by her husband, Paolo Giordano Orsini: her crime, an affair with his cousin. Isabella provided, if one were needed, a reminder of the dangers of Florentine life. Abandoned by her husband soon after their marriage, she was known, in her lifetime, for her love of literature and music, with her portrait even showing her holding a score. Paolo Orsini, on the other hand, was known for his love of prostitutes in Rome, women such as Camilla the Skinny, who describes finding Orsini with another prostitute, Pasqua, her rival's threats, the men with Orsini who 'had spurs in their hands', and the injuries she received when they 'touched her a little in the face with their spurs'. This not only reveals the more sordid aspects of the sex industry, but Orsini's propensity, whether in Rome or dealing with his unfaithful wife, to use violence to achieve his ends.

Since Isabella's murder, the villa had been abandoned. Now it glittered once more. Not only did Maria Magdalena cover the walls of her new palace with prestigious artworks, some such as Perugino's *Deposition* plucked from Florence's churches, but, as scholar Kelly Harness writes, she 'commissioned canvases and frescoes depicting heroines from history, hagiography, and the Bible, including precisely the same protagonists of the religious musical spectacles performed at the court during her rule'. To an extent, Maria Magdalena was simply doing what her Medici predecessors had always done, using art to legitimize her rule. Her extra challenge was to show that she stood in a long tradition of women who had drawn their power and authority directly from God.

As soon as Maria Magdalena's guests began their journey to the villa, they were witnesses to that power. As early as 1619, she had initiated a two-year, thirty-five thousand scudi project to widen the approach to the villa once travellers had left the city walls behind them. Now the road up from the Porta Romana was filled with hundreds of carriages. On arrival, guests were greeted by Cardinal Carlo de' Medici, arrived from Rome to support his sister-in-law. A lucky few might be permitted a 'private' audience with Maria Magdalena, whether in her audience room, antechamber or bedroom, all decorated with freshly painted frescos of exemplary, and powerful, women.

And then the spectacle begins. In only the first transformation of many, an aquatic scene morphs into the evil witch Alcina's garden, with trees rising from the sea. The good witch Melissa enters on a dolphin, and explains what is going to happen. Then, as the synopsis of scene five puts it, in the 'beautiful and luscious meadows' twenty-four 'maidens made their way dancing on sumptuously bedecked horses; and all the people gathered to watch them dance until Melissa, carried on a centaur, entered the site thus making the work's epilogue'. The Boboli Gardens of the Medici Palazzo Pitti in the heart of Florence would only gain its famous amphitheatre designed by Giulio Parigi some five years later. In February 1625, the audience of *La liberazione* enjoy their entertainment in an equally sophisticated and theatrical garden at the Villa Poggio Imperiale.

Around seventy-five minutes in length, and one of the few full-length works of early modern music theatre by a single composer to survive, *La liberazione* is, according to its title page, *un balletto composto in musica*, in other words an entirely sung, plotted entertainment meant to end in dancing. The success of the work lay in its fusion of moving, stimulating music with an inspirational plot line. There are playful nods to convention (Caccini uses four trombones in a scene featuring some enchanted plants, when her audience would have expected trombones to depict the under-world), suggesting the composer's confidence and wit. And with good reason: Caccini's skills are everywhere in evidence, but most notably in her demonstration of the possibilities for character expression through recitative. A generation later, the aria would become the dominant element in opera, but in Caccini's lifetime, moments of most intense passion were primarily created through dramatic and expressive recitative. Indeed, an envious French writer, writing in 1636, noted that the Italians succeed in representing:

> As much as they can the passions and affections of the soul and spirit, as for example, anger, furor, disdain, rage, the frailties of the heart, and many other passions, with a violence so strange that one would almost say that they are touched by the same emotions they are representing in the song; whereas our French are content to tickle the ear, and have a perpetual sweetness in their songs, which deprives them of energy.

The self-appointed spokesman for the Italian music had, of course, been Giulio Caccini whose *Le nuove musiche* included helpful, practical explanations of the techniques that a singer required in order to move the listener's soul, an aim that lies at the heart of any baroque artistic creation.

His daughter's achievement is to deploy a range of musical tech-niques (harmonic juxtapositions, chromaticism, dissonance and syncopation) to create a sustained illusion of emotion. Wladislaw Vasa, Poland's future king, was so impressed by Caccini's work that, on his return to his own country, he set about establishing opera there. Vasa had been to Vienna and Rome, had watched and listened to *Sant'Orsola* a week earlier in Florence, but Polish court accounts of the performance on 3 February reveal it was Caccini's work that day that 'evoked a bigger interest in the audience'. Vasa had the text of *La liberazione* translated into Polish, and, a further sign of his appreciation of Caccini, commissioned two works ('music dramas') from the composer.

But is *La liberazione* an opera? All too often it is described as such, in part to bolster Caccini's claim to a place in music history. In fact, *La liberazione* is hard to classify. The picture is complicated by the fact that the term 'seventeenth-century opera' encompasses a wide variety of music theatre from the earliest Florentine operas through the Venetian operas written for the public stage, Roman opera and Neapolitan opera to the French *tragédie lyrique*, English masque, English and Spanish semi-opera and Spanish *zarzuela*. Just as it is unhelpful to think of works in terms of a single definitive composer in an era of collaboration, generic definitions seem somewhat pointless in the face of this list. What is crucial is that Caccini is in at the start of something very exciting. As the musicologist and practitioner James Middleton points out, opera (whatever that may be) began as 'experimental theatre of the most radical kind'.

It was, however, experimental theatre in the service of powerful women who sought to maintain power despite outright hostility to their sex. To give but one example: the Venetian ambassador at the time when Cosimo II became grand-duke attacked the grand-duchess Christine's apparent desire 'to govern everything absolutely, without any thought to the reputation and the benefit of her son'. For the women rulers of the Medici state, *La liberazione* stood as a high-risk attempt to confront, head on, the sexually focused, but politically grounded, fears and fantasies that surrounded women in power. Christine de Lorraine was only too familiar with these myths, having been brought up in the court of Catherine de'

Medici in France, a court that was the subject of a feverish account of what would today be designated lesbian activity. The account may stop short of denunciation, noting that so long as dildoes were not used then the women's sexual activities were not a true threat to patriarchy, and might even, if one was being generous, prepare girls for marriage, but it was utterly indicative of the attitudes towards women and power.

La liberazione is a remarkable, and risky, assault on precisely these attitudes. Not only is its plot taken from what has been described as one of recent literature's great gynophobic stories, Ruggiero's rescue from the feminizing sorceress Alcina by the 'bi-gendered' (because she impersonates a man to achieve her goal) Melissa, but its performance at the Villa Poggio Imperiale was a reminder that the last woman to command entertainment in that house had been the murdered adulteress, Isabella. But both Christine de Lorraine and her daughter-in-law Maria Magdalena were clearly ready to take the risk. For years, they had sought to demonstrate that it was business as usual for the grand duchy of Tuscany. There was no dangerous interregnum; the (political) show would go on. *La liberazione* takes their message one step further. The final vocal scene of the work makes the crucial, and radical for its time, claim that men and women are fundamentally equal.

La liberazione was a political and musical triumph, whilst also serving as a reminder that Caccini's career depended on the existence of Christine de Lorraine and Maria Magdalena d'Austria in positions of power. Caccini could not merely serve, she could *embody* their political agenda. Put simply and powerfully by one musicologist: 'If Francesca got away with something in history, she did so in tandem with Christine and Magdalena.' What she 'got away with' was a huge body of compositions, only a fraction of which survive.

The Medici women did not only use music and spectacle to support their claims to (female) power. Prior to *La liberazione*, they had commissioned a massive literary work from Cristoforo Bronzini: *Della dignità, & nobilità delle donne* (Of the Dignity and Nobility of Women). Bronzini argued that the equality of men and women was not only an absolute value, but that it was politically necessary to the health of the state. More astonishing, the work pointed the finger of blame at men, whose 'most insolent tyranny' had resulted in their taking power 'unjustly in every sphere of life'. Bronzini offers a vision of a non-violent woman's world, epitomized by mercy, piety and compliance, and Caccini is none other than its poster girl. Twenty-three pages of praise extol her virtue, revealing a woman who, through her music, could heal the sick, transform violence into peace, evil into goodness and invite 'every breast (even if opposed to chaste intentions) to pure *continenza* and *onestà*'. There is even a spiritual dimension. Caccini's music, writes Bronzini, allowed her listeners glimpses of 'celestial things, such that she transformed (I dare say one could say) human beings into gods'.

A perfect, all-powerful, even God-like, Caccini becomes part of a sustained public relations exercise, designed to legitimize the power of the Medici princesses. So far so good, but Bronzini's insistence, over-insistence maybe, on Caccini's virtue, to include her *onestà*, *castità* and *continenza*, actually points up the elephant in the room: the fear of precisely the opposite qualities, which were traditionally located in the body of the music-making woman. As one contemporary put it, expressing a formula found throughout the writings of the time: 'When music combined with visual beauty, it served as a double invitation to the pleasures and dangers of love, for body and soul were thus twice besieged and rational man deprived of his physical senses.' Every female musician operated in the shadow of this image of the lascivious whore, who used music as a form of entrapment, destroying 'rational man'. This mindset might explain why Bronzini writes, distinctly unflatteringly, that Caccini was not 'favoured by the gifts of nature', but that she is:

> Nonetheless friendly and admirable, never tiresome or resentful but merry and charming, and presented herself first of all with sweet and graceful manners toward everyone. And whether playing, singing, or pleasantly talking, she worked such stunning effects in the minds of her listeners that she changed them from what they had been.

Caccini, in impressive style, breaks the still prevalent model whereby a woman is judged by how she looks, rather than what she does, but Bronzini's praise is motivated by his concern to show that the composer's powers of transformation are not dangerously linked to her physical beauty.

This mindset also helps to explain the cultural phenomenon whereby female singers were subjected to so-called virginity tests, all in an attempt to stave off the horror of the unchastity associated with their art. Physiological 'evidence' was drafted in to support these views. As one social historian explains, 'chastity existed as a moral category and as a physical state, both of which singing implicated'. It was, then, an easy step to imagine the throat 'as the sieve through which chastity leaked out in the world and which rendered singing an activity that could prove the singer anything but chaste'. A whole range of treatises dealt with the 'problem' of the female voice, even when the female in question was considered virtuous. Silence, it was believed and asserted, was a natural female condition, condoned by famous verses from the Old and New Testament. 'Let a woman learn in silence with all submissiveness. I permit no woman to teach or to have authority over men; she is to keep silent' (1 Tim. 2:11–12) was just one of the most explicit.

This is the powerful landscape of belief within which Caccini worked as a singer, teacher and composer. It is a landscape that will reappear in almost every chapter of this book, and it served to complicate the praise she received from Bronzini in 1622. If 'whenever it suited her' Caccini 'so ignited wonder and daring in the breasts of people that they would have done anything, no matter how difficult', then surely that made Caccini dangerously powerful, a woman entering the territory of the sorceress or courtesan?

On a more practical level, Bronzini's praise, not to mention his vision of male/female equality, makes a mockery of Caccini's everyday working conditions. Although she certainly benefited hugely, and possibly suffered silently, from being born a Caccini, and although her father undoubtedly provided her with a way in to the life of a professional musician, the reality was that, from the moment Francesca became *la musica* in 1607, the *famiglia* of the Medici court controlled her. To enter the court meant surrendering rights over one's art, one's marriage, the very place where one lived. In return, those who joined the Medici *famiglia* received favour in the form of assistance with dowries, jobs, pensions, housing allowances and income, not to mention the possibility of valuable gifts from visiting princes. It was not a glamorous life for any musical servant, who might, as one husband-and-wife team were, be commanded with half a day's notice to perform for two and a half hours at a certain palazzo. The couple complied, of course, but, as the husband reported to a friend, it was hard. His wife 'did as well as possible, sang a few things, although with very great difficulty, because she is in her sixth month of what has been a very difficult pregnancy . . . I can assure you that she could hardly breathe, and as a consequence could not sing at her usual level.' It was a world in which, just as the father was the head of the family, controlling the lives of his children, so was the noble at the head of the court in relation to the adults in his or her employ.

It is no surprise, therefore, that within months of Francesca's appointment as *la musica* back in 1607, a marriage had been arranged for her to a fellow musician, Giovanni Battista Signorini. Marriage could be, and was, the end of a professional woman's career. In a previous generation, a scandal led to the composer Laura Bovia losing her place at the Medici court. On her return to her home city of Bologna, 'her uncle-become-father arranged a nice marriage for her' (in the laconic words of one music scholar). She never composed again.* Marriage, far from marking the end of Caccini's career, would mark its true beginning, tied as it was to her appointment as *la musica*. From the little that is known of her husband, thirty-one at the time of the wedding, and from the artisan class, he was handsome and easy-going. It did not appear to trouble him that his wife's career was far more successful and lucrative than his own and, indeed, he acknowledged in his will the huge imbalance in their respective financial contributions, a document that expresses only goodwill towards Francesca.

Francesca and Giovanni probably lived in one of her father's properties at first, but eventually her dowry was invested, as was customary, in property. This was on the via Valfonda, now an unprepossessing road running behind the main railway station but, in its time, a street that encapsulated the subtle gradations within the class system in Florence, from patrician households with

---

* Laura is buried at the church of San Giacomo in the village of Castelfranco, sixteen miles from Bologna, where her husband's family chapel can still be visited, with its Madonna still wearing the silver crown that Laura's husband gave her, four centuries ago.

servants out to much smaller, poorer homes.* The Caccini/ Signorini house was their primary workplace and, if it was anything like other musician households of the time, it is likely that musical instruments (many on loan from the court), manuscripts and other tools of their trade were scattered throughout the building. One musician couple used their pantry to store about half their music books, alongside a larder full of food.

For the first fifteen years of the marriage there were no children. Since the vast majority of women had a child shortly after marriage in early modern Europe, this long period of childlessness is unusual. Francesca may have become pregnant and miscarried. Perhaps the couple used, discreetly, the limited contraception that was available, such as condoms made from animal intestines or bladders. It is impossible to know. Caccini certainly never expressed any regret about her prolonged childlessness, despite the prevalent view that procreation was the prime function of marriage, not to mention the equally prevalent view that childlessness was always the fault of the woman.

But then, on 9 February 1622, and with Caccini aged thirty-four, a daughter, Margherita Signorini, was born. Neither Margherita's arrival, nor indeed the pregnancy, appears to have had any impact on Caccini's life as a composer and performer in a culture in which advanced pregnancy did not stop women singers performing, and sending babies out to be nursed was standard practice for those who could afford it. Caccini, with her starring role in Bronzini's *Della dignità, & nobiltà delle donne* and her regular court commissions, could certainly afford a nurse, and there was no interruption of Caccini's professional career by the time of Margherita's third

---

* The city end of the street was drastically changed by the building of the Santa Maria Novella train station in the 1930s, whilst the coming of the railway some hundred years earlier destroyed the more rural part of the street.

birthday in 1625. Indeed, with the success of *La liberazione*, and commissions from Prince Wladislaw, the composer apparently had a glittering future ahead of her.

It was not to be. Giovanni Baptista Signorini died on 29 December 1626. His will, dictated just six days before his death, shows that he acknowledged to the last the talents of his wife of nineteen years standing, not least her ability to bring in the money:

> The entire cost and value of these [houses] and the improvements, decorations and other additions to them were all executed from the effects and the money of the aforementioned Signora Francesca his wife, and therefore as he said above he intends and wills that the aforementioned houses belong to her as her own property.

Caccini kept her own property, but Signorini also bequeathed her the responsibility for paying for the funeral, prayers for the dead and a dowry for an unnamed girl. This came on top of the need to provide a dowry for the couple's own daughter, Margherita, now four years old. The funeral, which took place the day after Signorini's death, saw him buried in the tomb kept by his burial society, the Compagnia del Santo Rosario della Gloriosissima Vergine Maria, in the church of Santa Maria Novella, close to the family home in via Valfonda. If his wife conformed to the usual practices of her place and time, she would not only have put on mourning clothes, but also shaved her head in readiness to lead the ritual laments that were the women's part in this final religious office. As so often, she would not have been seen in a public space, since the female mourners occupied a separate room, their laments filtering through to the men in the main body of the church.

Signorini's death would have far more impact upon Caccini's life as a composer and performer than had the birth of Margherita. As a widow, Francesca had, according to her society's conventions, three options: dependency upon the Signorini family; a return to her own Caccini family who would then arrange for a second marriage; or, risky, rare, but possible, to support herself and, as a working widow, to provide a dowry for Margherita.

It was a bad time to be seriously considering the challenging route of independent widowhood. The Italian peninsula was entering a period of economic decline, after a period of relative stability and, by the 1620s, the Florentine economy had slipped into depression, economic historians pointing to a deepening crisis in agriculture, the arrival of English and Dutch shipping in the Mediterranean, the competition of northern textiles, costs of production in Italian cities and a series of banking crises. More pertinent still, the young Arch-Duke Ferdinando was approaching his majority, and his mother and grandmother were focused on preparing their male heir for power. Just at the moment when Francesca's personal life was in crisis, so too was her professional world, with the shift from a female court to one that was unmistakably male, and masculine. The shift left little room for Caccini's particular kind of expertise. Why would Grand-Duke Ferdinand need, or want, an exemplary female composer to bolster up his claims to power?

In the end, a fourth option emerged, in part an indication of the value placed on Caccini by the Medici family, but also an indication that she was expendable in the new political climate. By October 1627, Francesca, together with, it seems, her daughter Margherita, had left Florence and the grand duchy of Tuscany, and were settled in the small, independent republic of Lucca, some forty-five miles west, and at least two days' travel. She was now the wife of Tomasso Rafaelli. This second marriage, probably brokered by the Medici, offered a new arena for her talents, and also a major step up the social hierarchy. Tomasso was a member of one of the 104 Lucchese families qualified by birth to serve in government. In sharp contrast to Signorini, ever and always the artisan musician, Rafaelli was a leading figure in musical and intellectual academies of Lucca, wealthy enough to be a collector and patron, rather than a mere performer. Indeed, a combination of dynastic and cultural ambition may have led to Rafaelli's decision to marry the forty-year-old Francesca Caccini. He was fifty-six and had never married. A contemporary describes him as a 'Ganymede' (a reference to the beautiful boy adored by the god Jupiter), an unsubtle term to describe a man who preferred men. But even a Ganymede needs an heir. Tomasso, a son, was born to Francesca and Tomasso in 1628.

Caccini offered her husband more than a son. Away from the Rafaelli Palace in that street of magnificent palaces, the via Fillungo in Lucca, out on the slopes of Monte San Quirico, there were 'many beautiful villas owned by gentlemen' in which there were 'very large gatherings for conversation'. Out in the hills, in those beautiful villas, Lucca was being 'transformed into a new Parnassus' by Rafaelli and his friends. That was the vision, anyway, and Francesca Caccini was the woman to help achieve it.

The dream was to be sadly short-lived, for Rafaelli at least. Already struggling with the fallout from the collapse of the Lucchese Buonvisi banking empire in 1629, by the beginning of the following year he was seriously ill. By 16 April 1630, Rafaelli was dead. He had dictated his will in February and, like Signorini, was generous to a fault. The difference was that Rafaelli had something to leave. He named Francesca '*padrona, donna, e madonna*' of all that he owned, expressed his respect for her, and conferred upon her, as far as he could, a place in Lucca's elite. He even made a bequest to his stepdaughter Margherita, in gratitude for her 'many kind gestures' towards him, gestures made as if he were her 'true father'.

At first sight, Caccini's situation in 1630 was enviable. As a forty-two-year-old widow with her own means she did not *need* to work again. And yet, Rafaelli's death did not signal the end of her career as composer, performer and teacher. The needs and desires that drove Francesca Caccini forward at this stage in her life had, it seems, very little to do with money. At first, indeed, she was driven by the very real fear that she would lose her daughter, Margherita, ironically to the Medici family who had previously promised to protect and support the girl. Medici protection might well have seemed like a valuable offer at one stage, but now, widowed and far from Florence, Caccini could not bear the thought that her daughter would be in 'the hands of strangers', her future determined by the whims of the Medici *famiglia*. Emotional and professional concerns are painfully entangled. Caccini does not want to have 'laboured in vain, in continuous study for forty years' without being able to pass this on to Margherita. Her daughter's achievements must be her true legacy. Alongside the anguish, some of Caccini's more familiar pride and temper seep through, when she writes that she is hurt that a Medici representative came to her house and 'spoke with my daughter as if I were not her mother, or were not even in the world'. Caccini also reminds her correspondent that she is 'absolute guardian' of her son, Tomasso, and 'free *padrona* while I live of all that there is'. Why can she not 'return if I want to my homeland'? After all, she has not 'committed crimes for which I deserve exile'. Lucca was exile; Florence was home.

Caccini's arguments worked. She was given permission to continue to raise and teach her daughter in Florence, but the journey was not made – because plague, the living nightmare of the seventeenth century, arrived in Lucca. Desperate attempts were made to placate an angry God, with St Antonio's remains borne through the city. Four hundred people were cured, but it was a temporary respite. Women and children under sixteen were forbidden to leave their homes, with just one person from the household permitted to go out for provisions, but only on Tuesday and

Fridays. There were to be no 'assemblies and gatherings of people in times of contagion', schools were closed, and all games and entertainments stopped. By August 1631, eight thousand people had died in Lucca alone, one-third of the population.

Francesca Caccini, and her son and daughter, survived. At last, in February 1633, almost three years after her husband's death, the quarantine was lifted, and a return home beckoned, only to be prevented by a further outbreak of plague, this time in Florence. More months passed. At last, probably late in 1633 or early in 1634, Francesca Caccini was able to return home, to her professional life as a singer, teacher and composer.

She was again immersed in a woman's world. 'Widow Francesca Caccini' was permitted to 'enter the *monastero* of La Crocetta, with her girl'. This rare glimpse of Caccini's name in the archives indicates that her new centre of female activity would be the Dominican Monastero di Santa Croce, a convent, not a court. La Crocetta was, however, no ordinary convent. Back in 1619, one of Christine de Lorraine's daughters, Maria Maddalena, had expressed a wish to enter La Crocetta. Accordingly, the Medici architects spent two years creating a suitable palazzo with an enclosed garden that could adjoin the convent, for the princess and her resident staff of four unmarried adult women and two seventeen-year-old *donne*. In addition, two of La Crocetta's resident servants were to cook and clean for the princess's household, and another three or four would be sent daily by Christine. Maria Maddalena's presence at La Crocetta led to the monastery becoming the urban home of a number of unmarried princesses and, by 1633, the now elderly Christine de Lorraine was using the convent increasingly as a retreat. Of course, the usual restrictions on nuns' movement did not apply to these Medici women or indeed to their servants, much to the dismay of the church authorities, but it was only after Christine's death that the passageways which connected the monastery with the new-built palace were sealed by Florence's archbishop.

The convent as it was in Caccini's time no longer exists, but a map from the period shows a substantial building, dominated by the chapel and with a large garden, one of the benefits of a location on the extreme edge of the otherwise overcrowded city. Two *caval-cavia* (covered walkways) do still straddle what is now the via Laura, providing the link between the former palace of the Medici princesses and the convent. Of the convent's interior, only a small part of the chapel survives, now part of the Hotel Morandi Alla Crocetta. When I visited in 2014, the charming hotel receptionist scurried off to check whether the chapel was being used. After a few moments waiting, envisaging the spiritual sanctuary that I was about to see, complete no doubt with candles and incense, the receptionist ushered me into a hotel bedroom, which was also one end of a chapel. It was a strange moment: past and present colliding, spiritual and secular colliding even more. Then again, that was what La Crocetta was all about, at least when Caccini was working there: a perfect example of what has been called the permeability between convent and the outside world.

The composer herself lived less grandly on Borgo Pinti, just behind the convent, in a neighbourhood of 'many households, few shops, some patricians, some households with servants, many households without surnames and many widows'. Caccini, the widow, joined their number, and continued to teach her daughter Margherita, now eleven, as she had wanted (young Tomasso, now five, would present a different challenge). Her move to La Crocetta was therefore far from a complete break with the outside world, let alone from the Medici family. Indeed, in some respects it was as if the years in Lucca had never occurred. She was working again with Michelangelo Buonarroti, another survivor. Despite having supported Galileo in his heliocentrism in the 1610s, and then again when the astronomer was condemned by the Inquisition at the very time of Caccini's return to Florence, Michelangelo had managed to keep himself out of trouble. Now in his sixties, he was flourishing, according to the evidence of a bust sculpted in 1630, which creates vividly in stone the writer's still-luxuriant hair, his sumptuous clothes, his expressive hands and, above all, an energy, even arrogance, of expression. Michelangelo had been commissioned to provide eight stanzas of verse 'at once erudite and witty' for a surprise birthday party 'the following Sunday' for Christine de Lorraine's granddaughter, Vittoria della Rovere. Vittoria, betrothed as an infant to her cousin, Ferdinando II, had entered La Crocetta with her mother as a baby in 1624. Along with entertainment, the cook had been commissioned to create a sugar palace for the thirteen-year-old princess. Chests would be filled with Christine's presents to her granddaughter ('gloves, handbags, and other *galanterie*'). The doting grandmother's secretary noted that 'the direction of the singing will be good, because Signora Francesca Caccini and her daughter are here, even though neither of them yet knows this thought of *Madama's*'. As ever, Caccini's ability to compose music at the drop of a Medici hat is utterly taken for granted.

Taken for granted or no, in La Crocetta Caccini may well have found a satisfying creative environment during her second widowhood. Convents are only now being understood as crucial creative hubs for many musical women in the seventeenth century. It is not simply a matter of numbers (in that more than half the women whose music was published before 1700 were nuns) but the nature of the music being produced, music that blurred the boundaries between spiritual and secular, music that revealed that the wall between convent and outside world was permeable, and not just for a Medici princess. Scholar Laurie Stras, an expert in composer nuns, has, for example, found convent music to be 'colourful, varied, witty, and sophisticated, continually resonating with practices and references from the secular culture the nuns had officially forsworn'. The witty interplay between the sacred and the secular is visible in one of the favourite musical devices of the time, the instruction 'cantasi come', which asked nuns to sing (in the words of Radio Four's *I'm Sorry I Haven't a Clue*) one song to the tune of another, and resulted in sacred words sung to popular melodies.* This kind of crossover between sacred and secular, most vividly demonstrated in the renowned, even notorious, concert series performed by some religious houses, was precisely the thing that led to severe condemnations from the church authorities.

La Crocetta embodied a number of these virtues – or vices, depending on one's viewpoint. It had been known as a musical convent for some years before Christine de Lorraine and her daughter became more closely involved. But with the arrival of the Medici princesses, La Crocetta stepped up and embraced most of the so-called abuses of female monastic life. Apparently, the residents still refer to the period as the 'epoch of the princesses'. The noble women would move in and out of the monastery at all times of day and night; have servants; receive guests; indulge in conversation, jewellery and secular books. Musical entertainments at La Crocetta even borrowed costumes from the court. As soon as Christine died, the nuns were told in no uncertain terms that the

---

* On at least one occasion, it appears the nun composer played a trick on her performers, inserting potentially crude references into her lyrics, which the unfortunate singer would have to perform whilst maintaining a straight face. The famous theorist of Renaissance social behaviour, Baldassare Castiglione, recommended that women should pretend not to understand the double-entendres so frequently present in elite carnival humour. How much more pressure was there upon a nun who had the misfortune to read aloud an equivocal text?

convent had become a 'court of princesses and ladies, and you became so many courtiers'.

Yet, for all this vibrancy, and the opportunities for music making and music teaching, for all that La Crocetta's corridors literally led, eventually, back to the centre of power, the convent was disconnected from matters of state. La Crocetta may have allowed Caccini to be musically active, and satisfied her desire to be with, and to teach, her daughter, but the composer would never, as Cusick points out, 'again make music in a way that was important to the public record'.

It is quite possible, however, that Caccini had a different agenda by this stage of her life. In January 1637, plans were being made for a series of entertainments to celebrate the prospective consummation of the marriage between Vittoria della Rovere and Ferdinando. (The marriage itself had taken place back in 1633, when Vittoria was only eleven.) Caccini's daughter Margherita was expected to sing. The composer refused. This seems astonishing at first sight: surely Caccini had worked all these years so that her daughter could replicate her own success as *la musica* to the Medici? Margharita was already recognized as a rare talent, chosen to sing to the ailing grand-duchess. What had changed? Now, 'the mother is the one who opposes it, on the premise that by being seen on a stage the daughter could lose her future and have that much more trouble either marrying or becoming a nun'. Another letter from the time mentions the potential detrimental impact on Tomasso Rafaelli from having his half-sister perform on stage. Caccini, as the widow of a nobleman of Lucca, and as the mother of his son, could not function as a professional musician without, to an extent, dishonouring the Rafaelli name. Indeed, Caccini made one final attempt on her own behalf to become a true *dama*, to complete the journey from artisan/servant to lady of the court, an attempt that, for reasons that remain unclear, the seventy-six-year-old Christine de Lorraine blocked. It was to be one of the duchess's last actions confirming, if confirmation were ever needed, that Caccini to the last remained a servant, if a very special, honoured servant. Her exceptional status, eventually frustrating for her, if rewarding to those of us who love her music, is captured in the inscription in the records of her name *between* the Medici gentlewomen and their servants.

Caccini's quest for other, and to her mind better, futures for her children was more successful. Margherita would enter a Franciscan monastery where she continued to be known for her singing: a safer, if more limited, path than the one taken by her mother. Then, in 1671, Tomasso's daughter, Maria Francesca Rafaelli, became a *dama* in the court of Vittoria delle Rovere, marrying a minor Florentine nobleman, fulfilling her grandmother's social ambitions but bringing to a close, after only two generations, the Caccini composing dynasty.

'La virtuosissima cantatrice di Giulio Strozzi'
('Giulio Strozzi's extremely virtuosic singer')

Chapter Two

STROZZI

Venice 1619. A baby girl is born to a woman, Isabella Griega, or perhaps Garzoni, but known as 'La Greghetta'. The register of births notes that her father is *incerto*, uncertain, unknown. Isabella's identity, beyond her name, is just as uncertain. A poem from the time celebrates a courtesan, *'la Grega detta anche* [known as] *La Greghetta'*. Perhaps it is the same woman. On 6 August, Isabella's daughter is baptized in the church of Santa Sofia, Cannaregio. The baby is given the name Barbara Valle, but she will not keep it. As a child, Barbara lives in the household of Giulio Strozzi. He may be her father, he may not. All she knows is that she, and her mother, are both dependent upon, and protected by, him. *La Greghetta* will be inscribed in Giulio's will of 1628 as his long-time servant, and will receive his 'Venetian effects' on his death. If she dies, then Barbara inherits Giulio's household goods. It is a start.

Giulio Strozzi is a man who knows how Venice works, despite carrying the name of one of the great families of Medici Florence, and he knows that although his own father was illegitimate, and that he himself is illegitimate, this does not matter in Venice, the more so since Giulio is an intellectual, a poet and a libertine. He belongs to the Incogniti, one of the largest and most prestigious intellectual and creative academies in Europe, a major political and social force in the city and beyond. The members, leading Venetian intellectuals (excepting women and musicians), discuss with

53

intrigue the latest development in music – public opera – and Strozzi is actively involved, writing the libretto for *La finta pazza* (The Fake Madwoman), a work that sets the standards for a generation with its spectacular stage machinery and a star performance from an early prima donna, Anna Renzi. Venetian opera has arrived and Giulio Strozzi is king of the librettists.

He has influential and wealthy friends – landowners, bankers, businessmen – and he flatters them with dedications, even building their names into his libretti. Amongst these men are the wealthy, ambitious Vidman brothers, distantly connected to the world of German banking, but now working their way up to the very heights of Venetian society.* Giulio is keen to keep the Vidmans on side so he makes provision that, if he dies, and if Barbara or her mother want to sell his portrait of him, then Giovanni Paolo Vidman, already honoured as the dedicatee of *La finta pazza*, should have first refusal.

Giulio is a dominant, but restless, figure in Barbara's childhood. He rents a ramshackle place on the island of Murano one year, but leaves within months because it is just too much work. Most of the time he is based on his home turf, the district of Cannaregio, and most of the time he pays the rent. He comes and goes. Barbara and her mother live in households of women. They do not succumb to the decimating plagues of 1630, and witness the building of Santa Maria della Salute, still a dominant presence at the entrance to the Grand Canal, and still hosting the Festa della Salute every 21 November, when the people of Venice give thanks for the survival of their city. Venice, it seems, is always in decline (and always, it

---

* The name is spelt in a bewildering variety of ways, including Widman, Widmann, Wildman and Vidiman, although it is most common now in Venice as Widmann. The family were based in the German quarter of Venice, near the Rialto.

seems, survives) but Barbara is born at a time when the city is threatened on all sides, and, worse still, is being sidelined within Europe: as one historian puts it, 'history was now being made in the capitals of other nations'. Even Venice's maritime mastery was being threatened by the navies of England and Holland. The city staggered from one crisis to the next in the early years of the seventeenth century: the papal crisis of 1606, internecine conflict between the Giovani (young) and Vecchi (old) political groupings, Balkan piracy, conflict with the House of Austria and then the devastating plague of 1630–31.

Barbara is twelve at the time of the very first Festa della Salute of 1631. She is reaching the end of her childhood, and her musical talent, in particular her voice, is becoming gloriously evident. She is a soprano, good at rapid passage work, even better at long legato lines and, like all singers, she accompanies herself on the lute or theorbo. Giulio is ambitious for her, arranging for Barbara to have composition instruction from one of the leading composers of the time, Francesco Cavalli. The music lessons pay off, for at age fifteen the young woman is described as '*la virtuosissima cantatrice di Giulio Strozzi*', *his* exceptionally virtuosic singer. She has no name, but she is most surely Giulio's product. By the time Barbara reaches the age of eighteen, Giulio has enough money in hand to rent an expensive house, 150 ducats a year, when he could have got, and usually did get, something for one-third of that price. That same year, 1637, Giulio Strozzi's virtuoso singer becomes known by the name she will keep until her death: Barbara Strozzi.

What will Giulio Strozzi decide for his *virtuosissima cantatrice*? Marriage or the convent are the most obvious options. The latter has the advantage of being cheaper: marriage dowries are rising fast in real terms. Whether one made a wife or a nun of one's female dependants, a dowry is needed, and Giulio is never financially secure for long. Even with all the money in the world, would a libertine, anti-clerical poet choose a conventional path for his protégée? Giulio decides on a third, ambitious and potentially dangerous route for Barbara.

Through the second half of the 1630s, from around the time of Barbara's sixteenth birthday, Giulio Strozzi began publicizing her musical ability, ensuring, for example, that musical works were dedicated to her, if necessary by providing the texts himself: two volumes of music by Nicole Fontei, the *Bizzarrie poetiche* (Poetic Oddities) appeared in 1635 and 1636, full of praise for Barbara's singing ability. Giulio went a step further the following year, initiating the Accademia degli Unisoni, an offshoot of the Incogniti, but unlike its parent academy, open to musicians. The Unisoni, invoking both musical and social harmony, has been described as 'a sort of laboratory for musical and dramatic experimentation', and operated from the Strozzi household. It provided an important showcase for the display of Barbara's talents as a musician and, on occasion, composer. More than that, she displayed her charm and intelligence as a hostess, presenting a prize, for example, for a particularly fine opera libretto. At each meeting of the academy, a debate took place ('does slander inhibit or increase virtue?' 'does love bring happiness or unhappiness?') complemented by appropriate musical interludes. Barbara would delight the Unisoni members by her presentation of the male-authored arguments on each side of the debate as to whether tears or songs were the most potent weapon in love. If this was, as one historian has suggested, 'a debate that might have been constructed for Barbara herself', the question remains as to whether having a teenage girl perform men's words about women's erotic strategies is an event 'for Barbara herself' or for her male audience.

The display of Barbara was Giulio Strozzi's first aim and he succeeded: *la gentilissima, e virtuosissima donzella, la Signora*

Barbara was becoming widely known. She was, however, becoming known not merely as a virtuoso musician. Satirists were quick to make the familiar link between musical performance and sexual licence: 'It is a fine thing to distribute the flowers after having already surrendered the fruit', sniped one. Here, 'the fruit' is Barbara's virginity, whilst the flowers are her musical performances. Another satirist wondered how Barbara avoided becoming pregnant. The answer: she had a predilection for a particular castrato. These claims prove little, since sexual slanders were the currency of literary and musical life amongst the Venetian academies, all part of their members' display of their libertine (and misogynist) credentials and, indeed, it has been suggested that the satirist behind these slanders was himself a member of the Incogniti, of which Giulio Strozzi was a prominent member. Then again, a portrait of Barbara, painted at precisely this point in her life, does not exactly play down her position as both a sexual object and musician. The portrait, by Bernardo Strozzi (no relation), an artist who painted Monteverdi and other members of the Italian academies, shows Barbara, as one critic puts it euphemistically, as 'impressively *décolleté*'. In fact, one of her breasts is fully exposed. She holds a viola da gamba (an early cello), whilst on the table next to her is some duet music and a violin. It is a remarkable picture, in part because of the almost world-weary gaze that Barbara, not yet twenty, fixes upon the viewer.

This portrait suggests that establishing Barbara as a musician was only the first stage of Giulio's plan for his protégée. If all went to plan, she would be musician, composer and courtesan. It was a very Venetian combination, with the figure of the courtesan epitomizing the contradictory gender politics of the city. When the English traveller James Howell visited Venice (also known as *La Serenissima*) in 1621 he, like so many travellers past and present, fell in love with the city, imagined as a virgin Maid:

> At my first landing I was for some days ravished with the high beauty of this maid. This beauteous Maid hath been often attempted to be vitiated; some have courted her, some bribed her, some would have forc'd her, yet she hath still preserv'd her Chastity entire.

The irony was that in this city, so old and so beautiful, 'with hardly a wrinkle' writes Howell, women were absolutely excluded from public life by the Republic's very constitution. And yet, Venice prided itself (herself?) on its tolerance and sophistication. The city was Europe's playground, it celebrated Europe's most famous carnival, it had Europe's best shopping opportunities whether for silk, wool or lace, soap, glass or sugar, and it offered Europe its most sophisticated sex workers. Venice's pleasures and liberties could be sampled without too much concern for the Inquisition, so powerful elsewhere in the Italian peninsula. Specifically, titillated visitors were at one and the same time excited by, and wary of, the fabled *cortigiana onesta* (honest courtesan).

In the previous century, the poet Veronica Franco epitomized the *cortigiana onesta* and exemplified the ironies of the elite end of Venice's sex industry. Her career could well have provided a model for Giulio as he considered Barbara's future. Franco's protector and patron had been Domenico Venier (1517–82), a Venetian poet and the head of the most renowned vernacular literary academy in Venice, who supported Franco in her exchanges of poetry with male poets. According to one critic, Franco was 'forthright about her profession; she is often erotic, even sexually explicit. Her frankness challenges the literary poses adopted by male poets who repeat the idealizing clichés of Petrarchan poetry that praises a reserved, unattainable woman, rarely represented as speaking in her own voice.' Franco's writing made her wealthy, and she was able to repudiate the 'wicked life' of a courtesan, instead encouraging mothers to place their daughters in marriages or the convent for the sake of both their souls and their bodies, and providing bequests in her will to finance dowries for such future wives and nuns. Despite these profoundly moral gestures, Franco was charged with witchcraft by the Inquisition, and would end her life an impoverished outcast. Whilst it is true that a *cortigiana onesta* was, in the words of one social historian, 'a socially and intellectually accomplished woman, known for calculated deception in love, artfully composing a public image, and dissembling in provocative speech and song', then it is also true that even the most accomplished *cortegiane* led precarious lives. Each courtesan knew that at the heart of their trade lay the age-old linking of female music making and sexual availability: playing music, singing and composing poetry comprised the honest courtesan's most essential, marketable skills.

What of Barbara Strozzi? Just over a year after her portrait was taken, she was pregnant with her first child. The father was Giovanni Paolo Vidman who, in 1641, accepted the twin gifts of Barbara's body and the dedication to Giulio Strozzi's *La finta pazza*. In a letter, written after Barbara's death, it is reported, laconically, that she 'was raped by the Count Vildman [sic], a Venetian nobleman, and had a son who bears the name Giulio Strozzi'. Whether he raped her or not, Vidman certainly did not marry Barbara since he was already married. But whether he raped her or not, Vidman certainly was the father of baby Giulio, and then two further children, Isabella in 1642 and Laura in 1644, and possibly a fourth, Massimo.* It has been suggested that the rape claim might merely have been a story circulated in order to protect Barbara's reputation. In other words, as an 'innocent' victim of rape (rather than a

---

* Strozzi's (probable) fourth child, Massimo, became a monk, taking the name Giovanni Paolo, suggesting that Giovanni Paolo Vidman was his father.

willing participant in a sexual act) she retains her honour, a reading of the situation that provides a perfect example of the twisted logic of patriarchy, certainly then, maybe even now.

The events of the early 1640s suggest that Barbara Strozzi was, in fact, more a concubine than courtesan. Concubinage, viewed as an intermediate state between the married and unmarried woman, was, according to social historian Federica Ambrosini, far from disapproved of in Venice until a couple of generations before the Strozzi/Vidman alliance, so long as (and it was often the case that):

> Men of high standing chose as their concubines respectable women of good families and endowed with all those virtues that could be required of good wives. Male partners might or might not cohabit with their companions, but between such couples mutual ties were still very close, and their offspring were usually lovingly cared and provided for.

This somewhat rose-tinted view of concubinage was being increasingly challenged by the 1640s. In public at least, a new, sterner morality was in play. God, it was said, had poured his plague-full wrath upon Venice for its licentiousness. Men were encouraged to find husbands for their concubines, or even to take the responsibility of 'saving' the woman by marrying her himself. Some of them even did so, although invariably in secret. Not only did Vidman not marry Strozzi, he did not arrange her marriage to another. He did not need to, because, despite the bursts of moral thunder, the Venetian authorities usually maintained a flexible approach to these matters, their primary concern being the maintenance of social order. So, as long as Barbara Strozzi presided over a stable household, so long as her children were not destitute, the Venetian state would not intervene in the sexual arrangements of its citizens.

Veronica Franco was eloquent on the human cost of those arrange-ments, even when they were dressed in the euphemisms of the *onesta cortegiana* or concubine:

> It is a deeply unhappy thing and too contrary to human
> nature to force one's body and behaviour to such a slavery
> which is frightening only to think about. To give oneself as
> a prey to many, with the risk of being deprived, robbed,
> and killed, of being able to lose in only one day what you
> had earned over a long time, with so many dangers of
> injuring yourself, of catching contagious and terrifying
> diseases; to eat with someone else's mouth, to sleep with
> someone else's eyes, to move according to someone else's
> desires, running always towards the inevitable shipwreck
> of your faculties and your life; what misery could be
> worse? What riches, what comforts, what luxuries can
> acquire so much weight?

The reality for the women involved was stigmatized single parent-hood. Regardless of whether the child had been fathered through rape, a false promise of marriage, prostitution or an affair, lone parenthood was, it has been said, a 'source of anguish, at times lead-ing women in this condition to long for their own death'. One such mother asked to be buried in the monastery of the repentant pros-titutes, the Convertite, wearing their habit.

Then again, so little is known of Strozzi's life during these years that it is hard to tell what her situation was, let alone what she herself thought about it. All that survives are a handful of financial dealings between Strozzi and Vidman. Surprisingly, it was *she* who lent *him* money. The loan would be repaid after Vidman's death and, perhaps, as one historian suggests, 'the nearly ten percent interest she received in December 1648 on the repayment of her loan is beyond what one would expect under normal circumstances and may reflect Vidman's desire to provide some extra income for Barbara and her children'. Count Giovanni Paolo Vidman did take his financial responsibilities as a parent seriously, at least towards his oldest natural son, bequeathing Guilio Pietro an annual income of about 200 piastre. The sum, just over 200 ducats, was hardly enough to provide bed and board for Giulio Pietro in Venice, but it was still ten times the amount paid out to his sister Laura in her convent. Martin Vidman, the boy's uncle, also contributed, although his bequest came with the proviso that Giulio Pietro had to find a suitable office, something the young man signally failed to do. The historical fact remains that, in the census of 1642, Barbara, in her early twenties and with two small babies, is back in her birth parish of Santa Sofia living with three adult women and no men. And it is her father who is paying the rent, not Vidman.

Had she been born a man, of course, the options open to her (and to her father) would have been very different. One has only to compare the progress through life of the baby christened Barbara Valle in 1619 and one Francesco Caletti, born in Crema in 1602. Like Barbara, Francesco revealed his musical talent early. Unlike Barbara, Francesco was adopted by Federico Cavalli, the Venetian governor of Crema, and, under his patronage, entered the *cappella* of San Marco, Venice, on 18 December 1616, as a soprano with an annual salary of eighty ducats. It was not just the money that mattered. San Marco was the territory of Claudio Monteverdi, the composer who retained musical control of the basilica for the first twenty-five years of Francesco's tenure there.* Francesco edited one of Monteverdi's works, and took the opportunity to publish

---

* San Pietro, in Castello, was the cathedral of Venice at this time, but the Basilica of San Marco was the real centre of political, ecclesiastical and, indeed, musical power.

his own six-voice *Magnificat* setting; he took a job on the side as organist at the important church of SS Giovanni e Paolo; he had wide-ranging freelance activity at church feasts; he was able to live in the house of a nobleman; and he married a wealthy widow in 1630, who brought a dowry of more than 1,200 ducats, plus land and capital. It was at this moment, 1630, that the married, financially secure and professionally established Francesco started using the name Cavalli in honour of his patron. It was also at this time that he started to become involved with the development of the most exciting new music around, opera. His debut as an opera composer occurred the day after his election as organist at San Marco in 1639, and only two seasons after the introduction to Venice of musical theatre for paying audiences. Cavalli, as investor, organizer and composer, would become crucial to the future shape of seventeenth-century Venetian opera. His work travelled beyond Venice, with touring companies performing throughout Italy, as far as Paris, possibly Vienna. Little Francesco Caletti therefore became the renowned Francesco Cavalli, composer, organist and singer, and the most performed composer of opera in the quarter-century after Monteverdi.

For a moment, in 1644, the year of the birth of Barbara's third child by Vidman, she herself entered Francesco's world. Strozzi's *Il primo libro de' madrigali* (First Book of Madrigals) appeared in print, complete with a dedication to twenty-one-year-old Vittoria della Rovere, Grand-Duchess of Tuscany, the former resident of Francesca Caccini's La Crocetta, and future patron of Caccini's granddaughter. For all the confidence of the claim, in one song, that she will be the new Sappho (*sarò Saffo novella*) – the Greek poet who epitomized female creativity – the volume is an anxious foray into public life. Strozzi extends the usual expressions of the composer's unworthiness to include fear:

Being a woman I am concerned about publishing this work. Would that it lie safely under a golden oak tree and not be endangered by the swords of slander which have certainly already been drawn to do battle against it.

Neither Giulio nor Barbara Strozzi could have been unaware that she was entering an existing 'battle' of and about the sexes, since many of the combatants were members of the Incogniti academy, led by the notorious libertine Giovan Francesco Loredan. The Incogniti were ranged against figures such as Archangela Tarabotti, the proto-feminist nun, who, like Strozzi, and in the very same year, dedicated her own contribution to the debate to Vittoria della Rovere. *Il primo libro* was, on one level, an attempt by Barbara and Giulio (who may well have written the lyrics) to stoke the fires of controversy, or at least capitalize upon them.

Giulio Strozzi had educated Barbara, musically and intellectually; he had created a setting to display her abilities, the Unisoni; and he had prostituted her to his patron, perhaps friend, Vidman. If Giulio Strozzi was behind the publication, it could have been a further act of display, designed to enhance Barbara's value, or even to rebrand her. This would make sense of the fact that, whilst in 1644 Barbara is still primarily known as a singer, *Il primo libro* contains no solo pieces, suggesting that it was designed to display her wide-ranging abilities as *composer*, rather than to foreground her own vocal ability. Then again, by 1644, and since 1640, Giulio Strozzi had been focusing his attentions on the promotion of another singer, Anna Renzi, who had been crucial to the success of a number of operas, including his own *La finta pazza*. A series of triumphs, including Renzi's performance in *La coronazione di Poppea* (The Coronation of Poppea) with music primarily by Monteverd, led to the publication by Giulio of the eulogistic *Le glorie della signora Anna Renzi romana* of 1644. Preoccupied with superstar Renzi, would Giulio Strozzi have wasted his energy on Barbara?

It is just possible that Barbara's first publication (her opus 1 of 1644), appearing after a period of four years during which she has either been pregnant or recovering from pregnancy, is, at least in part, an attempt by Strozzi to establish a new professional identity as a composer. As Cavalli's career suggests, a male composer could take up major musical posts in churches, courts and theatres. A woman composer would find it hard to secure institutional employment at all. If the publication of *Il primo libro* was indeed an attempt to establish Strozzi as a composer, it failed. If she continues to be mentioned at all, it is as a singer. And if she is mentioned as a singer, it is her beauty rather than her voice that is praised. She did not even have to fend off the 'swords of slander' she claimed to fear. Barbara Strozzi, composer, fell silent.

It is what happened next that makes Barbara Strozzi remarkable. From 1651 to 1664 she published seven collections of compositions, which went far beyond the achievements of her opus 1, demanding a higher degree of virtuosity from the performer, containing more and more drama in the music and, above all, revealing ever-growing ambition in herself as the composer. After some fifteen years of being little more than a pawn in a game played by powerful men – whether her father, Vidman or the Incogniti – Strozzi's publications from 1651 mark, to a degree, an attempt to assert her own voice as a composer.

That voice works in complex negotiation with many of the forces that had shaped her since a young girl. If, from the mid-1630s onwards, Barbara Strozzi had been directly involved in the somewhat queasy phenomenon whereby a girl or young woman sings for men, words by men, about the sexual desirability and yet fundamental falsity of women, then, by the 1650s that girl had become a mature woman, a composer seeking recognition through publication and, moreover, a composer willing to play some fascinating games with the erotics of performance.

It is not merely that Strozzi handles her erotic subjects, and viewpoints, with confidence and sophistication, although she does just that. (In one song, 'Cor donato', the sexual tension is heightened by the entwining of the two voices, each as powerful as the other as they cross and recross, whilst the sexual climax is expressed through a repeated descending major tetrachord in the bass, achieving an almost hypnotic effect upon the listener.) What is even more striking is that, in Strozzi's music of the 1650s, most particularly from opus 3 onwards, there is often a striking disjunction between the compositional voice and the misogynist text. The words of 'Moralita amorosa', from opus 3, for example, constitute a typical attack on women, who deceive men into desire through their clothes, make-up and hairstyles. The text ends by exposing these as seductive fictions: the woman, herself, is revealed to consist merely of 'dust and fumes'. The poem echoes, strongly, the terms of the debates about women in the mid-1640s that had so engaged the Incogniti. Ten years on, Strozzi chooses to set a text which argues that, stripped of her trappings, a woman is nothing. And yet, as a musical composition, the work is both complex and coherent, deploying techniques familiar to her opera-writing male contemporaries as the music moves easily along a continuum between recitative and aria. The song opens with a triumphant ascending melisma on the word sorge (rising). It sounds improvised: it is, in fact, carefully written. The irony is that a text that condemns women's adornment, shows that their beauty is illusory and that women's charms are a mere fiction that should not have power over man, is set to music by a woman who uses such adornments but in a controlled, sustained way to create a work of power and compositional coherence. In sharp contrast to the words, describing the collapse of woman into 'dust and fumes', the composition is formally robust and secure, and built to last in print.

Like many of her contemporaries, Barbara Strozzi uses predominantly 'Marinist' texts (from the poet, Marino) that, depending on one's view, display either sharp wit and linguistic virtuosity or tired clichés and pretentious conceits. In Strozzi's hands, the wit and edginess come to the fore, as she challenges the listener to consider her own status as singer, composer and woman. As early as her opus 2 of 1651, the song 'La mia donna perché canta' refers to a woman who sings (and, it is implied, has sex) only for money. The second strophe is the most explicit:

> She never sings if I don't 'count'
> Nor does her voice find the pitch,
> Nor does she have the quill ready to play
> If she doesn't hear the sound of gold.
> She is always teaching me
> That if I want to sing a duet,
> Before she'll sing the 'fa'
> I'd better give the 'dough.'

Elsewhere, gender lines are intriguingly challenged as in 'Voi pur, begl'occhi' in which a woman's body is described in explicit terms, as is its effect upon the speaker's body. (Breasts were something of a Venetian fetish, 'Italians most loving fat women', and women revealing their 'dugs' 'bound up and swelling with linen and all made white by art'):

> O yes, beautiful breast, you are living snow.
> Yes, how your gentle throat quells my passionate fire.
> Yet in the end so sublime is my delight
> that as it grows, little by little,
> my fire is spent among the snowflakes.

The only thing that is certain here is that it is a woman's body that is creating and satisfying desire. The speaker is at once male (if the poem is understood to describe an erection) and female (if the voice of the singer, not to mention the sex of the composer, is considered). Indeed, the majority of Strozzi's texts are non- or bi-gendered, allowing for maximum creative confusion, a reclaiming of the erotic as a knowing woman composer who is taking desire beyond traditional gender divides and stereotypes.

As such, Strozzi's music epitomizes yet another aspect of Venetian life, and one that fascinated visitors to the city, including the English traveller, John Evelyn. As was the case with many of his fellow tourists, Evelyn was intrigued by the women's high heels ('the noblemen stalking with their ladies on *choppines*'), but he went on to write that he had seen courtesans who were 'in plain English, whores', dressed 'like men, in carnation or light colored doublets and breeches, and so playing with the racket at Tennis with young men'. But it was not only whores, but 'honourable women in honourable company', who would dress like men, their identities concealed by their masks; they would go 'all about the streets, even from Christmas holy days to the first day of Lent'. Evelyn was shocked to note that the women's breeches were 'open all before, and most part behind, only buttoned with gold or silver buttons', and that the courtesans 'make all the forepart of their gowns in like manner open'. Whether in its explicit sexual content or its gender bending, Strozzi's music was merely another echo of the erotics of Venetian street life and fashion.

Yet, for all the wit, edginess and downright sexiness of her music, Strozzi is at her most compelling when she shocks the reader to attention with a raw evocation of emotion. In the opening bars of her song '*Lagrimie mie*', the singer lets rip an astonishingly doleful wail, from the very top of her vocal register, falling down and down, over a stationary harmony. The intensity is merely heightened by the faltering syncopated rhythm and some intentionally painful dissonances. As musicologist Russano notes, this kind of thing had been done before, but never in such an extreme way. And, although Strozzi only published one collection of religious pieces, her opus 5 of 1655 dedicated from 'the motives of my heart' to Anna de Medici, the Arch-Duchess of Innsbruck, the collection offers a similarly intense musical experience. Too intense, it seems, for some: Strozzi (barred from churches in her own lifetime) is still considered by some today as being 'too sexy for church': this phrase was allegedly used by a London concert programmer in 2015 when excluding the composer. The motives of her heart, then, and her suitability for church now aside, Strozzi was, as always, looking for a patron, and therefore the most significant work in the collection is the astonishingly powerful motet for solo voice 'Mater Anna', which, of course, honours both the arch-duchess and Sant'Anna/Saint Anne, mother of Mary and patron saint of Christian mothers. Scholar Robert Kendrick has noted that Strozzi would have been well aware of the nature of Anna de Medici's devotion to her namesake saint. At the age of thirty (in other words, very late for the time), the Medici princess had been married to a man of eighteen, and although she did successfully produce three daughters for him, a son remained elusive through a relentless series of miscarriages and stillbirths. The cantata to Saint Anne culminates in a final prayer, the voice ascending over a walking bass, in a heart-rending plea for mercy and succour, reminiscent in its intensely emotional religiosity of works such as the sculptor Bernini's *Teresa in Ecstasy*. All of the composer's ambition is evident here, with an iridescently beautiful melody alternated between voice and continuo, and each section designed to create a different effect by being structured in a different way. Her spiritual focus did not prevent Strozzi exercising the full array of her compositional skills.

That Strozzi understood how far she had come from '*la virtuosis-sima cantatrice* of Giulio Strozzi' is clear from the ways in which she writes about her own work over the years. Back in 1644, she had feared the 'swords of slander'. In opus 2, she is still writing that 'the lowly mine of a woman's poor imagination cannot produce metal to forge those richest golden crowns worthy of august rulers'. By opus 5, Strozzi claims to be liberated from 'feminine weaknesses' that might stop her offering the work to her patron, whilst never-theless bowing before him in devotion, since assertiveness can only be taken so far, by any composer, but particularly a female composer. In her final three works, Strozzi does not even mention being a woman. Having distanced herself from 'feminine weak-nesses', she is almost placing herself beyond gender.

It was an impossible dream. Strozzi's time, place and gender meant that she remained steadfastly a composer of musical minia-tures, such as arias and cantatas, and that she watched from the sidelines the triumph of public opera, and its promoters, in Venice.[*] For although the Accademia degli Incogniti may not have invented Venetian opera, 'the influence of its members on the new art form can hardly be overstated'. Not merely debaters of opera, not merely writers of libretti, it was the Incogniti who inspired the construc-tion of a brand-new building, the Teatro Novissimo, the fourth opera house to open in Venice, and one that promoted heroic operas rather than comic plays, thus establishing a distinctive Venetian operatic tradition. In all this, Barbara Strozzi had no part to play.

---

[*] These generic terms were far from fixed in Strozzi's time, but the arias (and ariettas, or little arias) are generally short, strophic pieces, with every stanza sung to the same music, while the cantatas are mostly longer sectional works, scored for between one and three voices, with a basso continuo, in which the music changes to suit the meaning of the text, moving between recitative and aria as appropriate.

All the evidence suggests that she did nevertheless find a way to engage with the musical debates of her time, in particular the phenomenon of 'sheer music' or 'pure voice'. Venetian operas were placing more and more emphasis on the aria at the expense of recitative, and less and less emphasis upon the words themselves, let alone their philosophical content. By the end of the century, nostalgic music lovers regretted the change: now the 'philosopher remains confined to schools, the poet to academies; and for the people what is left in the theatres is only pure voice, stripped of any poetic eloquence and of any philosophical feeling', wrote one disgruntled opera lover. Although Strozzi never wrote an opera, she is part of this transformation. Indeed, an unusually large proportion of her music does not articulate any word at all. All that is heard is voice. She creates thereby a 'languid, almost self-indulgent lyricism', taking the techniques developed by the previous generation of avant-garde Venetian composers, such as pungent chromaticism, awkwardly large leaps, persistent syncopation and sudden interruptions, and applying them not to word painting but to sheer sound. In the words of Strozzi scholar Ellen Rosand, Strozzi 'exploits the superior eloquence of the naked human instrument'.

Scholars have suggested that Strozzi's increasing interest in 'pure sound', and also her use of a feminine version of the Incogniti's insignia – *Ignotae Deae* (unknown goddess), not *Ignoto Deo* (unknown God) – signal her continued involvement with Loredan's academy. The Incogniti were certainly preoccupied with exploring the philosophical issues raised by the dissociation of word and music, and Loredan himself blasphemously reworked St Paul's reference to the unknown God (Acts 17:15-34) into an image of truth as a soon-to-be-unveiled female body. Strozzi's focus on the historical figure of Henri de Cinq-Mars, who is the speaker in the composer's *'Lamento'* (in yet further gender confusion, his first-person account of his own death is introduced by a tenor and delivered by a soprano) suggests an involvement with the Incogniti, for whom the executed Henri was a hero on account of his libertine life and anti-absolutist views. This eerie, appropriately haunting work draws attention to the idea of 'nothing', both the word and silence. Henri's ghost laments that fortune's wind has turned against him, concluding '*Onde ho provato, ahi lasso, / Come dal tutto al niente è un breve passo*' (alas, I have experienced how short is the step from all to nothing). Strozzi singles out the word '*niente*', and asks her singer to descend to her lowest note, middle C. The sentence itself is framed with two rests, which are both extended by a fermata (pause), an unsettling, indeed unprecedented, musical artifice, according to one musicologist.

For all the tantalizing hints that Strozzi was involved with the Incogniti, if only to capitalize on their influence, Loredano, the dominant figure in the Incogniti, may well have provided texts for at least one of Strozzi's collections, although the utterly conventional Marinist nature of the poetry makes it hard to tell the author. It appears however that there was little room for a female composer with her clothes on within the Incogniti 'philosophy', and no possibility of a woman composing, rather than starring in, an opera. There is certainly no evidence that her mysterious dedication to '*Ignotae Deae*' led to any tangible reward or commission, unless one counts the fact that Strozzi continued to get her work printed in a publishing world that was, it is said, dominated by the Incogniti. Loredano, seen as the society's most prominent member, did praise the composer, in a published letter of 1655: 'had she been born in another era she would certainly either have enlarged or usurped the place of the muses' but the praise was hardly original (he had used almost exactly the same phrases to celebrate Anna Renzi) and, what is more, despite the apparent acknowledgement that Strozzi's talent cannot be recognized fully in her own time or world, she remains cast as a female inspiration for male creativity, rather than a creator in her own right. Strozzi remained, at best, a 'muse', at worst, a ventriloquizing puppet of the libertines' misogyny.

That Barbara Strozzi remained enmeshed in a cultural economy that linked the provision of sex with the provision of music is only too evident from the few references to her in the historical archives. A letter from Strozzi to Carlo II, the Duke of Mantua, of 30 November 1655 reveals that, earlier in the year, the thirty-six-year-old composer had sent some music to the duke, who was visiting France at the time. He had already begun his journey back to Mantua by the time the music arrived, so Strozzi redirected her collection to him there, adding a covering letter:

> These poor compositions of mine, enriched by Your Highness's gracious ear, and in part by your own voice, should not enjoy the light of the world if not under those rays that shone on them previously. Sent to France in care of Ambassador Lolino, they have followed your return here to bow reverently before you. They bear on the cover a sun, certain not to find disfavour, all the more as they will have your gracious regard.

Strozzi's words suggest that the duke had heard the music before, and possibly even sung some of it himself. Carlo II was certainly a regular visitor to Venice, which was less than a hundred miles (fairly easy miles, at that) from Mantua, where he not only indulged his interest in music and gambling but also, in Strozzi scholar Beth Glixon's words, 'enjoyed the charms of Venetian women'. Put more bluntly, the duke led a separate life from his wife once she had provided an heir in 1652, and took lovers of both sexes wherever he could find them. Ten years on, there is another glimpse of the relationship between duke and composer in the archives. Strozzi is now composing *for* the duke, rather than presenting him with a finished publication as she had done in 1655:

> Only yesterday Marchese Santinelli gave to me the words to serve Your Highness, which I will immediately do with my weak talents. In the meantime, I found that I have some poetry by another Cavalier, that seemed to me suitable for a bass. In order to serve Your Highness, I have drafted the songs, and will send them to you.

These tantalizing glimpses of a connection between Barbara Strozzi and Carlo II, Duke of Mantua, are all that remain. There is no direct evidence of a sexual liaison (Strozzi was ten years Carlo's senior, and he had plenty of other men and women to choose from nearer to hand), although Beth Glixon believes one did occur. All that survives in the records are two instances of the duke receiving, and then perhaps commissioning, some music from Strozzi. Did the composer hope that the Duke of Mantua might emerge as Giovanni Paolo Vidman's successor? If so, she played a long game, and it failed. Ten years on from her first attempt, and just a few months after the promise to provide more music for his bass voice, the duke died.

The crucial issue raised by the Mantua/Strozzi correspondence is not whether they had sex with each other. They might have done so. Nor is it even if Strozzi's lost opus 4 is the book of compositions she sent to the duke in Paris. It may well be. The crucial issue is the one encapsulated in two words in a letter written to the duke on 14 April 1655. The writer is Antonio Bosso, the duke's man in Venice. The ostensible subject is Strozzi's opus 5, her only religious work, the one dedicated to Anna de Medici in Innsbruck. Bosso writes very much one man to another:

I will tell your most Serene Highness some curiosities that are not too serious. Barbara Strozzi dedicated to the Archduchess of Innsbruck some of her music; her Highness sent to her the other day a small gold box adorned with rubies and with her portrait, and a necklace, also of gold with rubies, which the said Signora prizes and shows off, placing it between her two darling, beautiful breasts (Oh, what tits!).*

It seems that at least two of Barbara Strozzi's contemporaries could not look past the breasts to the composer. An anecdote that could have been about a woman's composition (rewarded by another woman's act of generous patronage) becomes one about a shared knowledge of a woman's 'tits'. Maybe that suited Barbara Strozzi very well, but it is impossible to tell. It is certainly an insight into how Strozzi operated in the shadow of the courtesan, it seems always and for ever.

For ever because, ironically, this very chapter, which questions whether Barbara Strozzi was indeed Vidman's concubine, or Mantua's mistress, which questions what that might mean for her, as woman and composer, is complicit in the prurient fascination with the courtesan. Perhaps these are the wrong questions, because every woman in early seventeenth-century Venice, from servant girl to princess, existed to a greater or lesser extent as a commodity to be exchanged by men. Money was always involved, whether the dowry necessary for marriage or the cloister, or the payments made

---

* The final words, in Italian, are: 'et un gallano da petto pur d'oro con rubini, di che la detta Signora si preggia, e ne fa pompa, ponendo il gallano in mezzo alle sue due belle tettine (o che tette)'. Beth Glixon, whose painstaking research has been foundational to this chapter, found the letter in the Archivio di Stato di Mantova, Archivio Gonzaga.

to what a later era would call 'kept' women. Does it matter which particular sexual arrangements dominated Barbara Strozzi's life?

To seek out her house in the district of Cannaregio offers another perspective on Strozzi's achievement. Already some distance from Cannaregio's main street, and its main canal (let alone the splendour of San Marco and the Canale Grande, or the splendours of the Merceria, in Strozzi's time enticing buyers with gold cloth, rich damask and brightly coloured silks, all hung from the windows of Venice's central shopping street) one can still turn down a narrow, somewhat gloomy alleyway, which leads only to a small, dingy canal. Half-way along, one steps under a *sotoportego* (a porch between two houses, creating a small tunnel) into momentary darkness, and then into the Corte del Remer (now Cannaregio 4765A).

Strozzi would have walked, or rather tottered, to the Corte del Remer on the high platform heels, *pianelle*, that so excited visitors to Venice. Originally a practical solution for the avoidance of street dirt, the shoes became a mark of status (because one needed servants to support one when walking in them) and femininity (because of the swaying motion required to walk in them). The highest heels were those of the courtesans, 'three or four handsbreadths high' gasped one visitor, making it easy to see why a woman needed at least two supporters, usually old women – one to lean on, the other to 'bear up the train' of her gown. Even if we could measure the height of Strozzi's shoes, we would still be no closer to understanding her social position in Venice. Indeed, visitors to Venice were disconcerted by the fact that it was so hard to tell the difference between a whore and a lady, because both categories of woman dressed in low-cut dresses and *pianelle*. A woman who was not quite a lady could keep up appearances because of the vibrant trade in second-hand clothing in Venice: did Strozzi pick up the cast-offs of noblewomen at the guild-registered dealers in the ghetto or, more riskily, at a tavern or even from a pedlar on the streets of Cannaregio?

We do know that Barbara Strozzi paid ninety-five ducats a year to the Vidman family to live in six rooms in her courtyard. The records remain silent as to whether her children, still all aged under ten, lived with her, but there would have been space, just about, with living areas on two floors, each made up of two larger rooms and a smaller room: a '*studietto*' on one floor, a '*spazza cucina*' on the other. The house also provided storage areas, a washroom at entry level and attic spaces, all organized around, above and below a central portico or large hall. A stone spiral staircase led to the upper floors, a narrow staircase to the attics. It is a long way to the 'stupendious' glories of St Mark's Square, 'a market place of the world, not of the city' according to one visiting Englishman. Cannaregio is, and remains, a different Venice. It is, and remains, the home of the Jews of Venice, who had been forced to settle in the foundry area (*getto*) away from the city's heart in the early decades of the sixteenth century. In Strozzi's time, the ghetto had expanded and its social and cultural structure had metamorphosed into a microcosm of different Jewish subcultures, despite the desperate overcrowding and restrictions upon all aspects of daily life. Indeed, by the end of the seventeenth century, two new synagogues had been built, the Schola Levantina and the Schola Spagnola (Ponentina). The church where Barbara was baptized, Santa Sofia, still stands, now facing a more recent Venetian institution, the fish market. It embodies something of the city, and its foremost female composer. Santa Sofia's date of foundation is hazy, perhaps as early as 886, perhaps not; no matter, myth is powerful in Venice. By Strozzi's own lifetime the records show that the church had already been rebuilt twice, first in the early thirteenth century, and then again in the composer's great-grandparents' generation. Now, in the late seventeenth century, Strozzi saw her baptismal church once again restored. Santa

Sofia would then burn to the ground, be rebuilt, suffer suppression under Napoleon, be sold to the Jewish community and finally reopen again as a church. Despite or because of all the rebuildings, the church's facade remains unfinished. Not only that, it is hidden, now by the priest's house, but as early as 1500 by the encroaching buildings. The campanile, once taller and more elegant according to the evidence of a woodcut of 1550, is now chunky and the interior is plain by the standards of Venice, not least because on its suppression most of the church's riches were dispersed, amongst them a Veronese *Last Supper*. Santa Sofia, half-hidden by the buildings that crowd around it, stripped of its glories, such as they were, and with little obvious beauty to it, is hardly a tourist magnet, but it endures, rising from the ashes again and again.

'Barbara of Santa Sofia' is the name by which the composer is known in the document created by Giulio Strozzi, living in Corte del Remer, in which he finally made the relationship between the two of them legally explicit, if not transparent: *Barbara di Santa Sofia mia figliola elettiva pero chiamata comunamente la Strozzi* (Barbara of Santa Sofia, my chosen daughter, but called generally La Strozzi). Does *elettiva* mean adopted, or is this an acknowledgement that Barbara is his natural daughter? In practice, the biological relationship between Giulio and Barbara was irrelevant by this stage. Barbara was Giulio's creation. She had taken his name over ten years earlier, and he had, at least by his own standards, acted as a father towards her. From one perspective, his ambition led her to a life of rape, prostitution, the bearing and solitary raising of children, and the threat and reality of public ignominy. Alternatively, Giulio found a path for his exceptional daughter that allowed for the expression of her musical virtuosity, precisely because it avoided the gilded cages of church and home.

Giulio died unexpectedly on 31 March 1652. Barbara ignored his request for a simple burial and terse inscription, '*senz altro lode, o cirimonie'* (without further praise or ceremony), and provided an eloquent memorial that appeared on the wall of the chapel of Madonna della Pace, in the church of Santa Giovanni e Paolo where so many of the great cultural figures of Venice have been honoured over the years. (Sadly, the inscription no longer survives.) Giulio had bequeathed to his daughter *elettiva* all his unpublished writings. Barbara did not get much else: a few books, a bed with a canopy, some clothing, some silver (which would not weigh even a hundred ounces, according to Giulio's depressing and depressed commentary in the will) and a few paintings. Giulio was not even able to provide for his own burial, and asks Barbara to do so, from her own money. The following year, although it is hard to be certain given the gaps in the historical record, Barbara lost her mother: a Madonna Isabella Strozzi died in the parish of Santi Apostoli on 31 July 1653. If Barbara had been, de facto, the provider for the family, including in recent years her father, then now she truly was the head of her family.

Giovanni Paolo Vidman, the father of at least three of her four children, had died in 1648, leaving nothing, at least officially, to Barbara, although a secret codicil is mentioned in the archive. Its contents may be visible in the events of 1656, when Vidman's wife, Camilla, paid the necessary spiritual dowry of 2,000 ducats so that Strozzi's two daughters could enter the convent of San Sepolcro in Venice, which was, conveniently, run by one of Mrs Vidman's relatives. Isabella Strozzi died only six months later, aged fifteen. Laura survived, changing her name to Sister Lodovica, and then, some thirteen years later, taking the family name Vidman, and receiving an annuity of twenty-five ducats per year from her natural father's brother, Martin Vidman. Their convent, San Sepolcro, founded in 1409 as a hostel for pilgrims, was suppressed in 1808, so all that survives are the portal, from a renovation of 1570, on the Riva degli Schiavone (now the entrance to the Presidio Militare), and a rather lovely altar table, resting on four kneeling angels, which migrated to a dark corner of the church of San Martino, close to the Arsenale. Carlotta Vidman's own daughters, it should be noted, were placed in the most exclusive and richest convent in Venice, that of San Daniele.

Despite these personal losses, and her unconventional status, Barbara Strozzi does not seem to have been poor at any time. In fact, Glixon describes her as a 'savvy investor', handling her business dealings confidently from her own home and, when she did loan out money, demanding interest. (Anna Renzi, in contrast, would make three loans, none for interest, each one to individuals poorer than she.) That Strozzi had 2,000 ducats available to loan to Giovanni Paolo Vidman in the 1640s tells its own story. The amount was presumably small change to Vidman, who would pay the astonishing sum of 100,000 ducats in order to buy his way into the Venetian nobility in 1646, but the loan yielded a good return for Strozzi, almost ten per cent compound interest.*

However, on 11 December 1651, when Strozzi restarted her publication programme, she was claiming poverty. It might just be significant that she is responding to a demand for tax. For six years, Venice had been waging an expensive war against the Ottoman Turks, focused on the struggle for control of the island of Crete (Candia to the Venetians). The war would continue for almost twenty more years, 'alternating truces and merciless sieges, characterized by acts of heroism and by innovations in warfare, countered by military blunders and ignominious retreats. For Venetians this was seen as a way of redeeming themselves, as an opportunity to

---

* The Vidmans were one of the first families to take advantage of the opportunity to buy one's way into the Venetian nobility. Only in 1645 had it become possible to do so, part of the city's response to the twin pressures of plague and economic decline during the 1630s.

demonstrate to the world that their armies were still in a position to overcome a powerful enemy.' They were not: Venice lost the war. But in 1651 there was still hope, and the state desperately needed money. Strozzi is having none of it:

Most Serene Prince: From the time that this Most Benign country succumbed to the torment of war, even I, Barbara Strozzi, Your Most Serene Highness's humble servant, lamented Her misadventures. As my condition did not permit me to help Her with my blood, I gathered up all my possessions: I sold my belongings, and deposited all of the money in the Mint, well in agreement that the public calamity should become the calamity of private wealth. I believed that having, with this voluntary sacrifice, done my duty to the possible limit of my resources, I would never be constrained to do the impossible. Nonetheless, I suddenly see myself obligated by a mandate of the Most Excellent Governors of Income to pay into the Mint two taxes of 100 ducats each. These were imposed on me when I found myself far from the city, and thus I could not be heard. I am persuaded that if the Most Excellent Tax Assessors had reflected with justice that I have four children in addition to my aged mother, and on my miserable fortunes, this harassment never would have occurred. One can see clearly in the public books that I do not have anything listed in the property tax rolls, and God only knows that if the little interest that comes to me from the Mint were lacking, I would surely have to beg for my sustenance from some other charity. Kneeling, I implore Your Excellency not to permit the destruction of a household unable to pay, that has devoted to the Public as much as it had [to give]. Kneeling, I implore you to pity the miseries

of a large family, and grant me pardon, so that my arguments will be heard by some tribunal; so that even I might
achieve that charitable relief that in this Most Serene State
has never been denied to the tears of poverty. Thank you.

Strozzi's pathetic eloquence worked, although it took three years
for the state to express its pity for her vulnerable condition. By
then, the composer was back on her feet, if she had ever been off
them, and once again able to loan money to others, and all without
any cushion of inheritance or support from either Giulio Strozzi or
Giovanni Paolo Vidman.

Through these years in Cannaregio, years in which the father of
her children died, her parents died and her daughters were
immured in San Sepolcro, Strozzi continued to compose and to
publish. Her opus 2 was dedicated to Ferdinand III of Austria and
Eleonora of Mantua, on the occasion of their marriage. The couple
are styled as Austrian Mars and Gonzaga Venus, no less. Ferdinand
and Eleonora did not even notice. Nothing had changed by opus 8.
Presented in a handwritten copy to Sophia of Braunschweig (the
mother of George I of England), this final work proved equally
unsuccessful in gaining patronage for its composer.* And yet,
despite, or indeed because of, these repeated failures, Strozzi had
continued to publish and it is this that makes her unique for her
era. Astonishingly, Barbara Strozzi had more music in print in her
lifetime than any other composer of the era, achieving this feat
with neither the support of the Church, nor the patronage of the

---

* Sophie had married Ernst August in 1658. He was a regular visitor to Venice,
especially during carnival, but 1664 was the first time Sophie had visited the
city. The Dukes of Brunswick usually rented the magnificent Ca' Foscari on the
Grand Canal. Sophie, writing her memoirs, recalls her time in Venice, but fails
to remember Strozzi.

nobility. It helped that she was in Venice, a city with the most sophisticated and the most liberal publishing industry in Europe. In Venice, Strozzi, without a conventional sexual reputation to protect, could not only perform and compose, but publish and be damned. Each of her works was prepared with great care. They are remarkably free from errors or ambiguities, with the scores presented in unusual detail, nuances of dynamics, tempi and ornaments all carefully explicated. These remarkable documents show a composer who cared how her work would survive, and wanted to ensure that it would.

In this, she stands apart from the majority of her male contemporaries, some of whom were thoroughly wary of the new tendency to set down scores at all, let alone in print. A generation before Strozzi, Jacobo Peri, ironically in the preface to his published *Euridice*, argued that his trade secrets, the very things for which he was renowned, could not possibly be 'completely indicated in notation'. He reminded his readers that to learn properly one had to work directly with the master. A couple of generations later, Antonio Vivaldi would stop publishing his music because he discovered that there was little financial reward in doing so in a society without copyright. Strozzi could not hope to make money from publishing her work, but she could create a public. So, in contrast to her male contemporaries, whose work could and did often remain in manuscript because their reputations and livelihoods did not depend on publication, Strozzi actively embraced print. The numbers speak for themselves. Whilst almost every composer of the era wrote cantatas, the percentage that were printed remained very low. Strozzi's contemporary Carissimi, for example, wrote 135 cantatas, but published only five of them. What is more, the work of male composers that did make it into print appeared in joint collections. Strozzi stands out again, because all her works are single-author volumes. Above all, for male composers, there were other means apart from print to ensure one's posterity. An established, highly successful figure such as Francesco Cavalli may have issued only two publications that we know of but he made careful provision for the performance of his own music after his death. Twice a year, his *Requiem* for two choirs was to be sung by the cappella and canons of San Marco, along with a daily mass that would be celebrated by one Caliari, whom Cavalli himself had raised and trained. Moreover, he bequeathed his collection of opera scores to the same man, who ensured that the works passed into the Contarini collection, which now includes all Cavalli's surviving operas. It is thus that a composer enters the canon.

Strozzi's publication programme was very much a Venetian phenomenon, but in so many other respects the city proved to be a double-edged sword to a woman and a composer. Yes, it was the city of light, the city of wonder, the city of exceptional talents: 'Let him who cannot amaze work in the stables' wrote Giambattista Marino, capturing the city's hunger for the virtuoso. Yes, Venice was the home of the libertines, intellectuals and artists who challenged conventional social and political values under the tolerant eye of the government, which allowed the airing of most subjects, so long as Venice's own form of aristocratic republicanism was never questioned. Yes, palaces became academies, where libertines and poets debated with sceptical philosophers, and librettists tried out their texts for the new musical phenomenon, public opera. Sixteen regularly functioning theatres catered for a city with only 140,000 inhabitants. Venice itself was, in the words of one historian, 'a kind of ongoing performance, the setting for many ritual events engaging large numbers of actors as well as spectators, ranging from the procession of the True Cross to the anarchy of Carnival'. A piece of pre-performance publicity for *La finta pazza*, written by a member of the Incogniti, not only articulates the symbiosis of opera with

Venice itself but also recognizes that both opera and Venice are international commodities:

> May the eyes of those even in the most distant and secluded foreign countries enjoy in these pages what eyes and ears have enjoyed in this city, which in its every aspect surpasses the bounds of the marvellous.

No wonder opera found its true home there, and no wonder that singers became the most important force in the music industry, whether on stage, in private or, even, in church. According to music historians, individual singers were worshipped like rock stars today, and might be paid twice as much as the composers of their music. Anna Renzi, admired and promoted by Giulio Strozzi from 1640, the star of his *La finta pazza* in 1641 (and of the first performance of *Poppea* in 1643), the recipient of 750 ducats for just one opera run, had a seventeen-year career of opera performance, working in Rome and Venice, whilst also achieving a secure position at the court in Innsbruck.

This was not Strozzi's path. Her final three works appeared in 1657, 1659 and 1664. With each work, she was becoming ever more confident and sophisticated as a composer, embracing works of greater scale and even more drama. Significantly, each work was prepared with an even higher number of performance indications than before, Strozzi working to ensure as precise, and as authentic, a legacy of her art as she could.

Is it fanciful to see her publication programme as a quest for professional recognition – part of her self-definition as composer first, singer second? Could she have been seeking a fourth way, beyond wife (impossible), nun (implausible) and courtesan/ concubine (only too plausible)? As a professional, published composer she could bypass the prince, not to mention the prince's bedroom, and go straight to her public.

If this was her strategy, then it worked, at least in the long term. The world came to Venice in the seventeenth century, as it still does today. Strozzi's compositions were purchased by tourists and circulated throughout Europe. Her reputation was an international one, evident in the comments of the eminent English music writer Charles Burney, some hundred years after Strozzi's death:

> The first time, however, that I found the term CANTATA used for a short narrative lyric was in the *Musiche varie a voce sola del Signior Benedetto Ferrari da Reggio*, printed in Venice; which is twenty years more early than the period at which the invention of cantatas is fixed by some writers, who have given the honour to BARBARA STROZZI, a Venetian lady, who in 1653, published vocal compositions under the title of CANTATE, Ariette e Duetti.*

He recognized the composer as an important contributor to and, in the eyes of some (if not Burney himself), even a possible originator of the cantata form in Italy.

Thirteen years after her last known publication, in May 1677, Barbara Strozzi is still living in Venice. Some time later, it is unclear when, she travels to Padua, the second city of the Venetian Republic, for reasons unknown and then in late summer or early autumn she falls ill. The register of deaths ends her story:

> Barbara Strozzi, 70 years old, ill for three months. Having had the holy sacrament of penance, she was overtaken suddenly and died. Her body is buried in the *Eremitani*.

---

* Strozzi's opus 2 was in fact published in 1651.

Although she had been ill for some time, her death came more swiftly than expected, since she received only the sacrament of penance on 11 November, the day of her death, rather than the full last rites. The scribe gets her age wrong, suggesting that no one who knew Barbara Strozzi was with her when she died. Certainly none of her surviving children were present. Strozzi's eldest son, Giulio Pietro, custodian of her work, would do nothing to secure his mother's legacy, exposing her portraits and manuscripts 'to the ravages of time' in the words of one contemporary, before attempting to sell them off cheap.

Strozzi, just as so many other women of her time and place, was for much of her life a mere puppet, whether of her father, Vidman, the Incogniti, the Duke of Mantua, indeed of Venice itself. No noble household offered Strozzi a post as a *cantatrice*, let alone as a composer. Her children did not, perhaps could not, honour her. The shadow of the courtesan, present in the lives of all women composers, still present now in the way we seek to understand them, looms particularly large for Barbara Strozzi.* Yet I believe that Strozzi was on a quest for something like professional recognition as a composer. That she died alone, with no memorial, suggests she failed, at least in her lifetime. The record of her quest, those remarkable seven collections of music, means that, close on four hundred years after her birth, her ability as a composer is at last gaining the acknowledgement she sought, and that her music deserves.

* The idea seeps in everywhere. Strozzi is buried next to the Scrovegni Capella, 'which houses Giotto's superlative frescoes of the repentant courtesan Mary Magdalene', as one editor of Strozzi's music cannot resist pointing out.

'Elle est originale' King Louis XIV

Chapter Three

JACQUET DE LA GUERRE

Paris, as much as Venice, has a special place in our mythology of cities of culture. The American writer, Henry Miller, speaks for many who have visited the city in search of inspiration, or to escape the rigidities of their native land: 'I will write here. I will live quietly and quite alone. And each day I will see a little more of Paris, study it, learn it as I would a book. It is worth the effort. To know Paris is to know a great deal.' Miller, in the early 1930s, was not the first by a long way, nor would he be the last, to launch his career in Paris and be fed creatively by Paris before returning to his own land, renewed. But what of the artist who is not a visitor, but born and bred in Paris, whose life is focused on one small island on the Seine, the Ile Saint-Louis? What of an artist who is not free to travel from her own land? What of an artist who is dependant on the protection of an all-powerful king, the epitome of the absolute monarch, a man-god whose theatre state is maintained through surveillance and repression? What of an artist whose career starts in that same king's magnificent, if economy-breaking, palace, a 'synthesis of stagecraft and statecraft', and who must shape her every note to his tastes? This is the story of one such artist, the composer Élisabeth Jacquet de la Guerre, of her king, Louis XIV, and of Paris.

Jacquet de la Guerre knew Paris, which meant she knew a great deal. More precisely, she knew a particular corner of the city. Élisabeth-Claude Jacquet, as she was named at her baptism on

17 March 1665, was shaped by the island of her birth, the Ile Saint-Louis. Élisabeth's island on the Seine was itself shaped by the booming French economy during this first decade of the Sun King's long personal reign, a period of 'peace, prosperity, and cultural creativity'. As recently as her grandparents' time, it had been the *Ile aux Vaches*, pasture for the cows (*vaches*) of the cathedral of Notre Dame on the neighbouring island. By the time of Élisabeth's birth, the vision of successive French kings had been realized, and the masterpiece of urban construction, the grid of elegant townhouses that cover the Ile Saint-Louis today, had been created, the cows long gone. Strolling around what is today the exclusive, and unnervingly expensive, Ile Saint-Louis it would be easy to imagine that Élisabeth Jacquet was born into a Parisian elite. The reality was, however, somewhat different.

For decades, the Jacquet family had been master masons (what we would now call architects), musicians, composers and instrument makers. Jehan Jacquet, Élisabeth's grandfather, and her father, Claude, were both master harpsichord makers, working when Paris was becoming a centre for such luxury trades. Jacquet harpsichords retained their status and prestige right through the eighteenth century, and an inventory taken at Claude's death reveals a treasury of exquisite instruments: harpsichords (of course), epinettes (an ancestor of the dulcimer) and manichordions (a kind of clavichord), many ready to sell, some still being constructed, together with pieces of pine and beech wood, and all the tools of the instrument-maker's trade. Claude not only made instruments, he played them as well. Indeed, he was appointed organist of the new church of Saint-Louis, the foundation stone of which had been laid on 1 October 1664, just a few months before the birth of his daughter Élisabeth.

The Jacquet family's trades put them in close proximity to the nobility, who might require an architect for their latest project, or a luxury harpsichord for entertaining, but the family were far from noble themselves. They were, and remained, artisans, but artisans who operated within a vast web of alliances linking families and trades, facilitating business deals and creating job opportunities.* Claude Jacquet educated his sons *and* his daughters to survive, and thrive, in this world. Élisabeth and her older sister Anne would both become musicians. Élisabeth would go even further. She would be a composer.

Her journey started at a very young age. How young has been a matter of debate. She is often represented as a child prodigy, which neatly assimilates her into some very traditional ways in which women of ability and achievement are represented. If understood as a child prodigy, then Jacquet becomes a one-off, unique, a lone genius whose gift appears as if by magic, and who can be separated from the rest of her (imperfect) sex. The music scholar Suzanne Cusick makes the point about Francesca Caccini and her fellow female performers/composers in an earlier era, and a different setting, Italy of the 1600s, showing that these women were represented as angels or sorceresses, not truly human, 'never what they actually are ... formidably talented musicians'. To represent Jacquet as a dazzling five-year-old, as she is often depicted, or to talk about her in terms of the supernatural or magical world, as she was portrayed in her own lifetime, serves to diminish or distract from her status as a formidably talented, not to mention hardworking, professional adult performer/composer. This is not to say that Jacquet did not display exceptional talent at a very young age. But commentators in Jacquet's own time, perhaps Jacquet herself, emphasized or even exaggerated her feats as a child if only to

---

* Élisabeth's mother was Anne de La Touche, a widow when she married Claude. Her first husband had been in the service of the Duke of Orléans, the king's brother.

increase the glory and perspicacity of her king who, the story went, was the first to recognize the little girl's talent when she performed at his palace of Versailles, aged five. Élisabeth was twenty-two when the journal *Mercure Galant* wrote that 'she had always been regarded as a prodigy' and, in the same year, the composer put on record her own gratitude to the king for 'having taken an interest in her education' and for finding in her 'at the age of five, a certain disposition for playing the harpsichord'. There obviously was a Versailles performance from the very young Élisabeth, but other comments make clear that Jacquet's early career unfolded steadily over a number of years, and in less spectacular ways. She spends 'a long period of retreat' with her father, during which time she pursues 'continuous study', presumably including composition. The next time she surfaces in the court records, it is a July evening in 1677, and she sings a song in praise of Louis XIV to the delight of the court, and, most importantly, the king. The lyrics consisted of the kind of sycophantic drivel that fuelled the cult of the Sun King, but Élisabeth's freshness of performance was highly valued. She was twelve. Some eighteen months later, Élisabeth is mentioned again, as one of the musicians involved in the Thursday concerts at the residence of the lutenist, dancer and composer, Louis de Mollier. This was another stepping-stone towards a life as an adult professional musician. Mollier was well-placed at court, the master of the music for the dauphin, and of the children of the chamber and the chapel. The *Mercure Galant* records that the 'young Élisabeth Jacquet took part in these performances by playing the *clavecin* [harpsichord]', and goes on to suggest that it was on the basis of these performances that some of Mollier's musicians were taken into the service of the noblewoman Gabrielle de Rochechouart, who had apartments in the palace of the Louvre. This may well have been Élisabeth's formal entry into court service.

Neither anecdote suggests that Jacquet was a prodigy. She is simply another very talented young girl, on the cusp of womanhood, making her way as a musician in the court of the Sun King. In this, she was following a similar path to her older sister, Anne, who was employed in the service of Marie de Lorraine, Madame de la Guise, as a '*fille de la musique*', and a '*femme de chambre*', both traditional (and traditionally combined) court roles. Madame de la Guise, based in Paris, and, by the time Anne entered her household, the last Guise standing, was known for her love of music and her patronage of musicians. Since she had little left to fight for politically, Madame de la Guise devoted herself to the support of, amongst other things, the cause of Italian music, which set her at odds with the French musical establishment, led, of course, by the Italophobe Louis XIV. (In her youth, during the 1630s, Madame de la Guise had been exiled to Medici Florence, the same decade in which Francesca Caccini returned to her home city and La Crocetta.) The duchess's favoured composer was Marc-Antoine Charpentier and, by the early 1680s, she had developed a group of musicians that rivalled, in the words of one contemporary, the ensembles of 'several sovereigns'. Élisabeth's sister was, therefore, living and working at the cutting edge of music in Paris.

It did not take long for Élisabeth to make the crucial transition from her patron, Gabrielle de Rochechouart, at the Louvre, to her patron's sister at Versailles. She was in her mid-teens when she entered the service of Madame de Montespan, the principal mistress of Louis XIV.* In doing so, she entered a world fraught

---

* The prodigy stories refuse to lie down and die, with one story saying that Élisabeth was 'given' to the king's principal mistress, Madame de Montespan, when she was only eight, c. 1673, and another having the young Élisabeth noticed by Madame de Montespan, and brought into her entourage, or under her protection, again at a very young age.

with sexual politics, as much, if not more, challenging than those negotiated by Caccini in Florence or Strozzi in Venice. All servants of that most absolute of absolute monarchs, Louis XIV, had to operate in an environment in which keeping up with, but not being caught out by, the king's choice of mistress (or more precisely mistresses) remained a daily challenge, but Élisabeth joined the household of Françoise Athénaïs de Rochechouart de Mortemart, the Marquise de Montespan, at a particularly critical moment in her mistress's career.

Born in 1640, just two years after Louis XIV himself, Athénaïs had been introduced to the king at Versailles in the autumn of 1666, and became one of his mistresses the following year. It was a double infidelity. Both the king and Athénaïs were married: three years prior to her arrival at Versailles, Montespan had given birth to a daughter, Marie Christine, and then a son, Louis, born in 1664, by her husband. It was, of course, Montespan's marital status that presented a problem, rather than the king's. For eight years the situation was ignored, and Madame de Montespan's influence grew unchecked. By the age of thirty-four, in 1674, she had been elevated to the position of the king's official favourite, displacing Mademoiselle de la Vallière. Throughout these years she did as all Louis's mistresses did: bore his children (a daughter in 1669, a son in 1670, another son in 1672). All three were legitimized in 1673. Madame de Montespan remained married. By 1674, the king had engineered an official separation between his mistress and her husband, much to the disapproval of the Church. If only to placate Louis's Jesuit confessor, a temporary, strategic estrangement between the king and his mistress ensued, but by 1676 it appeared that Madame de Montespan's position was secure. She bore her king two further children, in 1677 and 1678, the ultimate sign of her intimacy with the king.

With intimacy, came power. Her apartments were next to those of the king, a proximity that meant everything in an absolute monarchy, in which all power was invested in the body of the king. Louis XIV may not have actually said '*L'État c'est moi*' but he might as well have done. No wonder, then, that at the height of Madame de Montespan's power it was said she was 'the centre of the court, and of the pleasures, fortune, hope and terror of the ministers and army generals'. Artists and musicians also depended upon her, amongst them the writers Molière and La Fontaine. If Élisabeth was taken up by Madame de Montespan, possibly via her older sister, Gabrielle Rochechouart, as early as 1677, when Élisabeth was twelve, then the young performer would have entered the service of a woman at the very pinnacle of her political and cultural power, newly freed from her marriage, and each year pregnant with a child of the king. If, as seems most likely, Élisabeth entered Montespan's service later, when she was about fifteen, c. 1680, then the situation was very different.

Already, in the earlier period, the warning signs had been there. Madame de Montespan had hired a woman of impeccable character to act as governess to her children by the king. Françoise d'Aubigne was excellent in the role, in effect raising the children herself. She became a good friend of Montespan, and then, more problematically, a good friend to the king, who gave her the title Madame de Maintenon in 1674 in recognition of the quality of her service to his children. As the years passed, Madame de Maintenon's influence over the king himself grew, to the dismay of her erstwhile employer, Montespan. By January 1684, the former governess reigned supreme for, although it remained a secret to the public, the king had married her some six months after the death of his wife, Maria Theresa.

It was not, however, the rise of Madame de Maintenon that was the most potent threat to Élisabeth's patron's security when the teenager began her stint at court. It was a young woman, only a couple of years older than Élisabeth, who did the damage: the Duchess of Fontanges, with whom Louis XIV became infatuated in the winter of 1679. The king's behaviour with his teenage mistress was extreme even by his own standards, and both Montespan and Maintenon were horrified both by the king's antics and the erosion of their own influence. Then, in June 1681, the nineteen-year-old duchess died.

It is now thought that she died due to complications connected with a miscarriage, but at the time there were those quick to point out not only that Madame de Montespan, in her desperation, had been directly or indirectly involved with sorceresses and necromancy, but even to suggest that she had poisoned her rival. A judicial enquiry, which had been precipitated by news of a plot to poison the king (rather than his teenage mistress), revealed, in the words of one historian, 'a vast criminal underworld in seventeenth-century Paris made up of the purveyors of secret and supposedly magical powers. Stranger still was that this underworld was frequented by Parisians from every level of society, including some of Louis XIV's most trusted and high-ranking courtiers.' Sordid revelations of torture, poison, abortions and witchcraft emerged throughout the enquiry's proceedings, but when, in 1782, the investigation seemed to implicate Madame de Montespan, Louis stepped in, and the enquiry was swiftly closed down. The damage, however, had now been done. The king, it was said, never visited Madame de Montespan alone after these revelations. Her years of power were effectively over.

Versailles was, and remains, a very special environment in which to come to maturity as a woman and composer. The palace may still have been under construction during Jacquet's time there, since the transformation of Louis XIII's hunting lodge had only begun in the year of Élisabeth's conception, 1664, and Louis XIV would not transfer himself, and therefore his government, completely to Versailles until 1782, but it was already an over-whelming architectural symbol of the Sun King's absolute rule.

Even the most functional of rooms, such as the *salle des gardes du roi* (the room of the king's bodyguard) had wall hangings of leather decorated with gold, high art on the walls, chandeliers complete with the king's monogram, all alongside the benches and camp beds used by the king's men. At its height, Versailles would contain three thousand courtiers and functioned as an immense theatre of power, within which, some argue, women occupied a central place. Since the king's body was the repository of royal and God-given authority, it followed that his mistresses, who had access to that body, wielded strategic political power even if they never held formal political positions. Some historians have even suggested that Jacquet's youth was a golden age for women since, if persuasion, negotiation and ingratiation were the only means of advancement in Louis's Versailles, then women became the power-brokers at court. Perhaps. But the Duchess of Fontanges was dead at nineteen. And Élisabeth Jacquet witnessed at close quarters the fall of her own patron, Madame de Montespan, if not her patron's physical destruction. In fact, she was discarded surprisingly slowly. It took until 1691 for Montespan to leave the court, with a golden handshake of a half-a-million francs with which she began her new life at the monastery of Saint-Joseph in Paris.

Like Francesca Caccini and Barbara Strozzi, in Florence and Venice, the young Élisabeth learned her trade in a world fraught with sexual politics, but Jacquet faced a further challenge since she was fated to come of age during the closing years of what can only be described as the cultural reign of the composer Jean-Baptiste Lully. By any measure of success, Lully was a winner. Born in Florence, he became the epitome of French culture, the right-hand man, musically speaking, of King Louis XIV. His appointment as *surintendant de la musique de la chambre de roi* in 1661 signalled the beginning of a remarkable decade during which Italian opera was imported into the French court. The same year, Barbara Strozzi's contemporary Cavalli was brought over to Paris from Venice to write an opera in celebration of Louis XIV's marriage to Maria Theresa of Spain. Cavalli's six-hour spectacle *Ercole amante* (Hercules in Love) was certainly enjoyed, although more in rehearsals at Cardinal Mazarin's palace than in the 'vastness of the theatre', but it was Lully's dance music that stole the show. Lully, already established as the foremost composer of the king's favourite art form, ballet, swiftly moved to establish himself as the king of French opera. Cavalli returned to Venice.

From the start, Lully understood the need, Louis XIV's need, to establish a recognizably French opera, one that catered not only to the nationalist agenda, but also to the cultural tastes of the Sun King himself. He duly injected substantial quantities of dance into the Italian opera format, together with elaborate political prologues and epilogues in praise of the monarch. Given his chance, Lully became a ruthless operator in the music world, systematically sidelining his competitors, by fair means or foul, all the time protected by his king. The founding of the Académie Royale de Musique, (created in 1669 as the Academie d'Opéra, soon to be known as the Paris Opera, and established by royal patent 'for the presentation of French prose set to music') merely gave Lully a new arena for his dominance. From 1673, and the king's attendance at one of the composer's 'tragedies in music' (as French opera was often known), Lully was unassailable. When the king permitted the composer to use the Palais-Royal free of charge, and Molière and his actors were removed from their own theatre in Paris, the knives started to come out for Lully but, although the hostility in Paris was such that opera performances were moved to Versailles, this merely consolidated Lully's position further.

But even Jean-Baptiste Lully could fall foul of the king, or, more precisely, his mistress. In 1677, at exactly the time when the twelve-year-old Élisabeth Jacquet was charming the court with her unaffected singing, Lully's most significant collaborator, the librettist Quinault, was being forced out of the court. Quinault's mistake (not Lully's, of course) was to insult Madame de Montespan in his *'tragédie en musique, Isis'*. As Caccini had found at the court of the Medici, libretti could be dangerous things, with everyone quick to spot a contemporary application for an old story. Quinault recovered his place fairly soon, no doubt helped by the waning of Montespan's power. Lully continued on his way, with the king – and therefore the court – turning a blind eye to the married composer's preference for young men as sexual partners. Only later, in the 1680s, and probably due to the influence of the morally correct, religiously minded Madame de Maintenon, did Lully's openly homosexual activities lead to a gulf between him and his king, most notable in Louis's absence from the premier of the composer's masterpiece, *Armide*. And yet, Lully had achieved a position of such power, and remained such a ruthless businessman, that even this sign of royal displeasure could not displace him from the control of the French music world, from the Paris Opera to the Palais-Royal.

Lully's Versaille. Lully's Paris. This was the world in which Élisabeth Jacquet continued, and enhanced, the musical education begun by her father, and in which she made the, what is for some, challenging transition from child performer to professional adult. Like her predecessors Caccini and Strozzi, Jacquet was a brilliant improviser and, like them, she made the leap from improviser/performer to composer, probably around the year 1680 when she was sixteen. Ironically, the fact that we know almost nothing of Élisabeth's life during these years at Versailles is a sign of her success. Despite the ubiquity of scandal of all kinds in the court of the Sun

King, Jacquet flew under the radar. What is more, she continued to function as performer and composer in the entourage of a woman whose own political career was on the verge of destruction. It is possible that the certain knowledge that Madame de Montespan was on the way out, and the glimpses of Parisian (rather than Versailles) musical life that Élisabeth would have gained through her older sister, Anne, made the next step in Élisabeth's life an easy one.

On 23 September 1684, and not yet twenty, Élisabeth was married to Marin La Guerre. The marriage returned her nominally, and then physically, to the creative and artisan dynasties into which she had been born. Within a few months, the couple were settled back on the Ile Saint-Louis, probably staying with or very close to Élisabeth's parents in the rue Guillaume (now rue Budé). Élisabeth would from now on use both her own and her husband's surnames. Not merely a sign of her pedigree, the double surname is a musical advertisement, an early sign of her determination to continue her professional career after marriage. Five years later, her older sister would take a different path. When Anne married a fellow servant of the Duchess of Guise (one Louis Yard, a *valet de chambre*) in 1689, it marked the end of her life as a professional musician. In 1684, when Élisabeth married Marin, the story would be very different. For Élisabeth's French biographer the reason for this lies in ability and personality. Élisabeth was simply more gifted, more self-willed and more ambitious than her sister.

Far from closing the door on a musical career, marriage actually increased the possibilities for Madame Jacquet de la Guerre. Two Ile Saint-Louis dynasties were joined in the union, and some might say that La Guerre's pedigree was even better than Jacquet's. Élisabeth's new husband came from a dynasty of organists. His grandfather had been appointed the organist of the cathedral of Notre Dame at the age of only fourteen and then, after fourteen years in that post, gained the even more prestigious position of organist at the magnificent Sainte-Chapelle. Marin's father was equally successful, and Marin himself began married life as the organist of the Jesuit church of Saint-Paul-Saint-Louis (where Lully had learned his counterpoint) in the Marais, and then moved to Saint-Séverin, on the other side of the river, four years later. Marin La Guerre reached his highest position in 1698, when his older brother, Jerome, gave up his post as organist at Sainte-Chapelle. Jerome, of course, requested that his brother be appointed in his place, and so it came to pass. With up to eight chaplains, twelve clergy, eight children in the choir and permanent precentors, La Guerre's life was a musically rich one. Indeed, Sainte-Chapelle has been described as almost a music college, with the Master of Music, supported by the organist, directing the singers, teaching them plainchant and counterpoint, and managing the players of the traditional church instruments of serpents, cornets and bassoons. Above all, of church organs, Sainte-Chapelle's was one of the best in the country, recently restored to all its glory.

Marin La Guerre's career through to his appointment at Sainte-Chapelle is visible to us now because, and only because, he held official positions within the church. Those posts, of course, were not open to his wife. But the silence of the archives is broken by Élisabeth Jacquet de la Guerre. In 1687, at the age of only twenty-two, and three years after her marriage to Marin, she published *Les pièces de clavecin: Livre I*. It is tempting to speculate that, with the downfall of Madame de Montespan, and her own removal to Paris, Jacquet de la Guerre was seeking an identity outside the world of court patronage. After all, the frontispiece to the work gives the composer's address on the Ile-Saint-Louis, and instructs the reader to go to a particular Paris bookseller.

But *Les pièces de clavecin* marked no simple rejection of the court and embracing of the city. Instead, the work positions Jacquet de la Guerre directly as a loyal subject of the king himself. Indeed, the music is published through royal authority, a hint that the pieces had been played, first, to the king and were now, through his majesty's kindness, being given to his grateful public. Jacquet de la Guerre may have lost her most powerful female patron, Madame de Montespan, but Louis XIV remained alive and well, and a fountain of plenty.

This first publication from Jacquet de la Guerre presents itself as the work of a young but also a confident composer, in demand and even internationally known. At the same time, the dedication, addressed to the king himself, is an expression of abject servility from 'the most humble, the most obedient, the most faithful, the most obliging servant and subject Elizabeth Jacquet' [sic], as she signs herself (hinting that the works themselves were composed while she was still Mademoiselle Jacquet at Versailles). Her dedication is followed by two poems in praise of the composer and, by implication, the king. She is a marvel, in this reign of marvels. She deserves a place on Mount Parnassus, with the Muses. She is 'learned Jacquet', her voice and her playing exemplifying the power of music to touch the listener.

The poems are written by a cousin by marriage of Élisabeth's, René Trépagne, and the one thing he does not exaggerate is the loveliness of this collection of pieces assembled by his relative. Unsurprisingly, as a composer, Jacquet shows herself utterly familiar with the work of both her predecessors and contemporaries (after all, she had been playing their music night after night through her teens) and as an expert in counterpoint, testament to her many years of education. Her pieces have been praised for their 'delightful melodic lines', the sense of balance both within and across the works, but also for their expressiveness, unpredictability and innovation. Most notably, Jacquet's unmeasured preludes, that is, movements composed without orthodox indications of rhythm and metre, are a striking example of her ability to capture the listener's interest. One gets the sense that this is a composer who wants to be noticed.

Was it merely coincidence that this glittering collection of keyboard pieces appeared just weeks before the death of the composer Lully, who had so dominated the Académie Royale de la Musique for the previous fifteen years? If Jacquet de la Guerre was signalling her readiness to take a prominent place in the post-Lully musical world, then she underestimated the composer's power even beyond the grave. Four years pass in which there remains little to indicate whether Jacquet de la Guerre lives or dies, let alone works. It is hard to believe she was inactive, but the records keep their counsel. Then, in 1691, there is a glimpse of her as composer. What is more, it is a glimpse which shows that, in this very year of Madame de Montespan's final exile from court, Jacquet de la Guerre is not merely surviving, but thriving, as the composer of an opera-ballet for the king. Sadly, the single surviving manuscript contains the libretto, the scenery, the dances, Jacquet's dedication to the king, and even the instrumentation for *Jeux à l'honneur de la victoire* (Games in Honour of the Victory), but no music.[*]

In the dedication, the composer acknowledges that she has been delighted to serve the king in a private capacity, but, now:

> [Those previous] signs of my devotion seemed to me insufficient and I longed for an opportunity to express my devotion publicly. That is what led me to compose this Ballet for the Theatre. Women have already given excellent pieces of poetry therein, which have been most

---

[*] Musicologists have traditionally seen the 1697 work of Antoine Houdar de la Motte and André Campra, *L'Europe galante*, as the first opera-ballet. Jacquet de la Guerre's *Jeux à l'honneur de la victoire* was composed six years earlier, meaning that the honours should go to her.

successful. But so far, none has attempted to set a whole opera to music; and I take that advantage for my undertaking, that the more extraordinary it is, the more worthy it is of you, Sire, and the more it authorises the liberty I take in presenting this work to you.

Jacquet de la Guerre knows exactly what it means for her, a woman, to 'set a whole opera to music', and, barely concealed by her humility towards her king, she glories in it.

Jacquet de la Guerre's reputation was growing stronger with each year. In December 1691, the *Mercure Galant* was once again extolling the composer's virtues, this time in the form of a long poem 'written' by the ghost of Lully from the Elysian Fields, addressing himself to the 'best musician in the world'. In response probably to *Jeux à l'honneur de la victoire* – although perhaps to another work, now lost, of which one has to assume there are many – Jacquet de la Guerre garners nine pages of praise, both for her '*opera nouveau*' and for being remarkable amongst her sex. She is crowned Lully's successor, and the king's support and admiration for her 'happy genius' is noted. The poem ends with the vision of Lully, together with Orpheus and Amphion, drinking a toast to Élisabeth Jacquet de la Guerre.

It all looks so plausible on paper. But the events of the next few years would show that the ghost of Lully could work in less benign ways. Lully had created a 'distinctive national opera', primarily because of his unassailable position from 1672 at the Académie Royale de Musique (or Paris Opéra), and his mixed model was so successful that it continued well beyond his death in 1687, consolidated by the publication of the composer's oeuvre, beginning in 1679, which 'essentially established a national repertory and a permanent tradition', according to one music guide. What has become known as the Lully effect was stifling upon new music. If you wanted audiences, you simply revived the works of Lully rather than commissioning new work.

In this stifling musical climate, Jacquet de la Guerre continued to compose. Seven years after Lully's death, and three years after her opera-ballet, she turned to writing a *tragédie en musique*. (Again, one assumes that she was busy in the intervening years, but, again, no works have survived.) The 'new opera from the little La Guerre' made her 'the talk of Paris', according to one correspondent. The word on the ground was that it was going to be a great success: 'I have seen two rehearsals; it will be excellent.' In the event, the opera was, at best, a 'semi-failure'. First performed on 15 March 1694 at the Théâtre du Palais-Royal, *Céphale et Procris* had only five or six performances. Various explanations have been and continue to be given for the disappointing reception of Jacquet de la Guerre's one surviving opera. Perhaps the most touching can be found in the *Histoire de l'Académie Royale de Musique*, which recounts that, the day after the premier, Marin La Guerre 'who tenderly loved and respected his wife' met with several of those who had criticized the new opera, told them to be quiet, and then said: '*Messieurs*, I assure you that my wife's opera is a fine work [*est fort bon*], it is merely that the overture is too long.' More damaging was the work's weak libretto in a musical culture, which insisted on the primacy of the

---

* The opera involved first a prologue in celebration of the glory of King Louis XIV, then a love quadrangle between Céphale, a warrior; Procris, the daughter of the King of Athens; Borée, Prince of Thrace (in love with Procris and Céphale's rival); and the goddess Aurora, in love with Céphale. Things do not end happily. Aurora, believing that Céphale has rejected her, casts a spell to make Procris believe that Céphale has been unfaithful to her, but then changes her mind and convinces Procris that Céphale has always been true to her. However, disaster awaits. Procris intervenes in a fight between her two lovers, Céphale accidentally wounds her with an arrow, and the opera ends with Procris's death, and Céphale inconsolable.

text in opera, to the extent that a work such as *Céphale et Procris* would be known as a *tragédie en musique* (a tragedy put into music) or even simply a 'tragedy', with opera remaining, in the words of one musicologist, 'French literary theatre recited musically'.

Jacquet de la Guerre's contemporaries also fell foul of a French musical culture that was wary of contemporary opera. Opera might flourish in Italy 'thanks to its ability to entertain tourists', but the French 'discuss Italian opera like a culinary object that was not a real alternative to proper food'. In Paris, a nostalgic cabal was devoted to perpetuating the Lully tradition beyond the grave – so much for the vote of confidence from Lully's ghost! – with composers such as Marc-Antoine Charpentier being deemed too modern, too Italianate. Unlike Charpentier, Jacquet de la Guerre does not venture too far away from Lully in her opera, showing more musical caution in *Céphale et Procris* than she does in her other works from this time. Could it have been simply the presence of a female composer in the halls of the Académie Royale that was enough to ruffle Parisian feathers? If so, it is ironic that *Céphale et Procris* and its composer get into the music history books precisely because Jacquet de la Guerre can be noted as the 'first woman in France to compose an opera', or, more precisely, the first 'tragedy in music written by a woman for the Académie Royale de Musique'.

The reception of *Céphale et Procris* tells us more about the world of opera, and about French music in the 1690s, than it does about the ability of the composer herself. What is frustrating for those of us who admire her music is that the lack of success with *Céphale et Procris* seems to stop Jacquet de la Guerre at least in her opera tracks. She would not compose another '*tragédie en musique*', nor indeed any other kind of opera.

She did, nevertheless, take the trouble to publish the work. As before, she addresses her monarch in the most humble, obsequious of terms, drawing attention to his long-standing support for her career. There is a fascinating hint that there has been a hiatus of some kind. Jacquet de la Guerre refers to a misfortune of fate (*malheur de mon sort*) that has made it impossible, for a time, to give her life to the king's service, to put her talents to work for his glory. She quickly moves on to remind the king, and her readers, that she has been active in his service for many years, indeed since her childhood, providing entertainment on many occasions. The dedication ends by insisting that the public, as much as the king, need to know the extent of her ardent and respectful zeal for the king's 'sacred person', and signs off, as before 'the most humble, most obedient, & most faithful servant and subject. JACQUET'.

What was the misfortune that prevented Élisabeth devoting herself to the service of the king? It is just possible that the preface is a veiled allusion to the fall of Madame de Montespan, whose name is tantalizingly associated in the records with the genesis of *Céphale et Procris*, and whose final departure from Versailles occurred in the year of the opera's performance. Earlier, in the year after Élisabeth's marriage, Montespan, at that time still just about clinging to her position at court, if no longer the mistress of the king, was offered three operas to consider for the winter season. One was *Céphale et Procris*. It was chosen, but would not be performed in 1685. This was hardly surprising, given the collapse in Montespan's cultural influence, and the concomitant rise of her successor, Madame de Maintenon, who was far from being an opera fan. When the opera that, apparently, Madame de Montespan had wanted back in 1685 was finally performed nine years later, it would be staged at the Palais-Royal, a building that epitomized the fraught world of high politics, or, more precisely, sexual high politics, and even more precisely, a building from which Montespan had recently been very publicly excluded.

At the time of Élisabeth's birth, Louis XIV's brother, the Duke of Orléans, was in residence at the Palais-Royal, busy transforming the gardens and buildings into the social centre of Paris, the city that the king had by now come to fear. The Palais-Royal nevertheless worked to feed the king's sexual appetites at Versailles. Both Louise de la Vallière and Madame de Montespan entered the court world by first joining the household of the Duchess of Orléans, before moving on to bigger and better things at Versailles. Later, the short-lived Duchess of Fontanges was in the service of the Orléans's daughter, Marie-Louise, before she too became the king's mistress. In 1692, two years before the eventual performance of Jacquet de la Guerre's opera-ballet *Jeux à l'honneur de la victoire* and one year after Madame de Montespan's final departure from Versailles, the king chose the Palais-Royal as the venue for the marriage of one of his children by Montespan, the fourteen-year-old Françoise-Marie de Bourbon. Her husband would be the king's nephew, Philippe d'Orléans, only son of the king's brother. The groom's father did well out of the marriage: he was deeded the Palais-Royal. The bride's mother, Madame de Montespan, did less well. She was not even invited.

Jacquet de la Guerre, in her hints about misfortune and her restatement of devotion to Louis XIV, could well be reminding the king that his favourites may come and go, but she, the composer, remains loyal to him only. This might explain why she again signs her work JACQUET, the name by which Louis XIV knew her first. However, despite the brave words in the dedication, and despite some archival evidence that Jacquet de la Guerre's opera continued to be played, if only in the houses of amateurs, *Céphale et Procris* marked the end of an era. For thirteen years, the composer published nothing.

When Élisabeth emerges again from the historical mists in 1698, she is living very well. She and Marin had a large reception room, three bedrooms, a small office (*cabinet*), a kitchen and an attic in the Palais de la Cité, now the Palais de Justice. Their home can be glimpsed in a contemporary engraving of the Cour du Palais. They are on one side of the courtyard; on the other, the reason they were there: La Sainte-Chapelle.

The *salle* was the heart of the apartment for the two musicians, perhaps more so for Élisabeth than for Marin, whose main responsibilities lay in the church opposite. The room was richly furnished. Along with her harpsichord, there were at least six armchairs, four couches and four chairs. It is easy to imagine gatherings for concerts, the walls draped with tapestries celebrating the power of the king. The room also contained something of a library, including six folio volumes containing the works of the ubiquitous Lully, and numerous other works of theology, history and other equally learned subjects.

The nature of Jacquet de la Guerre's reception room, with its instruments and seating, makes it tempting to imagine her presiding over a salon. It is probably an inappropriate vision, for a number of reasons. It is one thing to describe the literary and musical gatherings initiated and bank-rolled by courtiers such as the Duchess of Guise in their lavish *hôtels* as salons. It is another to describe a concert held by petit-bourgeois, artisan-class Jacquet de la Guerre as a salon. Class matters, even in the etymology of the word *salon* itself. It means, literally, a large reception room (from the Italian *sala*), but during Jacquet de la Guerre's working life the word was first used in Versailles to connote the musical performances that took place in certain architectural spaces, specifically courtly, noble, architectural spaces. The women who did preside over salons used them to generate and maintain bonds of private patronage, whether of literature, art or music, and had the means to support and champion the work of protégé composers. Jacquet de la Guerre's older sister, Anne, had direct experience of this in her position as a musician in the service of Marie de Lorraine, Duchess of Guise, the patron of Charpentier. Even in these noble salons, music often remained a secondary element. Musicians were hired and works were commissioned, to provide background entertainment in most cases, or interludes between conversation, as had been the case in Venice in Strozzi's time and would be the case in many so-called salons well into the eighteenth century.

Perhaps not a salon, therefore, in the beautiful *salle* at the Palais de la Cité. Perhaps something even better: an apartment where Jacquet de la Guerre performs, hears others perform, where up to a point the classes could mingle, and in which she could maintain her practice and identity as performer, teacher and composer, a place to make music and connections.

Into these rooms we can, tentatively, put our image of Jacquet de la Guerre as depicted in the rather lovely portrait on the cover of this book. Tentatively, because uncertainties abound: the painter is probably François de Troy; the painting was probably exhibited in the Louvre in the summer of 1704; and it is probably of Jacquet de la Guerre.* Circumstantial evidence does link the portrait with the composer, since the instrument that appears in the painting is very similar to the 'large Flemish dual-keyboard harpsichord' in Jacquet de la Guerre's possession, and, what is more, the artist, Troy, had in his youth produced tapestries for Madame de Montespan. Even if one accepts (and, believe me, I want to) that this is a portrait of Jacquet de la Guerre, there remains a final question, one provoked by the artist's reputation. François de Troy was known for, and apparently sought after, for his ability to make 'any woman look

---

* Dominique Brême, an art historian specializing in French portraits, is responsible for the identification of Jacquet de la Guerre. The original exhibition note has Madame de la Guette (sic).

beautiful'. The composer in the portrait certainly is strikingly beautiful, but she is also confidently appraising the viewer, her quill
ready to do its work. Whether it is Jacquet de la Guerre, or (if it is
her), whether it is an accurate depiction of her, remains impossible
to know. What is certain, is that Jacquet de la Guerre commissioned, for professional reasons, a number of portraits of herself, as
well as other pictures, such as one showing her with her father.
These have all now been lost, but the existence of such a picture
gallery demonstrates that, just as her sovereign made sure that his
image was circulated throughout his kingdom, so did the composer,
albeit on a much, much smaller scale.

But what of the human being? The records show that in August
of 1698, Élisabeth's mother, Anne de la Touche, died. They show
that Élisabeth's father died in November 1702. Did Élisabeth
mourn her parents? The records show that the floods of the winter
of 1689–90 destroyed the lower windows of Sainte-Chapelle. Was
she afraid? Historians note that by 1700, some two hundred 'hospitals' participated in what the social historian Michel Foucault has
called 'the great confinement'; 'within their walls resided 100,000
people considered outcasts: Gypsies, Protestants, beggars, the
unemployed, the transient, the insane, and those deemed to be
witches, prostitutes, and juvenile delinquents'. Political historians
note that 'from 1688 until his death in 1715', Louis XIV's 'ambition
far exceeded his power, and his reign ended on a note of frustration'. And yet we have no idea at all of Jacquet de la Guerre's
response to the changing world around her.

The records are less mute when it comes to money. In 1702,
Élisabeth and her husband received 1,666 livres and sixteen sols
from her father (about £125). It was not a fortune, bearing in mind
that Lully had been able to invest 10,000 livres into the Paris-
Opera, but it presumably made life even more comfortable for the
professional couple.

Their life together did not last much longer, for, in July 1704, Marin died. The immediate impact upon Élisabeth was the need to leave the apartment in the Palais de la Cité. Unsurprisingly, she returned to the island of her birth, signing a three-year lease for an apartment in the rue Regrattière, just a few steps from her brother Pierre on the quai Bourbon. The annual rent (300 *livres*, or £22 10s) suggests that she was not dependent on the legacy she had received from her father two years earlier. In fact, the widowed Élisabeth appears very well-off. Her apartment consisted of two *chambres* (one small, one large), two offices, a small kitchen overlooking the courtyard, a little room 'at street level' and a pantry. Above, on the third floor, were rooms for the servants and a small attic.

The rue Regrattière would be the setting for a remarkable re-emergence of Jacquet de la Guerre, composer. It took months, even years, but in 1707, the year of Madame de Montespan's death, and with the composer herself now forty-two years old, Jacquet de la Guerre published her *Pièces de clavecin qui peuvent se joüer sur le viollon* (Pieces for Harpsichord which can be Played on the Violin). That innocuous word, '*Pièces*', masks the commitment and audacity of their composer. The commitment is evident in the meticulous production values of the publication, which demonstrate the composer's active supervision of the project, her determination that every performance indication, from tempo marks to ornamentation to blank pages to ensure easy page turns, would be just right. The composer's audacity lies in the form she uses, for these 'pieces' are radical: they are sonatas.

Now, in the twenty-first century, we know what to expect from a sonata. In the early years of the eighteenth century, the form was still tantalizingly fluid, cutting-edge new music. The composer Corelli may have established certain key characteristics, such as the sonata's slow–fast–slow–fast sequence of movements, but Jacquet de la Guerre did her bit for the new form, deploying the viol (or the cello) in both a melodic and harmonic role within a single piece. She was the first French composer to do so.

Jacquet de la Guerre's sonatas are considered triumphs of the genre. Not only does the composer develop the role of the violin in important ways (she may not have played the instrument, but she knew how to write for it), but she blends French traditions with Italian innovation, the latter evident in elements such as the expressiveness of the slow movements, the innovative harmonies and the use of modulations. One of her secrets is to give the listener a conventional framework, making the formal shapes of each dance – whether the four beats of the stately allemande or the livelier three beats of the courante – easily identifiable. Within this formal exterior, Jacquet de la Guerre mixes things up, creating movement and variations through ornamentation, melodic motion, rhythmic activity or variations of phrase length.

Delightful as they are, Jacquet de la Guerre's 'délicieuses' sonatas, in the words of one contemporary copyist, were explosive stuff for their time because French attitudes to the sonata made any forays into the genre at best avant-garde, at worst, unpatriotic. What made the sonata so suspicious? The form had been born in Italy (a bad start in life from the French point of view), and most official pronouncements denounced the Italian sonata as impossible to understand, and entirely against French taste. The king's taste, of course, was the French taste, and dictated what could and would be heard in the court and beyond. To make matters worse, the violin, the vital ingredient of the new form, was viewed as a lowly instrument in France. As one contemporary wrote scornfully, 'one sees few men of rank who play' whilst there are many 'low musicians who live by it'. The violin might have been good for providing dance music but the lute and the viol remained the instruments of elite choice. The sonata therefore represented a threat to those seeking to prevent the contamination and debasement of French culture by foreign influences. It was extremely exciting for everyone else.

Through the 1680s, Jacquet de la Guerre's apprenticeship years, there had been discreet musical meetings for those who wanted to know more. It was during those years that Corelli's trio sonatas became known in Paris, and in which many fell under the new music's spell, and began working, in the words of one admiring contemporary, 'in a more brilliant fashion'. One such was François Couperin, three years younger than Jacquet de la Guerre, and the composer who claimed (in work published in 1726) that he had written the first *sonade français* (sic) in 1692. If music history is reduced to a first-past-the-post competition, then it seems Couperin has a rival. A recently discovered manuscript shows that Jacquet de la Guerre had been working on the form long before 1707. Twelve years before, in fact.* Her sonatas, copied by hand in 1695, were some of the first in France. The manuscript's title, *Sonnatta della signora de la Guerre*, with its Italian words, seems a declaration of intent. Possibly in the composer's own hand, it consists of four little booklets, each of eight pages, with the music elegantly transcribed.

Let us for one moment consider the achievement not of the music itself, but the creation of the manuscript, for, as the scholar Heather Wolfe puts it, 'the truth was that writing was laborious, messy and tiring for both genders'. First, Jacquet de la Guerre needed a quill, the writer's tool for a thousand years before 1700, made from the four or five outer-left-wing feathers of a living goose, or a swan when there was money available, plucked in the

---

* The 1695 manuscript was owned by the composer, lute player and advocate of Italian music, Sebastian de Brossard, the man who had appreciated Jacquet de la Guerre's *Céphale et Procris* when few others had.

spring. As a child, Élisabeth would have been taught to clean, harden and trim the shafts of her feathers, then make the five or six cuts necessary to create the nib. She would have learned how to hold the pen, how much pressure to exert, how to reshape the nib and how to avoid 'botching', that is, sloppy corrections. The correct posture (erect), and the correct surface (sloping but flat) all helped to enhance the quality of the manuscript. Every day, as an adult, Jacquet de la Guerre needed to sharpen her quills, or send them out to the professional 'stationers' on the streets of the Ile St Louis. Every week, she would have to replace her quill pens, buy paper and make her own ink, since that was traditionally women's work, the female-compiled receipt books from the seventeenth century containing time-intensive recipes for making black ink out of rainwater (or beer, wine or vinegar), gall nuts and copperas (iron sulphate or vitriol). In addition to ink, Jacquet de la Guerre required either pounce, sandarac or Calais sand in order to prepare the paper for writing if it were too 'spongy' and to dry the ink on the page, whilst under her desk a coal stove would burn so that the ink dried as quickly as possible. In the seconds before the ink dried, there was a moment when the composer could erase an error, simply by wiping it with her thumb. There could not be, and there was not, anything casual or spontaneous about the process of composition. 'Laborious, messy and tiring': it is even more disappointing therefore that so few manuscripts survive, and equally exciting when new work is found.

Jacquet de la Guerre stayed true to form in 1707 when she, yet again, dedicated the printed version of her sonatas to the king. Many others, by that time, were looking beyond the old, increasingly withdrawn and resolutely traditionalist Louis XIV. Jacquet de la Guerre remained loyal to her original and most powerful patron. And, astonishingly, Louis XIV, who disliked new music and particularly disliked Italian music, seemed to like Jacquet de la Guerre's sonatas. He liked them so much that over the summer of 1707 she was summoned to the *'petit couvert'* of the king to perform. This was to enter the inner sanctum of Versailles. Tall windows provided views to courtyards to the north and south; impressive canvases depicted military victories; Jacquet de la Guerre simply added another sensory pleasure as the king took his lunch. A brave courtier pointed out to the king that he did not normally appreciate this kind of music. In response, Louis insisted that Jacquet de le Guerre's work was like nothing that had come before: *'Elle est originale'.*

The composer's next project engaged with a genre as Italian – and therefore resisted and contested by all true Frenchmen – as the sonata: the cantata. In one respect, the cantata had less of a mountain to climb in order to conform to French taste. As has been seen when considering opera as *'tragédie en musique'*, French music in the seventeenth century could not be conceived without reference to a text or at least an occasion, such as a victory in battle. This was yet another reason that the sonata, merely music, was resisted. With the cantata, there were at least words, and indeed for some it was understood as a minor literary, rather than musical, genre. The problem with the cantata was the marriage of Italian music with French words. As is clear from Strozzi's work in the genre in the 1650s and beyond, the cantata was well-established in the Italian peninsula by the mid-seventeenth century but, in France, vocal music, although present in a theatrical context, still invariably shared the stage with Louis XIV's preferred art form, dance. By composing her *Cantates françoises sur des sujets tirez de l'Écriture* (Sacred Cantatas) using texts by Antoine Houdar de Lamotte, the composer was therefore entering the culture wars once more.

For some, these twelve sacred cantatas surpass even her sonatas: 'no other composer of the time handled the genre so consistently'.

In fairness, not many composers were writing cantatas, but she was onto something. The king, closer and closer to death, more and more under the influence of the devout Madame de Maintenon, was the ideal audience for Jacquet de la Guerre's sacred cantatas and, once again, the composer offered her work to her monarch, acknowledging (could there be a hint of irony?) that she does so out of 'long habit'. She can almost do no other. In a typical display of modesty, she hopes that the beauty of the (religious) subject and her own desire to please her king will make up for the lack of genius. She remains 'La très-humble, & très-obéissante Servante, & très-fidèlle Sujette. Élisabeth Jacquet DE LA GUERRE'.

Amongst Jacquet de la Guerre's biblical subjects was that of Judith's slaying of Holofernes, popular in both art and music for its intense drama and its marked eroticism, of which Veronese's treatment of the subject adorned one of the most sumptuous of Louis XIV's personal rooms. To create a cantata for solo voice out of such an essentially dramatic text was a challenging task for any composer. Moreover, as scholar Michele Cabrini asks, how could Jacquet de la Guerre use the form to 'give agency to Judith'?* His answer is to suggest that the composer bypasses the libretto (written by La Motte), and instead uses instrumental 'accompaniments and independent symphonies' to give voice to Judith, 'despite a text that downplays her character'. Not only that, but instrumental music is used to heighten tension, as in the passage where Holofernes is sleeping, unaware of the threat from Judith. For Cabrini, this makes Jacquet de la Guerre 'innovative and forward-looking' in her move away from the dominance of text that is usually understood to be the hallmark of her period. At the same time, she reveals herself as an innovative text-setter, always

* Cabrini draws comparisons between the cantata and the well-known Judith paintings by Caravaggio and Artemisia Gentileschi.

117

concerned to express intense emotion, for example underlining the violent emotions of her character with multiple changes of tempo in 'Le coup est achevé?' As Strozzi had done in her time, and as Jacquet de la Guerre herself had done earlier in Céphale et Procris, the borders between airs (arias) and recitative are creatively blurred. Throughout the religious cantatas, as the musicologist Mary Cyr points out, the composer's decades of experience come into play, as she entertains her listener with sudden major–minor harmonic shifts; active melodies featuring syncopations; and brilliant runs and imaginative changes of texture all contained within a clear, but flexible, vision for the overall design of each cantata.

Once again, Jacquet de la Guerre pulls off the trick of being innovative, possibly even un-French, whilst remaining firmly traditional. What is more, there is a sense of confidence in her dedication to Louis XIV. She writes that she has composed 'a musical work worthy, dare I say it, of YOUR MAJESTY', that the texts contain the 'most significant deeds of Holy Scriptures' and that she as composer has 'tried by my melodies to do justice to their spirit and to support their grandeur'. Most commentators agree that she succeeded.

Jacquet de la Guerre had clearly not forgotten how to compose musical drama. These late biblical cantatas can be seen as creative substitutes for the operas that she did not, perhaps could not, write in her lifetime. She followed up her Cantates françoises sur des sujets tirez de l'Écriture with three secular cantatas in 1715, works that retain their Frenchness (the work is entitled Cantates françoises to leave no one in any doubt of that) but also integrate all the composer's knowledge and practice of Italian styles: the vocality of the melodies, the harmonic developments, the diversity of rhythm and, overall, a sense of contrast and diversity. The secular cantatas are ambitious works, unusually long, which explains why she published three rather than the usual six, and use instruments prominently and powerfully: 'compositional perfection' according to Cessac's notes to the 2000 recording, which also celebrate the 'distinctly theatrical dimension' to *Le Sommeil d'Ulisse* (The Sleep of Ulysses) most notable in the slumber scene (*Sommeil*) and the storm scene (*tempête*), both common scenes in French stage works of the seventeenth and eighteenth centuries. As close to opera as she would get after *Céphale et Procris*, the secular cantatas are Jacquet de la Guerre's last known major works.[*]

There is a sense in the dedication to the published version of the secular cantatas, which appeared together with a duet, that it was time to move on. For the first time, Jacquet de la Guerre does not offer her work to King Louis XIV. Instead, she turns to the Elector of Bavaria, Maximilian-Emmanuel II, who had been offered a home in France by Louis XIV after his defeat in the war of the Spanish Succession. Despite the change of addressee, Jacquet de la Guerre's dedication appears to use all the old familiar phrases but there is something new, something disconcerting, in the phrase or two that pick up on her earlier hints about a crisis survived some twenty years earlier. Jacquet de la Guerre writes that it was necessary to her very survival to be able to offer Maximilian-Emmanuel her music. Without the chance to do so, she would not have been able to resist some unspecified '*maux*' (evils). A narrowly political, although rather obvious, interpretation of these *maux* could be the imminent or actual death of Louis XIV in 1715. He had been her supporter for over forty years. Jacquet de la Guerre's French

---

[*] The secular cantatas were published together with a piece that edged the composer still closer to the world of opera, but also marks a move in the direction of popular culture: *Le raccommodement comique de Pierrot et de Nicole*, a duet written for *La ceinture de Vénus*, a play by Alain-René Lesage performed at the Foire St Germain in 1715.

biographer sees melancholy in the dedication to this final work, and there is certainly a sense of lurking *maux*.

There is also the pragmatism of the survivor. In an *Avertissement* written by Jacquet de la Guerre, she not only writes about her art, but also gives practical advice to those who are going to interpret or perform her work. She highlights her commitment to variety in her music, primarily so that her listeners do not get bored. She draws attention to the ways in which she responds, sensitively, to words, but also aligns herself clearly with the French belief in the primacy of the text: her aim has been to make her music correspond to the words, since 'melodies that don't express the words, no matter how well-wrought, can only be displeasing to connoisseurs'. And, realistic about her audience as ever, she reassures her readers that they can detach the 'airs' from the 'symphonies', in other words that they can sing the songs without needing the orchestra. Jacquet de la Guerre shows her willingness, yet again, to adapt to the tastes of her time. God forbid she should bore anyone. Needs must, whether the king or the public drives.

Whether the composer was driven by melancholy or pragmatism in 1715, the music represents the culmination of the journey that Élisabeth Jacquet de la Guerre had made since her teenage years at Versailles. She was the composer who could incorporate Italian innovations but retain her Frenchness, who could balance the past and present, even for that most demanding, most conservative and most powerful of listeners, Louis XIV. She did far more than merely adapt Italian styles to the traditions of French music. As did her much more famous contemporary, Couperin, she explored, energetically, the new musical territory of the sonata. And, unlike her contemporaries, she breathed new life into the cantata, possibly as a surrogate for the operas she did not write.

After 1715, whether precipitated by the death of the Sun King, or her own old age, Jacquet de le Guerre's public appearances slowed and finally stopped. Occasional, short pieces appear in publications until 1724. Tillot, writing some years later, claims that her last work, now lost, was a *Te Deum* giving thanks for the young King Louis XV's recovery from smallpox. It was performed in the chapel of the Louvre in August 1721, a fitting symbol of Jacquet de la Guerre's enduring place at the very heart of the French establishment.

Five years later, in the autumn of 1726, and at sixty-one years of age, Élisabeth Jacquet de la Guerre prepared her will from her home in rue Regrattière. She was not ill at the time, and thus the will reveals a woman who sought to put her affairs in order, her order, while she was still in control. In both form and content, the document provides hints as to the character of the woman who prepared it. First and foremost, it is a lengthy document, not least because Jacquet de la Guerre has a lot to leave. The will is thorough, explicit, precise. There are lengthy expressions of a strong if conventional religious faith. She nominates her cousin by marriage, René Trépagne, the author of the two poetic eulogies that prefaced her first publication back in 1687, as executor. René also receives a good portion of her estate. He does not, however, receive her musical legacy, because, as Jacquet de la Guerre points out, he is no musician.

The will makes no mention of Élisabeth Jacquet de la Guerre's child. Indeed, without a solitary reference in a work published some years after her death we would not know that she and Marin had ever been parents. Élisabeth's son was apparently as talented a harpsichordist as his mother at the age of eight. Two years later he was dead. Nothing more is known: no birth date, no date of death.

This silence is only to be expected. There are no letters, because this was a family who were never apart, even if someone had thought their letters important enough to save. There are no records because the boy was not significant to his society. As has been seen, even the death of his father, organist to Sainte-Chapelle, does not get a mention. This particular gap in our understanding of Jacquet de la Guerre's life is frustrating, even heartbreaking: how can we understand the woman if we do not know about her child? But this profoundly post-Romantic view of woman is anachronistic to early eighteenth-century Paris. Élisabeth's status as a mother was irrelevant to her world, if not to her. She did not live in an era in which bearing children was a badge of proper femininity, nor in which the raising of children had become the *raison d'être* of the bourgeois woman. She could be the marvel of the age without being known as a mother. Yet to recognize this is not to dismiss the experience of Élisabeth and Marin as parents who lost their only child. Just because we have no record of their grief, just because their public identities did not, and could not, incorporate an emotional life, does not mean that neither the grief nor the family life existed.

Within a year of making her will in 1726, the composer moved to the parish of Saint-Eustache (the church at the entrance to Les Halles, the Paris market) in what is now the 1st *arrondissement*. On 19 July 1727, she signed a lease of five years in the rue des Prouvaires, a street now almost entirely obliterated by the modern Les Halles development. The move was perhaps not such a significant one, since she exchanged one cultural heart of Paris for another: Saint-Eustache was the church in which Molière had been baptized, and later married.

Jacquet de la Guerre did not survive the five years of her lease. As spring turned to summer in 1729, she sickened. On 24 June, close to death, Élisabeth decided to write a new will. Her writing is weak, and many of the earlier pious passages are gone, but the message remains clear. René Trépagne disappears and, instead, Élisabeth names her two nephews, her sister Anne's children, as her universal legatees. Three days later, on 27 June 1729, she died. She was buried the following day in Saint-Eustache.

Catherine Cessac, Jacquet de la Guerre's biographer, chooses as her epigram, words from the philosopher and moralist Jean de La Bruyère's *Les caractères ou les mœurs de ce siècle*, first published in 1688: '*Si la science et la sagesse se trouvent unies en un même sujet, je ne m'informe plus du sexe, j'admire*' ('if skill and wisdom are found united in one person, I no longer inquire into their sex, I simply admire'). La Bruyère is not writing about Jacquet de la Guerre, but Cessac wants her reader to see the achievement of her female composer of the seventeenth century in terms that transcend our modern-day, and reductive, focus on her '*sexe*'. In doing so, Cessac picks up on one of the more remarkable aspects of Jacquet de la Guerre's life. More so than any other composer in this book, Jacquet de la Guerre was understood in her own time as an exceptional individual, rather than an exceptional woman. Furthermore Jacquet de la Guerre was simply a professional musician in a world that, up to a point, permitted her to be just that.

Up to a point. Simply being born a woman meant that certain things were straightforwardly denied to Élisabeth, such as being appointed as organist, or a court post as a composer or musical director. Other aspects of life, other dangers, other constraints, were equally determined by her *sexe*: the very real risk of death in childbirth; the pressure for the married woman to step away from public roles; the lack of access to any formal advanced musical education.

It is only up to a point that Jacquet de la Guerre can transcend her chromosomes. When Titon du Tillet wrote his sustained eulogy of her, published in his 1732 *Le Parnasse françois*, he accompanies his words with an image of a medallion showing the composer, with the motto 'I contended for the prize with the great musicians'. Tillet describes Jacquet de la Guerre's genius for composition, her excellence in the creation of both vocal and instrumental music, her breadth of genres. So far so good. Then the house of cards tumbles: 'One can say that there has never been someone of her sex who has had as great a talent as she for composition and the manner in which she executes her music on the harpsichord and the organ.'

For reasons best known to themselves, Jacquet de la Guerre's nephews, who inherited her unpublished compositions, made no attempt to publish their aunt's work. Tillot writes: 'her last works have not yet been printed and are in the possession of her heirs'. Occasionally, and more often in recent years as people have become more aware of her work, a score is found such as the 1760 manuscript copy of the sacred cantatas, which was unearthed in 2008. This suggests that her music did circulate but not extensively, and not in print. And so, once again, a female composer's work fades into oblivion. Once again, a female composer's work is allowed to slip out of the classical canon because, after all, she only won the women's race.

And yet Élisabeth Jacquet de la Guerre operated successfully, and for many decades, within the glittering, if fickle, world of late seventeenth-century Paris and its surrounding royal palaces. That city, where I write these words, was truly hers. Paris permitted her to be what she was, a formidably talented performer and composer, and it provided her with the possibility to have her music, whether small-scale or large-scale works, performed, circulated and published. Then again, she could not have done any of this without the direct support of the Sun King, Louis XIV. There is no indication whether she felt that the servility necessary to survive was an imposition or a restriction. There is, however, the record of her achievement as a composer of opera, cantata and, most significantly, of the new sonata. Louis XIV, Versailles and, above all, Paris, provided the opportunity to be that rare thing, a successful female composer. Élisabeth Jacquet de la Guerre took that opportunity with both hands.

'I shall continue with unceasing application to exert my
limited talents in the study of music.' Marianna Martines

Chapter Four

MARTINES

It is fifteen years since Jacquet de la Guerre died in Paris, nearly thirty years since the rule of the Sun King came to an end. Now, 750 miles to the east, a great empress rules over a great nation with a great city as its capital. At the heart of the city, and protected by its encircling walls, stands a great church. In the house by the church, lives a young girl. She will be a creation of the imperial city, and will never stir from this, its very heart. The young girl is Marianna Martines, born on 4 May 1744; her home, the Michaelerhaus; the church, the Michaelerkirche; and the city, of course, is Vienna, where:

> In the Imperial Royal Court-Parish Church of St Michael on the name day of the Holy Archangel Michael, a High Mass was celebrated, for which the Mademoiselle Martines, a virtuosa just sixteen years old, composed the music, by the excellence of which all those who understand the art were amazed.

Complete with clarinets, oboes, flutes and trombones, the ambitious *Mass in C* was not even the teenage virtuosa Martines's first work and, over the following decades, 'all those who understand the art' will continue to be amazed by her compositions across a range of musical genres, from oratorio (her *Isacco figura del Redentore* contains, according to one critic, 'musical riches'), to psalm settings (such as the

Miserere mei Deus for choir, soloists and basso continuo, a 'study in harmonic fluidity' written when she was twenty-two) and keyboard sonatas, of which she wrote thirty-one, although only three survive.

The English music historian Charles Burney, visiting Vienna, could not find the words to express his delight in Martines. From the moment he saw her, she fulfilled his notion of the ideal woman musician, someone who was 'received by the whole company with great respect', well dressed, elegant and compliant. Burney asks her to play and she does so:

> In a graceful manner, without the parade of diffidence, or the trouble of importunity. Her performance indeed surpassed all that I had been made to expect. She sung two airs of her own composition, to words of Metastasio, which she accompanied on the harpsichord, in a very judicious and masterly manner; and in playing the ritornels, I could discover a very brilliant finger.*

Burney goes on to praise Martines's 'perfect intonation' and 'touching expression', her 'excellent shake' (trill), her ability to divide 'tones and semi-tones into infinitely minute parts'. It was not only her singing that impressed him. Having dazzled him with her improvised cadenzas, Martines went on to play one of her own sonatas, and Burney admires a psalm setting, which he sees as revealing a 'most excellent contrapuntist'. He had only one concern, with the physical toll that composition took upon Marianna's body as she stooped over her manuscript or sat for long hours at the harpsichord. It is a pity, he wrote, 'that her writing should affect her voice'. Gender is not an explicit issue here but, nevertheless, Burney

---

* A ritornel, in chamber music, is the repetition of an instrumental introduction to a song.

would prefer Marianna the singer to continue at the expense of Marianna the composer. But Martines, like Caccini and Strozzi, would continue to be both performer and composer.

Unlike them, however, Marianna Martines's life appears untroubled, with enough money and the right social connections to ensure a life of security and leisure. Not for her the frightening dip in income experienced by her contemporary, Mozart, in 1789–90, when Emperor Joseph II's Turkish war led to a mass exodus of the nobility from Vienna and the doubling of prices. As a female composer, Martines did not have to endure the more distressing aspects of a public, professional career that were faced by fellow male composers, whether it be hostile critics savaging one's work in music journals, publishers rejecting one's latest piece because they believed it would not sell, or paying audiences shouting down a shoddy or an unfamiliar performance. Instead, Martines's apparently untroubled life was centred on her home, the Michaelerhaus, at the southern end of the bustling Kohlmarkt, looking over the Michaelerplatz and adjoining the imperial church, the Michaelerkirche, where, according to one satirical contemporary, 'the beautiful people go to mass'. It was, and remains, the elite heart of the city. If Martines were to look out of her window today, she would see the imposing main entrance to the Hofburg and the Spanish Riding School, where on 9 September 2008, for the first time in its existence, two young women started their training. Vienna does not embrace change swiftly.

By the time of her birth in 1744, her father, Nicolo, with his Spanish surname and his relatively humble origins in the city of his birth, Naples, was securely established in Vienna, successfully maintaining his position as Master of Ceremonies, something akin to a modern-day Chief of Staff in the Papal Embassy, despite the arrival and departure of five different nuncios. He had wisely taken 'to himself a German wife of the most respectable birth and character'. Twenty-four years his junior, Maria Theresa produced thirteen children for Nicolo, six of whom survived into adulthood. Marianna was the fifth of those six. Her older brother Joseph was the most obviously successful, a brilliant linguist, who had mastered twelve languages by the age of twenty. He rose rapidly in the library system in Vienna, recataloguing both the Court Library and Imperial Coin Collection. Further advancement came when he was appointed tutor to Empress Maria Theresa's children, including the future Emperor Joseph II, who particularly enjoyed his Italian lessons with Joseph Martines. The family's rising status was signalled by a move, c.1785, to the first floor of a house in the Herrengasse. This was hardly a major upheaval, simply a move offering another perspective on the Michaelerplatz.

Marianna, now past forty, lived with two of her brothers, Carl Boromeus, *Hof-Concipist*, the official responsible for the proper protocol and legal precision of official documents in the Austro-Bohemian Chancellery, and Joseph. The fourth member of this household of unmarried, middle-aged or elderly siblings was Marianna's sister, Antonia Johanna Theresia, two years her junior, and about whom almost nothing is known beyond her name. If anything, life was even more privileged than it had been before. According to Marianna, the new house provided 'much more beautiful and convenient' accommodation. The four had ten rooms between them, plus a kitchen, access to a stable, a cellar with firewood bins and, on the ground floor, a small room for a servant and another kitchen.

This privilege had an important consequence for Martines. If one was a Viennese woman of the upper classes, and Martines indeed became such, then one would be expected to devote one's time to entertaining or furthering the arts. This social convention created a vital space in which it was possible for Martines to pursue her music with ambition and rigour. She followed a formidable daily programme of composition and study: 'My exercise has been, and still is, to combine the continual daily practice of composing with the study and scrutiny of that which has been written by the most celebrated masters such as Hasse, Jommelli, Galuppi and the others who are famous today and who are praised for their musical labours.' Visitors were 'delighted and astonished' by her keyboard playing, singing and compositions. Her arias, composed predominantly for her own soprano voice, were particularly admired by her contemporaries: 'neither common, nor unnaturally new. The words were well set, the melody was simple, and great room was left for expression and embellishment.' Of her larger-scale works, an exceptionally lively *Overture in C* survives, using horns, oboes and flutes alongside strings. The opening and closing movements are marked *Allegro spiritoso* and *Allegro con spirito*, and they are indeed spirited, epitomizing the energy and grace of Martines's music. The meticulous and elegant autograph score, signed *'Originale di Marianna Martines 1770'*, and with indications that Martines was revising the score right up until the moment of (private) performance, suggests not only the composer's thoroughness, but also her pride in her work. Wealthy and protected, assiduous and committed to her art, Martines would become the most prolific female composer of her place and time.

As the years passed, her reputation would spread far beyond Vienna. An ambitious young poet, Saverio Mattei, two years Martines's senior and a rising star in Naples, approached the renowned composer Johann Adolph Hasse in the hope of a collaboration. An attack of gout put paid to that idea, and Mattei ended up using Martines. He was not disappointed, although he might have been surprised by the composer's quiet determination, despite the constant need to assume a pose of compliance and submission to the male poet. Mattei, for example, wanted the fashionable salterio, originally from Asia, and an ancestor of the spinet/harpsichord with its finger-picked single note strings. Martines wanted violins. Her compromise was to write a salterio part, but also to ensure that the piece could be performed as she preferred in other settings. The salterio was conspicuous by its absence in all her future work with Mattei. As a composer, the greatest challenge she faced was the almost complete absence of variation in metre in Mattei's texts: sheer 'poetic monotony' in the words of one critic. With a typical expression of modesty, Martines recognized the problem, but ascribed it to the nature of the penitential psalms themselves and her own weakness as a composer: 'the consistent character of a contrite and downcast heart that asks ever for mercy and pardon requires such chapters of knowledge and imagination as I do not possess to avoid the pitfalls of sameness'. This is disingenuous at best, since Martines, by now in her mid-twenties, possessed more than enough 'knowledge and imagination' to avoid 'the pitfalls of sameness', and her settings were in due course highly praised. They were performed during Lent in Naples, as soon as the population had recovered from the carnival and could once again, in Mattei's words, turn their attention to 'celestial harmony'. The Queen of Naples herself (Maria Carolina of Austria, the thirteenth child of Empress Maria Theresa of Austria, and Queen of Naples and Sicily through her marriage to King Ferdinand IV and III) was delighted with Martines: the queen's copy of *Scelta d'arie composter per suo diletto da Marianna Martines*, complete with an autograph title from the composer, still survives in Naples. No wonder that Mattei now praised the originally second-choice Martines in the highest terms, as a modern Miriam, the Old Testament prophetess and musician: a 'divine metempsychosis has given us, in Signora Marianna, if I may put it this way, the sister of Moses'. Amazement at the 'divine' Martines was tempered by disbelief in some quarters. Could 'a person of her sex and of her years' achieve so much? Did Martines compose her own music, or was she merely a cover for someone else, someone more male, perhaps? Mattei insists that what he calls the 'phenomenon' of Martines:

Is truly extraordinary; but there are plenty of witnesses of it, and her progress in the art grows so vividly from day to day that it would be a manifest injustice to wish to suppose a useless imposture in soil from which none has ever grown.

Possibly prompted to the invitation by the questions being asked, Mattei asked Martines to travel to Naples. She did not go.

The reason given was that she wanted to maintain a 'separation' because it was 'necessary to the preservation of what she has achieved'. From what did Martines need to maintain a 'separation'? How could a visit to Italy threaten her life in Vienna? It is not made clear, but the caution and conservatism implicit in the refusal to travel to Naples run like a seam through Martines's story.

A couple of years later, in 1773, further international recognition came for Martines when the eighteen committee members of the prestigious Accademia Filarmonica in Bologna voted unanimously to grant the composer the title *Accademia filarmonica Onorata*. No woman had been elected to the Accademia in any capacity during its 108 years of existence. Martines was being honoured not only for herself, but also as 'an honour due to the Royal Majesties of Vienna', 'from whom the said Madame Composer comes deservedly protected'. She was a symbol of German supremacy, and it was therefore not well received in Vienna when the *Gazetta di Bologna* reported that 'Signora Marianna Martinez, of Spanish [sic] nationality' had been elected to the Accademia. The Viennese press quickly moved to claim Martines as one of their own, reminding their readers that her triumph was that of the 'German nation':

> How much patriots must rejoice as every day they see ever
> more how the German nation takes pains to distinguish
> itself in all the arts with such fine progress! And what rare

and special honour it is to the fair sex here, to be able to count as a member a woman for whom so many cities have reason to envy them. Thanks be to the glorious reign of our most honourable queen, under which all the sister arts have soared so high, and will soon lead us to expect a certain level of perfection.

That 'most honourable queen' was the politically strong-willed, religiously conservative Maria Theresa, who ruled the Austrian Monarchy for the first thirty-six years of Martines's life, her increasingly disjointed empire stretching from the North Sea to the Adriatic, from the borders of France to those of Russia and the Ottoman Turks. As with the Medici women, an exemplary female composer did no harm to the public image of an exemplary female ruler.

The work Martines produced for the Accademia, as all new members had to, was a setting of *Dixit dominus*, Psalm 109 (numbered 110 in the King James Bible) for performance at the annual celebration of St Anthony of Padua, in the church of San Giovanni in Monte. The Accademia members, gloated the Viennese press, could not 'express sufficiently their amazement at the combination of beauty, ingenuity, nobility of expression, and an astonishing correctness in the compositions of the new candidate'. Martines's setting is, according to the more measured, but equally appreciative words of a modern musicologist, her 'masterpiece'. It could and should be a mainstay of the choral concert repertory, he argues, with its vigorous choruses, exciting counterpoint and melodious solos:

> Everything about the *Dixit dominus* bespeaks Marianna's mastery. In it she organized tonality, textural variety, contrapuntal technique, and melodic imagination into an exciting, expressive, and impressive work.

Martines's own assessment of her achievement was suitably modest. The work, a product of her 'feeble powers', only had the merit of proving her 'obedience'.

Crucially, just as she had declined Mattei's invitation to Naples, Martines did not travel to Bologna to receive her award. Every other figure honoured with election, including one Wolfgang Amadeus Mozart who had been invited to join in 1770 at age fourteen, had been required to appear in person for an examination. The Accademia agreed to accept a formal letter from Martines in lieu of the woman herself. She, in turn, explained just how flattered and honoured she was, how much she hoped she would be worthy of their faith, and how full she was of respect and gratitude. She adds, in one of those rare moments when one glimpses the *naiveté* that was perhaps a product of her protected existence, that she has been advised to keep her letter simple, but if she has done wrong, to instruct her 'in the manner with which it should be written, and you will receive it rewritten by return mail'.

The decision to remain in Vienna would have lasting repercussions for Martines the composer but, in 1774, the year of her *Dixit dominus*, her social position in the city became, it seemed, impregnable. Marianna's brothers were raised by process of *Ritterstand* to the Austrian minor nobility, the whole family gaining aristocratic rank in perpetuity. From now on she would be Marianna *von* Martines. Although the decree mentions the accomplishments of the four surviving Martines brothers, and does not even name Marianna, it cannot have done harm to the family that she had, only a year earlier, received her 'rare and special honour' from Bologna as an exemplary product of Empress Maria Theresa's rule. In the words of one contemporary:

Martines, Fraulein Nanette [sic] von, is one of the most prominent connoisseurs among our many amateurs [in

Vienna]. She reads at sight, accompanies from the full
score, and is an excellent singer. Rigorously correct in
composition and execution, her taste is largely after the
older Italian style . . . She has written masses and a large
number of arias, which sometimes come close to Jommelli's
style, and is in every respect a great supporter of music.

Wealth, a secure social status, discipline, a rare talent: these are still
not enough to explain Martines's achievement. What enabled
Martines to rise above the 'amateurs' of Vienna and become a
'connoisseur'? What allowed her not only to be a performer, as
expected, but also to compose? And not only to compose works
for her own performance, but for large-scale forces, whether oratorio, mass or overture?

One answer lies in the remarkable household into which she was
born. The Martines family occupied the third floor of the
Michaelerhaus, some fifteen rooms in total, with kitchens, pantries,
stables, a closed coach space, room for hay storage and cellars. The
ground floor, as it still is to this day, would have been given over to
'shops, taverns, stables, workshops, storage places, apothecaries,
coffee-houses', in the words of one contemporary, who advised
against living on the first floor in Vienna, since the rooms were 'hard
to heat on account of the vaulted ground floor below, also because
they are affected by dust from the street, the smells of stables and
sewers, and the noise of wheeled vehicles passing outside or entering and leaving' the courtyard. On the dust-free, noise-free, third-
floor of the Michaelerhaus, the most important person in Martines's
household was not a family member, but an elderly family friend,
Pietro Trapassi, known as Metastasio, in his time the foremost
librettist in Europe and now Poet Laureate of the Austrian Empire,
a role he had fulfilled for ten years before Marianna's birth.

Born in 1698, Metastasio was approaching fifty when it started to become clear that the little daughter of the house had an exceptional musical talent. His own experience suggested a way forward. Trapassi/Metastasio, as boy and then man, had been taken up by wealthy powerful individuals who had financed and facilitated his success as a poet. The second instance of patronage proved to be more fraught than the first, blurring, uncomfortably, the social boundaries between married female patron (the singer Marianna Bulgarelli) and young male protégé. The relationship did not end well, although not from lack of generosity on Bulgarelli's side. She took the whole Trapassi family into her own house, and left Metastasio her fortune.

Now, in Vienna, Metastasio had his own opportunity to take on the role of patron and mentor, doing so at a time when, according to some, he himself was past his prime. Not only that, enemies represented him as something of a misfit in Vienna (excluded from the city's noble circles on account of his humble birth), not to mention something of a sexual opportunist, quick to become intimate with well-placed women. It is true that, as a poet, Metastasio wrote only about twenty works between 1741 and 1782, primarily intended for, and tailored to, Habsburg court occasions. Whilst he wrote no new libretti for oratorios, and only a handful of new *opera seria* libretti, his lack of productivity, particularly after 1755, may in fact signal that his energies were now focused elsewhere. For, as Metastasio approached sixty, and Martines approached womanhood, she became his project. Marianna was an opportunity for him to test his enlightenment belief in human potential, just as he had been an opportunity for others to test their beliefs, for good and for bad. Indeed, his Marianna project was a continued expression of the values that Metastasio espoused in his work because, as a so-called Arcadian poet, he, in the words of one critic, was 'much more concerned with what humanity might be than with what it actually is'.

An early biographical sketch of Martines suggests that Metastasio noticed Marianna's 'special gifts of both body and mind', 'even in her earliest childhood', and goes on to describe the way in which the elderly man developed those special gifts into 'complete artistic mastery':

> He took the greatest pleasure in the scholarly instruction he gave her personally, and he even directed the musical education in keyboard playing and singing she received from the still very young Joseph Haydn (who lived in a little attic room in the same building) and then from the composer Nicolò Porpora (with whom she also had lessons in composition), and later from other teachers: several years of the finest training that she, supported by the ripe counsel of her fatherly friend, strove ceaselessly to reinforce with the most zealous study, in order to form fully that complete artistic mastery with which she later shone so brilliantly.

With a little help from a teenage Joseph Haydn, out of a chorister job due to his voice breaking and living in the attic of the Michaelerhaus, and the eminent singing and composition teacher, Nicolò Porpora, who may well also have lived in the house, Metastasio's ambition to create a model artist succeeded magnificently. Although it is unclear whether Porpora, a product of the Neapolitan system of musical education and best known as a singing teacher, taught Marianna voice or composition, up to a point the question is irrelevant, since in the eighteenth century there was often little difference between the training of singers and of composers. Singers needed to understand harmonies in order to develop and improvise from scores, and composers needed to be able to write effectively for the voice. All musical training therefore concentrated on the interpretation of *partimenti*, a sketch written on a single staff, whose main purpose was to be a guide to the improvisation of a composition at the keyboard. A sound knowledge of *partimenti* was essential, providing a fund of musical gestures on which the composer could draw. Like Caccini, Martines would be particularly fond of the romanesca, in which the bass descends from the first to the sixth and then down to the third, using it, for example, in the final 'Alleluia' of her *Regina caeli* of 1767 and in her *Dixit dominus* of 1774.

For all the contribution made (perhaps) by Haydn, and (more likely) by the elderly Porpora, Martines's 'mastery' served to endorse 'in most emphatic terms', as one contemporary put it, 'the praise due to this famous master', Metastasio. Not for the first time in this book, a woman's compositional career has been, at least in part, engineered for the glory of her teacher.

And not just the glory: when Martines played with 'astonishing mastery' her 'own compositions', then Metastasio 'felt again the emotion that he had been able to excite in the human heart with his inimitable librettos [sic]', wrote one eyewitness, Charles Burney. Burney goes even further, describing Marianna as Metastasio's *alter idem*. Literally, the phrase means 'the same but somehow different', but it suggests that Marianna existed as another self, a (young, female) expression of Metastasio's very essence.

On a more mundane level, Metastasio, an experienced professional writer, could and did support Martines with the practicalities of life as a composer. He admired and encouraged her remarkable work ethic and 'diligence', and was stern with those who were to perform her work, insisting that her music be 'rehearsed several times by an expert, careful, and sympathetic conductor, so that none may attribute to the defenceless composer the defects of an inaccurate performance'.

Martines certainly never ceased to acknowledge the significance of Metastasio to her as composer. Writing in December 1773, she asserts:

> But in all my studies, the chief planner and director was always, and still is, Signor Abbate Metastasio who, with the paternal care he takes of me and of all my numerous family, renders an exemplary return for the incorruptible friendship and tireless support which my good father lent him up until the very last days of his life.

The 'paternal care' for the Martines family extended into the social and financial realm as well as the musical. Some have seen him (even in alleged decline) as the puppet-master behind their social advancement, the man to thank for brother Joseph's enviable access to the imperial family as tutor to the empress's children and thus for the 1774 *Rittersand*. What is more, when Metastasio died at the age of eighty-four in April 1782, he left his substantial estate to the Martines siblings with Marianna, approaching forty, receiving, in addition to her share of his money, her mentor's harpsichord and musical scores, a final gift to the composer he had created.

Metastasio's highly successful Marianna experiment was not conducted in a vacuum, however. Quite the opposite: it was conducted in Vienna, the centre of empire, the city of music, home during Martines's lifetime to composer greats such as Haydn, Mozart and Beethoven. Vienna's music world was not without its problems, with traditional histories of the period indicating a moribund era of political stagnation and musical conservatism, in which the Habsburgs clung to power in the face of encroaching revolution, and concert life stuttered in comparison with the burgeoning public scene in other German capitals or in London. The Viennese concert structure was 'inadequate and haphazard', and there was no specially designed music room or concert hall in the city before 1831. Worse still, socializing was often as important as, if not more important than, the music at the private concerts that dominated cultural life. These are not usually the best ingredients for creative achievement and international renown, as Martines's composer contemporaries, who disappeared off for stints in Prague, London or elsewhere, knew only too well. Vienna was enough, or had to be enough, for Martines, who spent the vast majority of her life in two houses within metres of each other, and never experienced anything other than this 'inadequate and haphazard' music world.

Ironically, however, the nature of the music scene in Vienna was, in some senses, helpful to Martines as a female composer. Empress Maria Theresa's conservatism, most notably her 'Norma edict', which closed the theatres for longer periods than ever before, served to boost other forms of music in Vienna. By the 1760s, it was possible to attend concerts three times a week during Lent. If you were lucky, their imperial highnesses might even be present. Crucially, elite women who might not enter let alone perform at a theatre or opera house, could and did circulate in the private homes where concerts, growing precisely at this time in number and prestige, were held. Indeed, women presided over such musical events in many cases, providing them with an opportunity to see and be seen, hear and be heard, without the 'problem' of public exposure. By the 1790s, there were at least twenty private concert patrons holding regular concerts, including a raft of princes, a baroness, four counts and one 'Mlle Marianna v. Martines'.

This concert series of the 1790s was merely a formalization of a process of private music making that had been going on for more than three decades. From Martines's teenage years through to her middle age and Metastasio's death, his name and her reputation ensured a steady stream of visitors, musicians, composers and connoisseurs to the Michaelerhaus. The singer Michael Kelly, in his delightfully unreliable memoirs, remembers, or thinks he remembers, musical evenings at the Martines house. Kelly describes Martines as being of a similar age to her brother (she was actually ten years younger): 'she was reckoned a deep blue [ie an intellectual?], and very well versed in all the arts and sciences', but still played with 'the gaiety and vivacity of a girl'. It is Kelly who makes a direct link between Martines and her most famous contemporary, Wolfgang Amadeus Mozart, who was, according to Kelly, 'an almost constant attendant at her parties', where he played duets with Marianna, 'a great favourite of his'. Mozart first stayed in Vienna between 1767 and 1769, together with his sister Nannerl who was closer to Marianna in age than Wolfgang, and Martines's biographer writes that it is very likely that the two composers met, since, by the time of the Mozart family's next visit in 1773, Leopold, Wolfgang's father, referred to the Martines family as if they were old friends. Vienna then was a much more intimate place than it is today: 'within the walls', according to one music historian, it would have 'been difficult for professional musicians and musical amateurs not to know each other'. The fact remains that all other records remain silent as to whether Mozart was 'an almost constant attendant' at Marianna's house.

What is clear is that, by the 1790s, Martines was the mistress of ceremonies at her concert series, with one contemporary noting 'a very grand social gathering at the home of this skilful musician', at which a great deal of music is sung and played, where foreigners are welcome and where sometimes a wind ensemble plays throughout the entire evening. Vienna's private concerts privileged participation and intimacy, offering performers the chance to make music with others, composers the chance to hear his or her works, and all with friends and acquaintances as listeners. This was the world in which Mozart had appeared in the mid-1780s, maintaining a punishing schedule of private appearances. Mozart, always concerned to earn money from his talent ('Believe me, my sole purpose is to make as much money as possible; for after good health, it is the best thing to have', he wrote to his father from Vienna) used these appearances to good financial effect. It was an atmosphere far removed from the cold, impersonal atmosphere of a public concert hall, with its rigid division between professional artist and paying audience. And it was a world that would disappear, almost without trace, during the following century.

It is hard to over-estimate the importance of this vanished world to Martines. The phenomenon enabled her to function as a composer and performer without the stigma of public or professional engagement. No accounts of music making at the Martines household survive, but something of the atmosphere, somewhere between amateur and professional, private and public, can be glimpsed in a diary entry from the composer's English contemporary, Susan Burney, daughter of the musician and music historian Charles Burney, who had so admired the young Martines. Almost a thousand miles from Vienna, but in a similar social sphere, the music 'was very excellent, & the Concert delightful tho' without any singing'. Susan Burney offers a critique of one performance: 'His tone & execution are perfect — & his style in general good — *Manca l'anima* [the spirit is lacking] alone! — a little word, which prevents me from ever enjoying delight in hearing him, tho' I never fail to admire his powers.' She notes that her father played one of his recent compositions, followed by a duet with 'his dear wife' (Susan's stepmother), a performance by one of Mr Burney's 'scholars', one Miss Frye, and there are 'sweet Quartettos between almost every performance'.

In Vienna, private concerts came in many guises, ranging in scope from profoundly amateur offerings to large-scale programmes of orchestral music, the latter sometimes supported by imported professional wind players, not to mention performances by visiting musical virtuosos such as Mozart, bank-rolled by wealthy patrons.

More often than not, however, music would be just one of a series of activities during the evening, or it would be merely an accompaniment to another activity, whether courtship, conversation or dining. In a society in which girls especially were encouraged to learn to sing or play the keyboard in order to make them more attractive to potential husbands, it is no surprise that, at times, musical standards slipped:

> If there's a young lady in the house, she has to bang out something on the keyboard and sing, so that the ladies and gentlemen don't fall asleep. Then you have to stand around the keyboard and cry bravo, even when the young lady howls like a little dog. Finally the card games starts and everyone gets lively again.

Elsewhere, there were other forms of dismay about standards of performance. Mozart's *Piano Quartet*, a work that 'demands the utmost precision from all four voices' and can only delight 'connoisseurs of music in a chamber [atmosphere]' has become fashionable, notes one diarist. The word gets out: a celebrity princess is playing the piece, and so it is played in 'grand noisy concerts' by 'mediocre dilettantes'. Audiences hear an 'unintelligible muddle of 4 instruments that were never together [for] even four beats'. The result? A Mozart masterpiece is dismissed. Obviously, many amateur performers at private concerts barely rose above the mediocre. Some were as good as the professionals. Some, like Martines, were better.

The private concerts of Vienna would prove to be a cultural dead end. The future lay elsewhere, in the meetings and then regular concerts, for example, of a select group of (male) musicians at the residence of Prince Lichnowsky, then at Prince Rasumofsky's. From these concerts, there emerged the first professional string quartet. Nothing so significant, at least to the music history books, emerged from Martines's concerts.

The composer remained, at least publicly, ambivalent about even a limited degree of involvement with what she calls the 'larger world' after Metastasio's death, anxious that, in pursuing a concert series, she has 'abandoned the methodically ordered way of life of my great teacher (of mournful memory)', now that she finds herself 'with many new acquaintances'. The 'larger world' is being experienced at the cost of 'time' and the 'neglect' of her 'other duties'.

The sentiments expressed here by Martines are just the tip of an iceberg of self-effacement, modesty and duty that set the tone for her life. Countless examples can be found, but they all sound the same note. Prompted by the Bologna honour, a portrait of Martines was commissioned from Anton von Maron, recently returned from Vienna after seventeen years in Rome and, in 1773, the painter of Empress Maria Theresa. When Martines (reluctantly, of course) sent the portrait of herself to her contact and supporter in Bologna, the composer Giovanni Battisti Martini, the occasion provided yet another opportunity for humility, being of 'limited talents', and her sex full of 'weaknesses'. Martines expresses in turn obedience, gratitude, esteem, respect and humility towards Martini.[*]

In Habsburg Vienna, Martines's ability to exercise her 'brilliant finger', to be a 'most excellent contrapuntist', depended upon these kinds of expressions. Did she truly believe in them? It is impossible to know. As her biographer astutely points out, Marianna von Martines's position in society 'imposed on her a total public

---

[*] This is the painting on p. 126: the inscription is not shown. The portrait sent to Bologna has disappeared, but a painting that still survives in Vienna has the inscription: 'Maria Anna Martines. Pupil of Pietro Metastasio Born in Vienna, on the fourth day before the *Nones* of May 1744, [member] of the Academic Philharmonic Society' (original in Latin).

acceptance of contemporary values. The woman's *compositions* might make light of those restrictions, but the *composer*, as a woman, could not.' This 'total public acceptance of contemporary values' (and there is no indication of a private rebellion) was crucial to the success of Martines as a Viennese *compostinin*. But the necessary narrowness of her world becomes all the more apparent when compared to that of her more famous contemporaries. Joseph Haydn lived in Lukavec, Eisenstadt and London. Vienna would not be the dominant factor in his career from 1761 to 1795, and London would be the city in which he made his serious money. Mozart only lived in Vienna for the last ten years of his life. Prior to that, his base was Salzburg, leavened by Milan, Mannheim, London and Paris.

Martines the composer paid a high price for her caution and conformity. Remaining in Vienna led to the non-performance of her masterpiece, *Dixit dominus*, written for the Accademia Filarmonica. Yes, there was some mismanagement in that the score was not prepared properly for private performance, a problem compounded by Martines unwittingly missing a deadline. Yes, her supporter in Bologna, Martini, had a falling out with the Accademia. But the truth was (and Martines was apparently never told it) that the Accademia passed a new law that stipulated that they would not perform any work by an academician unless that composer was resident in Bologna for the occasion. The ruling made good music sense. If the composer had prepared a shoddy or inaccurate score, then he or she had to be there to supervise the performance. Martines's decision not to leave Vienna ensured that her music would not be heard.

This missed opportunity was not an isolated incident. Martines's *Miserere* was performed on 1 April 1772 at one of the Accademia degli Armonici of Florence's Lenten concerts. The event attracted a large audience to hear words set to music 'at the request of Sig. Abate Metastasio by the famous Sig. Marianna Martines of Vienna'. It was this concert that really launched Mattei's career as a librettist, and which prompted him to invite Martines to his home turf, Naples. She did not go. Other composers took her place as Mattei's collaborators, and their settings of his texts made their way into print. Martines remained unpublished.

Martines's need for decorum and respectability infuses her compositions, which remain works of propriety, if highly spirited propriety. They reveal not only her tutelage at the hands of an elderly man who was proudly traditionalist, not to mention idealistic, in his outlook when it came to art, but also Martines's own preference for an aesthetic that privileged refinement and balance between ancient and modern practices, her desire to create a music 'neither common' nor 'unnaturally new'. In an era during which Haydn and Mozart would explore new forms, such as the rondo and the theme and variations, Martines continued to write in older styles, creating works with 'charm and instant appeal' but which are far from 'heaven-storming', in the words of one modern, but honest, admirer.

It was also an era in which composer/performers such as Mozart would enthusiastically embrace the new, more powerful, more expressive, fortepiano. As early as 1777 Mozart made the journey to Augsburg, where Stein the instrument's inventor, worked. Together the men put on a concert to showcase the pianoforte and Mozart's own recent compositions, including his triple-clavier concerto (*Concerto No. 7 in F*, K.242). Martines may not have been in a position to travel to Augsburg, let alone organize a professional showcase for her talents, but she certainly had an opportunity to learn more about the fortepiano when Stein brought his instruments to the Viennese court. Within months, workshops sprung up in the city to produce instruments for forward-looking musicians. Indeed, according to the Metropolitan Museum of Art's website:

> Rising popularity of the piano in Vienna caused a great demand for the instrument, which manufacturers were

only too pleased to fill. By 1800, there were approximately sixty known makers building pianos in Vienna. The new musical styles of the time, which we now call 'classical music', were well suited for the Viennese action piano and composers were beginning to write a great deal of music for the instrument. Musicians such as Mozart, Joseph Haydn, Johann Nepomuk Hummel, and the young Ludwig van Beethoven played these early Viennese instruments and helped drive the demand for them.

Mozart was so committed to the pianoforte that he had his own instrument transported to private concerts, whether driven by a desire always to perform on a familiar instrument, or by the fear that most private households would not have the new instrument. Martines remained resolutely committed to the harpsichord.

By the time of the only public performance of a major work by Martines, her oratorio *Isaac figure del Redentore* (Isaac, Figure of the Redeemer), performed in March 1792, by Vienna's Tonkünstler-Societät, with an orchestra including paired trumpets, horns, oboes, flutes and bassoons, timpani and strings, and a choir of around 200 singers, and thus deploying forces as elaborate as any of her contemporaries; her style of composition, most notably her continued use of galant voice-leading schemata, was rooted firmly in the past. Vienna, with its 'strongly evolutionary' musical culture, may have moved more slowly, and more cautiously, from the baroque to the classical styles than other cities such as Paris or London, but even in Vienna Martines falls clearly into the conservative rather than the progressive camp.

And yet, even if she, say, had composed a groundbreaking string quartet in the 1790s, it would not have been enough to move from the margins to the centre of traditional music history because she wrote neither an opera, the dominant genre of her time, nor a symphony, the form that would become the benchmark of any composer's achievement in the nineteenth century and beyond. Through most of the eighteenth century, 'the symphonic repertoire was written as entertainment music for private concerts' and, if played in church services, theatres and public concerts, symphonic music was of 'secondary importance to respectively the mass, the play, and concertos and vocal numbers'. That was the world that Martines knew. Would we now know of Martines if she had realized that her future reputation as a composer might be reliant on embracing the possibilities of the symphony, in the way that her contemporaries Haydn and Mozart did? Even though the notion of the emergence in the 1780s of the 'Viennese classical school' – with its megastars Haydn, Mozart, Beethoven and Schubert – has come under fire in recent years, Martines is still judged by its standards. It is hardly surprising that, in this cultural context, Martines's supporters have sought to make her into a symphonist, with someone, not the composer herself, adding the title '*Sinfonie*' to the score of her *Overture* of 1770. Opera presented another challenge, more obviously connected to Martines's gender. She may have composed numerous beautiful arias, which rival anything her fellow composers were producing at the time for the opera houses of Europe; her mentor may have been the foremost opera librettist of his era, albeit the traditionalist on one side of a famous culture war, with Gluck and Calzabighi, the modernizers of opera, on the other; she certainly studied, assiduously, the operatic scores of the great composers; but, Marianna von Martines never wrote an opera, for the simple reason of her gender and social class. It would not have been proper.

As her biographer notes, by the age of forty, in 1784, Martines had achieved 'everything that was open to a woman of her rank and station. It is difficult to imagine what she could have done with propriety to win further recognition of her musicality and creativity.' And that was the problem. Martines's conservatism and caution in both her life and work (or the conservatism and caution imposed upon her) merely served to compound the constraints upon her as a woman and composer. And yet, paradoxically, Martines only achieved what she did achieve as a composer precisely because she remained scrupulously, rigidly, relentlessly proper.

In the one portrait that survives (shown on p. 126), the composer gazes calmly at the viewer, resting her hands on stonework that bears an inscription explaining when she was born and by whom she has been taught. There is no quill in her hand, not even a musical instrument in sight. She wears a simple cap, ornamented with a few flowers, the epitome of bourgeois 'private simplicity' rather than aristocratic excess, and thus existing to embody the values of her empress, who forbade her duchesses and court ladies to wear rouge and cultivated 'bourgeois intimacy' in her private life, whilst nevertheless perpetuating a Spanish formal etiquette in public. Never forget that for all the apparent informality of this portrait, Martines lived and worked in a society in which women of her class spent their days in enormous hooped petticoats, restricting even the simplest of movements. In the years after this portrait, during the final quarter of the eighteenth century, there would be a slow move towards more freedom in dress, but still women, according to one historian of dress, moved 'like puppets', their feet sticking out, splendid but inaccessible.

Reading the few letters written by Martines herself (few, because until Metastasio's death, he handled her correspondence), she rarely moves beyond formal expressions of courteous humility. There are occasional glimpses of something akin to friendship. The one correspondent with whom she relaxes, just a little, is Aurelio de' Georgi Bertola: five letters from Marianna survive, spanning the years 1784 to 1793. Marianna had turned forty in 1784, the year of Metastasio's death: Bertola was nine years her junior, a historian, poet, literary critic, translator of German poetry into

Italian and, from that year, professor of history at Pavia. Martines writes warm letters to him, or as warm as she is able, calling him 'my most amiable friend Bertola, whom I will never forget as long as I live: nor will I forget his most delightful company, which I would like to enjoy again very much indeed.' It is in this same letter, of 21 June 1784, that she uses the only words of German to appear in all her writing. They appear in a teasing postscript:

> PS *bacia mani della Babiola* (kisses to Babiola)
> *nichts Tropfen? Nichts* (Not a drop? Nothing)
> *schon widerum? Nein* (Again? No)

At a guess, Marianna might be teasing Aurelio about his use of German, or perhaps his (or her) refusal to take another drop of wine, when he visited her in Vienna. It is about the closest Martines gets to flirting. Martines's biographer hints, indeed hopes, that the handful of works that she wrote for bass voice, in contrast to the solo vocal pieces written for, in her own words, 'her own pleasure', were personal gestures. Are the large leaps, the 'singing coloratura' something special for one particular bass singer? Do they offer glimpses of a 'hidden personal life?' he asks. The search for Martines's personal (sexual?) life continues, but it is stony ground, for the remaining letters to Bertola are more cautiously friendly, mentioning the kind regards of her siblings, talking about health and the weather as much as books and music. Propriety is restored.

Martines never married. The absence of any form of romantic involvement, let alone marriage, may have been yet another example of the need to maintain propriety, to remain perpetually an innocent. She is described in late middle age as having 'the gaiety and vivacity of a girl'. There is never any suggestion that she is a mature, let alone sexually experienced, woman. There is, of course, another way to see her single status: as something that allowed her to continue her work as a composer in ways that, as a married woman, would have been denied to her. What is certain is that the only constant figure in Marianna's life was her sister, Antonia Johanna Theresia, two years her junior, from whom she never parted, and about whom nothing is known except her name: because the sisters were never apart, there are no letters.

Remaining single did not, however, protect Martines from fulfilling the traditional female roles of carer and housekeeper. She cared for Metastasio until his death, a task presumably not made easier by the man's hypochondria (which nevertheless did not deprive him of the 'enjoyment of company, of sleep, of appetite, of work, or of the other activities of life', according to one acerbic contemporary). Metastasio had undertaken Marianna's 'rearing and education with all the warmth of a careful father'. It was only proper that 'she never left his side' until his death. Only proper that, even then, she kept house for her older brothers.

It was still not enough. The shadow of the courtesan loomed over even this most respectable, this most proper, of women. One of the most pointed attacks came a generation later from the writer of patriotic historical novels, Caroline Pichler, whose childhood in the 1780s had been spent in Martines's Vienna. No matter that there was a clear conflict between Pichler's conservative views about women in general, and her own role as a politically engaged author. No matter that Pichler argues, in the same breath, that there has never been a tradition of women composers, whilst grudgingly acknowledging that Martines did indeed exist and had produced compositions. The quick and dirty way for Pichler to diminish Martines's achievement is to sexualize it. Martines was the 'pupil of the celebrated Metastasio who lived with her parents and undertook the education of this in many respects distinguished woman, which was for him a pleasant task'. Pichler's point is clear, at least to an early nineteenth-century readership: Martines was Metastasio's mistress.

By 1846 Martines needs defending, so her last surviving relative, Anton Schmid, in true Martines family tradition the curator of the court library, offers a riposte:

> Evil tongues in Vienna really wanted to attribute the friendly relationship between Martines and Metastasio to sordid motives. However, when one considers, on the one hand, the noble character of the great poet, and remembers, on the other hand, that when Marianna reached the loveliest years of her young womanhood, Metastasio had already reached old age, even the faintest breath that would cloud the mirror of that pure relationship must come to naught.

The full weight of Empress Maria Theresa's approval is brought to bear, in order to establish Martines's 'moral purity' and irreproachable reputation:

> This sublime queen very often had Marianna summoned in order to enjoy her artistic talents in various ways: and Joseph II, recognized as no insignificant friend of music, was accustomed to turn pages for Martines. These signs of favour are further proofs of the moral purity of our artist, since the strictly moral empress never consorted with any females whose reputations were not absolutely irreproachable.

Even in 2010, her biographers feel the need to suggest that Metastasio might have been more interested in the 'men of the family', as they tactfully put it, than he was in Marianna. The fact that Metastasio has to be outed in order to protect Marianna von Martines's sexual good name says more about the enduring need to police women's reputations than it does about who actually had sex with whom back in the eighteenth century.

Pichler's *ad feminam* attack on Martines, unpleasant though it is, can be, and has been, challenged by asserting Marianna's virtue. It has proved much harder to challenge Pichler's more general views about women and art, primarily because those views had become musical orthodoxy by the end of the eighteenth century. Pichler claims that:

> Not a single woman has yet succeeded in distinguishing herself as a creative musician. There are successful women painters and poets, and if not a single woman in any art or science has ever achieved as much as men have, they have nevertheless made significant strides forward. But not in music. And yet one would think that this art, which demands the least preliminary study and more feeling and imagination than the other arts, would be the proper medium in which the female spirit might express itself.

Pichler asserts, devastatingly, that women may be able to perform but they cannot compose. She claims to be bemused by women's inability to produce good compositions, 'resting as it does on instinct, on inner impulses, on feeling, and on imagination', and states that there has not been 'even a somewhat significant woman composer'.

These claims, predicated upon what has been described as a clear shift in the understanding of the categories 'woman' and 'composer', and driven by an increased essentialism (women were innately and therefore 'naturally' capable only of certain things), would soon come to dominate the world of music. In the nineteenth century, the phrase 'woman composer' would be used in a new way, as a conceptual scandal, a self-evident absurdity, as the musicologist Matthew Head reveals. Up until this point, certain exceptional women could be, and were, celebrated as proving the, admittedly, rare, capability of the female sex. It helped if those exceptional women's abilities could be harnessed to a celebration of female power in the political world, whether in the form of a Medici grand-duchess or an Austrian empress. But now, there was no room even for an exemplary Habsburg woman. Indeed, it was the German-speaking world that led the charge against women as composers, part and parcel of claims to the universality, and supremacy, of German music. As Head notes, it was now argued that:

> Not all music and musicians were of equal value; patterns of exclusion and hierarchy served the economic interest and cultural capital of a professional, male elite. Exceptions and ambivalence notwithstanding, there were clear losers, among them women, amateurs, dilettantes, and non-Germans.

This hardening of ideology surrounding women and music may account, to an extent, for the forgetting of Marianna von Martines. More immediately, the world that created, sustained, and indeed protected her, would be destroyed in her final years. In terms of her family, all of her brothers were dead by 1797. Only Antonia remained. The sisters received their brother's wealth, but money could not protect them from what was to come: war.

Habsburg power had been eroding throughout Martines's life, albeit slowly. Austria had already suffered territorial losses in the decade before her birth, when in 1797 Joseph II had been forced to cede the Austrian Netherlands and northern Italy to France. But now the Habsburg world was not merely under threat. It was being destroyed at its very heart, Vienna. In 1805, Napoleon took the city. In 1809, the Battle of Aspern-Essling left forty thousand corpses rotting on the Marchfeld. According to a contemporary Austrian account, thirty thousand wounded were lying in hospitals in Vienna and its suburbs. 'Many were carried to St. Polten, Enns and as far as Linz', wrote an eyewitness, whilst 'several hundred corpses floated down the Danube and are still thrown daily on its shores'. The battle was the first major victory against the French in a decade, but it only served to delay Napoleon's final assault on Habsburg power. Six weeks later, the French were victorious in the Battle of Wagram and, by the peace that followed, Austria ceded territory that included most of Croatia, Dalmatia and Slovenia. The Habsburg Empire lost three and a half million subjects and its army was reduced to 150,000.

A year after Napoleon's occupation of Vienna, Marianna and her sister, both now over sixty, moved to the fourth floor of a house in Freyung Square, a building known popularly as the *Schubladkasten* (the chest of drawers) because it resembled a piece of furniture. Another move, yet further from the world of the Michaelerhaus (although the distances are still a matter of a few hundred metres, no more) would follow, the world of the Martines sisters narrowing still further. On 11 December 1812, Antonia Martines died, so suddenly that no diagnosis was possible. She had lived for sixty-six years and all that remains of her life is a name. Two days later, Marianna followed her sister. The cause of death was noted for the second death in the household: *Lungenbrand* (tuberculosis). There is something poignant, even telling, in Marianna surviving Antonia by only two days.

Marianna von Martines's twentieth-century biographer, a man devoted to her memory, and who sadly died before he completed his homage to the composer, spent long summer days searching for the sisters' graves in the St Marx Cemetery. He could not find them. Some fifty years before her death, Martines's *Mass in C* had been performed to acclaim in the Michaelerkirche. The same church was the setting for the first performance of Mozart's unfinished *Requiem*, K626, his wife Constanza's memorial for the recently deceased and, at the time of his death, impoverished composer. Martines's life might have been a charmed one, but her death prompted no memorial. There was no one left to mourn.

Martines's world is visible to us, and her music is, wonderfully, available to us now that it has been unearthed from the archive. Marianna (or Anna Catharina, or Nannerl, or Maria Anna – she appears under all these names) simply is not.* The living, breathing woman is difficult to see behind an emblem of female achievement contained within a frame of propriety. Her life was a narrow, circumscribed, albeit comfortable one. Every bar she wrote, ever hour she lived, was informed by notions of propriety. It is easy to see now that this was the price she paid for being a woman and a composer, although it is impossible to know whether she herself understood her life and work in these terms. And yet writing this chapter has also been revelatory of Martines's achievements as a composer. As I write, the utterly exhilarating opening bars of her *Overture in C* ring out. She is, indeed, Haydn 'in athletic mode', in the words of one admirer. Her music, always poised and elegant, but packed with energy and joy, perhaps must be allowed to tell its own story.

* Martines was christened Anna Catharina, named as Maria Anna in her Bologna award, but chose to be called Marianna. Whether conducting traditional archival research or a Google search, tracing Martines is further complicated by the variant spellings of her surname, coupled with the presence or absence of 'von'. Marianna and her brothers replaced the 'z' of the Spanish with an 's', but both spellings continue to this day, along with Martinetz. Above all, however, Martines leaves little trace in the public historical record because her life was lived within a private sphere. Even when an event impacts strongly upon her, such as the award of the *Rittersand*, only her brothers appear in the records, despite their sister's celebrity. Scholars still believe, or hope, that if her nephew, and heir, Sigmund von Martines, an Imperial-Royal mine surveyor in what was then Schemnitz (now Banská Štiavnica in Slovakia) could be tracked down in the Czech or Slovak archives, then more of her music might be found.

'I still would like to have a bit more time' Fanny Hensel

Chapter Five

HENSEL

Early in the nineteenth century, the century that left Martines behind, a wealthy family from Berlin travel to Paris. It is not much of a holiday for the two eldest children, who are already marked out as musical prodigies. The girl and boy take lessons in ensemble playing from the eminent Pierre Baillot, and on the pianoforte from the renowned Marie Bigot, the pianist and composer who had been given a manuscript of the *Appassionata* sonata by the great Ludwig van Beethoven himself in recognition of her interpretative powers. By the time the girl is eleven, she is 'really something special'. At thirteen she is able to perform the twenty-four preludes from Bach's *Well-Tempered Clavier* for her father's birthday – from memory. It is clear that something remarkable is going on. Her father continues to push the girl and her younger brother to excel and, back in Berlin, the girl learns about composition, admittedly from a somewhat old-fashioned tutor, but her love of 'early' music is secured by this education, just as her love of Beethoven's music is inspired by Marie Bigot. An aunt worries that the pressure on the children, particularly the girl, is excessive, and writes to their mother: 'the thing is decidedly blameable: the exertion is too great, and might easily have hurt her. The extraordinary talent of your children wants direction, not forcing.' Their father is branded 'insatiable': the 'best appears to him only just good enough'. And yet both children appear to thrive, looking for opportunities to please their father with their achievements. Witnesses of the girl's 'extraordinary talent' believe she has the capability to rival even the father of German music, Johann Sebastian Bach.

The girl reaches the age of fourteen and suddenly everything changes. Her banker father returns from another business trip to Paris, carrying special gifts for his talented daughter and son: for her, a necklace of Scottish jewels; for him, the writing implements so that he might compose his first opera. The boy will find a public stage for his talent. The girl will find bejewelled happiness at home.

And so it came to pass. The boy, Felix Mendelssohn (or Felix Mendelssohn Bartholdy as he was to become) would be celebrated as one of the century's great composers, conductors and performers. The girl, Fanny Mendelssohn (or Fanny Hensel as she was to become), would remain a private figure, lost to music history for a century and a half.

Fanny Mendelssohn's story is, however, not merely another tale of female creativity doomed by patriarchal strictures. Despite these strictures, and they were powerful, Fanny Mendelssohn composed more music and, moreover (some would say), more music of a higher quality, than any other composer in this book. Not only that, but she performed and conducted on a regular basis throughout her life. She was able to do this because musical activity was embedded into the Mendelssohn family's life, and Fanny was loved and admired for her ability. As her mother wrote, Fanny is 'musical through and through'. More specifically, she was able to do this because her father, Abraham Mendelssohn, enjoyed, appreciated and encouraged his daughter as a musician, even as a composer. It was Abraham who hired Carl Friedrich Zelter to teach Fanny the complexities of double counterpoint, and it was for Zelter that

Fanny, by December 1824 and just turned nineteen, composed her thirty-second fugue.*

What Abraham objected to was his daughter performing in public or assuming any kind of professional identity. His reasons were many and would profoundly shape the complex landscape of belief in which Fanny Mendelssohn lived and worked. Fanny's gender was, of course, one of the most significant. When she wrote to her father, alluding to, but taking care not to challenge, the disparity between her future and that of her younger brother, Felix, Abraham responded by telling Fanny that she was right to admire Felix, and correct not to wish to enter the public sphere: 'Music will perhaps become his profession, whilst for *you* it can and must only be an ornament [*Zierde*], never the root [*Grundbass*] of your being and doing.' Abraham praises Fanny for always showing herself to be 'good and sensible in these matters' and urges her to remain 'true to these sentiments and to this line of conduct; they are feminine, and only what is truly feminine is an ornament to your sex'. Most crushingly, perhaps, Abraham casually acknowledges that Fanny might, in Felix's place, 'have merited equal approval'.

Abraham's ideas about proper femininity imbue his critiques of his daughter's compositions. He enjoys, for example, one particular song and has been singing it to himself all day: it is 'bright, and has an easy, natural flow, which most of the others have not; some of them are too ambitious for the words'. The more ambitious work is dismissed, and

* R. Larry Todd, author of the fascinating *The Other Mendelssohn*, upon which I draw heavily in this chapter, explains double counterpoint. The student sets, against a given melodic line, such as a pre-existent chorale melody, a second, newly devised part, conceived so that the two can be 'inverted', or flipped (i.e. with one part transposed an octave above or below the other), without infringing the rules of voice leading and dissonance treatment. It is a hard discipline, as Fanny found. One of her early attempts, in her mid-teens, includes the exasperated note, '*O du schlecter Kontrapunkt*' (O, you wretched counterpoint).

Fanny is advised 'to keep as much as possible to this lightness and naturalness in your future compositions'. Abraham's understanding of femininity naturalizes brightness, lightness and being pleasing to others, and makes unnatural ambition and complexity.

Her father's objections to Fanny entering upon any form of public, or professional, musical career were not, however, merely grounded in his views about the nature of women. Class also played its part. As a wealthy banker Abraham Mendelssohn struggled for some time with the idea that any of his children would be anything but amateurs: there was no *need* for his children to earn their bread by prostituting their talent. One of the many ironies of Fanny Mendelssohn's life is that, had she been from a lower class, she might well have had a professional career. Indeed, her brother Felix supported the composers Josephine Lang and Clara Wieck (soon to be Clara Schumann) in the public performance and printing of their work. The irony was not lost on a near-contemporary, writing in 1854: had Fanny 'been a poor man's daughter, she must have become known to the world'.

Gender and class were powerful considerations, but Abraham Mendelssohn had yet another concern, that of religion. As a Jew, he was acutely aware of the presence of anti-Semitism in his native Prussia, whether the sporadic outbreaks of physical violence against Jews, the laws curtailing most Jews' business dealings or the casual jibes of everyday life. The recent anti-Semitic Hep Hep riots in Bavaria were not close enough to home to provide a direct threat, but generated increased anxiety amongst the Jewish communities in Prussian Berlin. Closer to home, Zelter, Felix and Fanny's composition teacher would in future years be revealed as a virulent anti-Semite, when his correspondence with no less a figure than Goethe was published, much to the whole family's distress. In his letters, although not to the Mendelssohns' faces, Zelter articulated his and many of his compatriots' prejudice, peddling all the familiar stereotypes. Abraham 'treats me very favourably and I can dip into his cash, for he's become rich during the general wretchedness without, however, damaging his soul'. Felix is Zelter's 'fine young lad, merry and obedient', crucially 'a jewboy [*Judensohn*], but no Jew. By way of real sacrifice the father didn't have his sons snipped and is bringing them up on the right lines; it would really be *eppes rores* [*etwas Rares*, something rare, in mock-Yiddish] if for once a jewboy became an artist.' Zelter's defenders in our own time argue that 'the context makes it perfectly clear that, with his own little *Jüdeln*', Zelter 'was in his elephantine way writing humorously to Goethe'. The Mendelssohns did not see the humour, elephantine or not, and an anecdote in one of Abraham's letters reveals the extent to which he was oppressed by the ubiquity of these attitudes. He was being introduced to Goethe, when the great man asked Abraham if he were a 'son of Mendelssohn'. It was the first time that Abraham had heard the name of his father, the eminent philosopher Moses Mendelssohn, mentioned 'without an epithet', that is, without the addition of the word 'Jew'.

At precisely the time that Abraham was advising Fanny to keep music as 'an ornament', rather than part of her fundamental being, let alone a profession, he was also taking steps to protect his daughter from his society's prejudice. Fanny would enter the Protestant church. Abraham wrote to her that Christianity:

> Contains nothing that can lead you away from what is good, and much that guides you to love, obedience, tolerance, and resignation, even if it offered nothing but the example of its Founder, understood by so few, and followed by still fewer.

He powerfully articulates his own humanist belief:

> I know that there exists in me and in you and in all human beings an everlasting inclination towards all that is good,

163

true and right, and a conscience which warns and guides us when we go astray. I know it, I believe it, I live in this faith, and this is my religion.

In 1820, when Fanny was confirmed and gained her middle name Caecelia (fittingly, the patron saint of music), and then two years later when Abraham together with Fanny's mother, Lea, also converted to Christianity, gaining a second surname, Bartholdy, Abraham clearly believed that full assimilation into German Lutheran culture was possible. One day, not too far off, the tell-tale name of Mendelssohn would lapse, and the family would be known simply as Bartholdy. He was wrong, but his efforts are yet another example of his desire to protect his children, especially his daughters, from a world in which the 'good, true and right' were sometimes hard to find.

Although Fanny would be haunted by her fourteen-year-old self in later years, at the time she seemed to accept the path chosen for her. After all, performing often made her sick with anxiety ('trembling' led to, in her own mind at least, 'failure', such that 'I could have beaten myself, and all the others, with vexation'), so it may have been no hardship to take a step into the shadows.

She did not, however, stop composing. Her family would have to, and did, constitute her creative environment. Again and again, she would write pieces for a special occasion, as did her brother Felix, who would compose something every year for Fanny's birthday. Again and again, often in collaboration with her siblings (Felix, four years younger; Rebecka, six years younger; Paul, seven years younger), beautiful presentation scores would be prepared as gifts for family and friends. Mendelssohn family holidays were simply an opportunity to make yet more music, often in rarefied company. Thus, in the summer of 1822, when Fanny was sixteen, the family visited the composer Louis Spohr in Kassel, the capital of the Electorate of Hesse.

Within these elite circles, Fanny gained just as much recognition as her younger brother. Ignaz Moscheles, the Bohemian piano virtuoso, was present at Fanny's nineteenth birthday celebration on 14 November 1824 and was mesmerized by both the Mendelssohn offspring:

> This is a family the like of which I have never known. Felix, a boy of fifteen, is a phenomenon. What are all prodigies as compared with him? Gifted children, but nothing else. This Felix Mendelssohn is already a mature artist, and yet but fifteen years old! ... His elder sister Fanny, also extraordinarily gifted, played by ear, and with admirable precision Fugues and Passacailles by Bach. I think one may well call her a thorough 'Mus. Doc.' [guter Musiker].

As Hensel's biographer, Todd, observes, Moscheles signed Fanny's album with a mark of his most 'deep esteem': a 'conundrum-like duet, condensed onto one line of music notated with a treble clef. To derive the second voice, one turned the page upside down and read the same line of music, now inverted, and fitted with a bass clef.' In her mid-teens, the challenge of double counterpoint had both exasperated and daunted Fanny, but now it is offered as a badge of her expertise.

Moscheles was not the only visitor. The Mendelssohns could, and did, attract a wide circle of excellent musicians to their house, enabling Fanny to interact with the finest musicians of the day in her very own home. The family's move, on 18 February 1825, to a vast mansion on Leipzigerstrasse 3, merely served to establish further the protected environment in which Fanny, 'musical through and through', could develop. The house was not just an expression of the Mendelssohn's wealth, but also their intellectual and cultural life. How many Berlin mansions had an eminent scientist using their garden to conduct experiments into the magnetic mapping of the geosphere? And how many eminent scientists could call on a composer such as Felix Mendelssohn to compose a cantata for the opening of an academic conference, as Alexander von Humboldt would do? Beyond Leipzigerstrasse 3, the world was changing, from the development of railways to the sporadic flares of revolution throughout Europe. It was not that Fanny Mendelssohn knew nothing of railways or revolutionaries, since she marvelled that a machine might one day 'take a person to Dusseldorf in 4 hours. O hypercivilization, when will you reach us?' and she witnessed an attempt on the French king's life in Paris which shocked her deeply. But these things had little or no direct impact upon her day-to-day life. Her parents had made sure of that.

Domesticity and marriage were the roles designated for Fanny, but not only would they be enacted in a remarkable setting, Leipzigerstrasse 3, but according to the values of that remarkable family, the Mendelssohns. So, when Wilhelm Hensel, an aspiring painter, fell in love with a teenage Fanny her parents stepped in quickly, protective and demanding as ever. It was not only that an unestablished artist was unsuitable husband material, but also that (so her mother believed) Fanny was 'very young and Heaven be praised, hitherto has had no concerns, no passion . . . I now have her before me blooming, healthy, happy and free'. Hensel was packed off to Rome, for five years, during which time he might become worthy, and Fanny would remain 'free'. Wilhelm's departure prompted passionate musical outpourings on the part of Fanny, a compositional frenzy that continued through 1823, her most prolific year, including thirty-two lieder, many on the theme of separation or loss of lovers, and into 1824, with more ambitious works for the piano, including her *Piano Sonata in C minor*. Wilhelm in turn, forbidden to write to Fanny, sent her sketches, so it seems that distance and prohibitions merely pushed the couple towards self-expression through their respective art forms.

The real challenge for Wilhelm Hensel was not, however, to be the winning of Fanny Mendelssohn's affection, but to achieve integration into the rarefied life in Leipzigerstrasse 3. The house, on his return to Berlin in 1828 after some success in Rome, was dominated by the intense, almost febrile, activities of the young Mendelssohns. Fanny and Felix were the primary movers in a year-long and visionary for its time project to perform Bach's *St Matthew's Passion*, but that was only one aspect of life in the house, which saw a steady stream of young men passing through – poets, philosophers, scientists, drawn (or so believed Fanny) by the presence of Felix and her younger sister Rebecka. Fanny somewhat gleefully notes that Eduard Gans, 'a man of intellect and knowledge', comes often and 'has a great friendship for Rebecka, upon whom he has even forced a Greek lesson, in which these two learned persons read Plato'. She goes on to suggest that it 'stands to reason that gossip will translate this Platonic union into a real one'. Fanny stirs things up further by mentioning 'Dirichlet, professor of mathematics, a very handsome and amiable man, as full of fun and spirits as a student, and very learned', who was also, it seemed, interested in Rebecka. Meanwhile, composer Fanny was, much to Hensel's dismay, setting an awful lot of poetry by Edward Droysen. But it was the closeness between Fanny and Felix that most disconcerted Wilhelm on his return from Rome. He asked himself, and with good reason, whether there was room in Fanny's life for a husband, when her relationship with her brother was so intense.

Felix and Fanny were long-standing musical intimates. Back in 1821, as she approached her sixteenth birthday, Fanny wrote to her brother, who was away from Berlin being introduced to Goethe: 'Think of me when I turn 16 . . . Don't forget that you're my right hand and my eyesight, and, without you, therefore, I can't proceed with my music.' (The letter, full of playful touches, is signed off from 'Your truest, coughingest Fanny.') Twelve years later, she would notice how 'certain small incidents, coincidental and otherwise, recur between us, even across the miles', and goes on to list the musical coincidences that seem to unite them, wherever they are in the world. Musicologists now recognize that, in strictly musical terms, the relationship was founded on reciprocity, regardless of the social circumstances that meant that Felix operated on a public stage, whilst Fanny remained essentially a private figure. In the words of one contemporary, who met the siblings, there 'existed between the two a *mutual* appreciation and affectionate esteem, which were certainly unusual' (my italics). R. Larry Todd, expert on both brother and sister, sees Felix as almost as dependent upon Fanny as she upon him. That dependency is expressed, musically, in the frequent exchanges of pieces between the siblings, and, even more strikingly, the way in which each responds to the others' ideas within their music, even to the extent of quoting phrases. The process continued for decades. Todd explains its workings in 1838, when Fanny was composing an etude in G minor. This strikingly virtuosic and dramatic piece opens with a tumultuous *fortissimo* passage in G minor. There follows a pause, and the work begins again, *pianissimo*, in a totally unexpected key, B minor. Ranging through dazzling modulations, the work returns to G minor, only to spring another surprise: rushing arpeggiations 'give way to a reflective interpolated passage that cites material from the first movement of Felix's *Second Piano Concerto*, op. 40, composed in 1837 for the Birmingham Music Festival' and were thus on Fanny's mind in the summer of 1838. The work ends with a brief elaboration on Felix's theme, before a return to arpeggiations and a G minor conclusion.

Such an intense musical relationship, the unusual and mutual 'appreciation and affectionate esteem' that he noted, certainly gave Wilhelm Hensel pause for thought. He responded with his own vision of creative collaboration with Fanny. On Christmas Day

1828, he presented her with a miniature album in the shape of a heart, into which Fanny would transcribe her compositions, which would then be decorated with Wilhelm's artwork. It was yet another way for Wilhelm to communicate to Fanny his desire that she continue to be an artist, and that they continue to collaborate.

Two months later, Fanny and Wilhelm were engaged. Droysen remained an object of jealousy for Hensel, to which his fiancée responded by volunteering that she would 'no longer compose for voice, at least nothing by poets I personally know, certainly least of all Droysen. Instrumental music remains to me; I can confide to it what I will, it is discreet.' Fanny even claims that she will give up music entirely, since it is fit only for girls, not for married women. Wilhelm's response was delightfully indicative of the man: the 'unlimited practice' of Fanny's art must remain a fundamental of their relationship.

At around this time, Felix was ostensibly removed from the emotional equation, heading off on a fully funded, three-year Grand Tour in April 1829. But he remained in a portrait, painted by Wilhelm, and described by Fanny:

> A beautiful keepsake we have of him, his portrait by Hensel, three-quarter life size, the likeness perfect – a truly delightful, amiable picture. He is sitting on a garden bench (the background formed by lilac-bushes in our garden), the right arm reposing on the back of the bench, the left on his knees, with uplifted fingers. The expression of his face and the movement of his hands show that he is composing.

This image of Felix became something of an icon for his sister. She had a similar bench made for the garden, life being made to imitate art, and by mid-June Fanny, and her sister Rebecka, were 'spending hours before the painting, waiting for it to move them'. At the end of the month, Fanny would write to Felix, responding to a new work by him, telling him it was:

> Really beautiful. How do I arrive at that conclusion? I've been alone for two hours, at the piano . . . I get up from the piano, stand in front of your picture, and kiss it, and immerse myself so completely in your presence that I – must write you now. But I'm extremely happy and love you very much. Very much.

A similar, unnerving intensity is present in a letter written by Fanny to Felix on the very morning of her marriage. She is looking at the sketch of her brother, produced by Wilhelm, of course, on her desk:

> I am very composed, dear Felix, and your picture is next to me, but as I write your name again and almost see you in person before my very eyes, I cry, as you do deep inside, but I cry. Actually, I've always known that I could never experience anything that would remove you from my memory for even one-tenth of a moment . . . Your love has provided me with a great inner worth, and I will never stop holding myself in high esteem as long as you love me.

Whatever the potent emotional cocktail created by her imminent wedding, Fanny married Wilhelm. She even, in a deeply character-istic step, ended up writing the music for the ceremony herself, because Felix, at the last moment, was unable to do so.

In many respects, Fanny's wedding to Wilhelm Hensel in the Parochial Kirche in Berlin changed very little. She remained at Leipzigerstrasse 3, the newlyweds setting up home in the grounds of the mansion, in the *Gartenhaus*. No meagre annexe, a sketch from 1851 shows this garden house to be an extensive building, fronted with columns worthy of a small Greek temple, with every detail designed to create, in urban Berlin, the illusion of country life, from the artfully placed shrubs in their pots to a half-glimpsed footstool placed next to a comfortable bench on the porch. It looks a very pleasant place in which to start one's married life.

Somewhat disconcertingly, Fanny notes, almost prosaically, in her diary that sex was difficult at first, but then much improved. On 6 March 1830, she felt the first stirrings of a baby and then about ten weeks later she was confined to bed. In late May, a delightful letter from Fanny to Felix offers a glimpse of her apparently comfortable life:

> My little arrangement here is very nice. The blue inkpot is on a small table next to my bed, a splendid sunny rose cutting is nearby, and the balcony doors are open and admitting glorious fresh air for the first time. I munch on strawberries every day, with which [. . .] my very prudent husband spoils me.

This domestic idyll (complete with ink, perhaps for composition) masks a much darker reality, of which Fanny herself may well have been unaware. She had been confined to bed because her amniotic sac had ruptured. On 14 June, she went into labour. Two long days later a baby boy was born. No one expected the premature baby to survive, and his mother's health was precarious. The two men in her life did what they could. Wilhelm sketched the baby as if in doing so he could keep it alive. Felix sent music, wrote about music, to Fanny. Each sketch, each note, communicates their love for wife and sister.

To everyone's surprise, the baby not only survived, but flourished. He was named Sebastian Ludwig Felix, honouring the composers Bach, Beethoven and, of course, Fanny's own brother, and a letter to Sebastian's new uncle, dated just three weeks later, reveals Fanny's high spirits:

> The 7 of July. You heard from us directly yesterday. I had an extremely happy day. We ate at Mother's at noon with Droysen, whose birthday fell on the same day as Hensel's, just as it did last year . . . I remained in the hall until 9 and it did me a great deal of good . . . Sebastian, whose progress you must follow in great detail, was dressed for the first time today, but not with jacket and boots. Rather, he's grown into a regular child's outfit (vulgarly called *Stechkissen*) from a little package that was bundled up and put into a tiny bed almost too pathetically. I've just received permission today to go walking in the garden because the weather is beautiful.

Fanny Hensel had become what her father had wished her to be. Abraham, in a letter to his daughter on the occasion of her twenty-third birthday, just months before her marriage, exhorted her to prepare for her 'real calling', 'the state of a housewife', reminding her, in terms that constituted the foundation stone of family values in the nineteenth century, that women had a difficult task in that they had to be constantly occupied with 'apparent trifles, the interception of each drop of rain, that it might not evaporate, but be conducted into the right channel, and spread wealth and blessing'. Felix, a couple of months earlier, added his voice to Abraham's, singing the praises of the angel in the house: 'live and prosper, get married and be happy, shape your household so – that I shall find you in a beautiful home when I come . . . and remain yourselves, you two, whatever storms may rage outside'. Both men subscribed confidently to the new bourgeois gender ideology that naturalized the placing of women within the domestic realm by insisting on feminine nature.

One thing had changed, however. Frau Hensel may have been allowed to be up and about again, after six weeks of bed rest; she may have been very happy with her 'chubby, splendid, healthy boy!' as she wrote to Felix; but Frau Hensel found it very hard to compose. Given the landscape of belief in which she lived and worked, it would not have been suprising if, at this moment, young wife and mother to lay down her pen.

And yet, slowly but surely, the composer returned to work, completing a piece for her parents' wedding anniversary, then her *Cholera Cantata* during the epidemic of 1831 (a 'remarkable achievement', writes Todd, involving over thirty minutes of music, with a taut unified design, and completed three years before Felix Mendelssohn would write his first oratorio), more songs and then an overture, her only large-scale orchestral work, in the spring of 1832.

By the summer of that year, Fanny was well-advanced into her second pregnancy. 'Bapsen', as Sebastian was called, had just turned two when she was confined to bed, as she had been two years earlier. This time, there would be no happy ending. As she notes, carefully, in her diary: 'From the end of September on I was confined to bed rest, and now began a very sad time for me . . . On November 1, I delivered a dead baby girl.' The studiedly neutral tone of the diary has perplexed some readers. Nancy Reich, more familiar with the gushing Clara Schumann, believes that Hensel is merely 'recording in her diary because it is the proper thing to do'.

More likely, the apparent detachment is a form of self-protection because the stillbirth hit Fanny Hensel, woman and composer, harder than anything had done before. Months would pass before she engaged with any form of sustained musical activity. Felix tried to encourage her, but it was only in March, some five months into the 'very sad time', that there is a glimpse of an appetite for anything other than grief. Predictably, the occasion was a show put on for her parents. Fanny dressed up as none other than J.S. Bach. Felix was Frederick the Great.

Once again, she returned to the old familiar ways. She continued to perform, privately, and to compose, sometimes intensively, despite the impossibility of any formal professional recognition, and she did so alongside all the domestic and familial responsibilities she undertook, apparently with great pleasure. The births, marriages, deaths, pregnancies, illnesses, courtships and journeys (not to mention the need to order the dinner, or sew coloured ribbons into Sebastian's baby clothes) sometimes disrupted her compositional activity, but never entirely stopped it. She may have only two days to write the music for a celebration of the feast of St Cecilia, Fanny's own saint, on 22 November 1833; she may be working in 'such haste that the accompaniment hasn't been copied yet'; she may need to ensure that her vision of the singer Pauline Decker (a new friend and musical collaborator) in a dress modelled on Raphael's *Caecilia* – 'the two taller girls' holding music in their hands 'in the manner of the angels' in the old paintings – becomes reality; and she may need Wilhelm and his students to put together the 'entire exhibition' 'without the help of a single craftsman' – but on the night a 'magical, beautiful' performance took place, although the unfinished piano part suggests that Fanny had to improvise. The Caecelia music would be heard once, then never again.

The hidden toll paid by Caecilia's composer can be glimpsed in a handful of almost elegiac phrases in the letters from this period, as if Fanny can only look back, not forward. Writing to Felix, on 27 February 1834, she compares her life now with a past idyll of collaboration:

It's really quite a different situation from when we used to sit together at home and you would show me a totally new musical idea without telling me its purpose. Then, on the second day, you would have another idea, and on the third day you would undergo the torment of working them out, and I would comfort you when you thought you couldn't write anything more. And in the end the piece would be completed and I used to feel that I had a share in the work as well. But those lovely times are of course a thing of the past.

Elsewhere, Fanny writes, with characteristic self-mockery, that her 'lengthy things die in their youth of decrepitude'. She even expressed, cautiously, frustration with the way she has to work, and the people with whom she has to work:

Recently I've been rehearsing and performing a great deal of music. If only once I could have as many rehearsals as I wanted! I really believe I have talent for working out pieces and making the interpretation clear to people. But oh, the dilettantes!

Fanny's reference to 'the dilettantes' is absolutely of her time. Musical dilettantes were a feature of 'Damenmusik' ('women's music'), the phenomenon discovered and more importantly despised by serious journals such as *Allgemeine musikalische Zeitung*. Reviewers gained easy laughs when writing of their 'feeling of dread' when faced with yet another composition by a dilettante female, yet more 'Damenmusik'. Fanny Hensel, understandably, did not wish to be known as a dilettante. She was better than that. But if she was not a dilettante, what was she? A trip to Paris in the summer of 1835 did little to help clarify the matter. Fanny found that she was received as Felix's sister, rather than in her own right.

These hints of ambivalence, loneliness, even despair, came as Fanny approached her thirtieth birthday, although Felix did not have the eyes to see this. He did note a change in his sister, and expressed concern, but only up to a point:

> It makes me sad, that since her marriage she can no longer compose as diligently as earlier, for she has composed several things, especially German lieder, which belong to the very best which we possess of lieder; still, it is good on the other hand, that she finds much joy in her domestic concerns, for a woman who neglects them, be it for oil colours, or for rhyme, or for double counterpoint, always calls to mind instinctively the Greek from the *femmes savantes* ['learned women': the phrase is taken from Moliere's comedy of 1672] and I am afraid of that. This is then, thank God, therefore not the case with my sister, and yet she has, as said, continued her piano playing still with much love and besides has made much progress in it recently.

Felix believed that Fanny took great joy in her 'domestic concerns', and other letters from this period, lively, even breathless accounts of family life, seem to confirm his view. 'Seem to confirm', because, as one historian notes, the Mendelssohns 'must have been well aware that correspondence from a family such as theirs would very probably, in German nineteenth-century sensibility, one day be considered public property'. As if to prove the point, Fanny's letters only survive in large numbers because Felix collected his correspondence together in 'The Green Books', which were then passed down through the family and eventually made their way to the Bodleian Library in Oxford. How honest were Fanny's letters, when one considers that many were co-written by numerous family members? No wonder, then, that the letters reveal a woman delightedly immersed in domesticity: 'Dear Felix, it's 9am. Sebastian hasn't gotten washed yet and my menu hasn't been ordered. I merely wanted to start the letter and instead the quill got carried away.' For Sebastian's birthday he received a 'real live lamb' from his aunt Rebecka, which Fanny believes is 'a horse in disguise'. Her ideas, and her quill, rush on again, ending abruptly, since her mother is waiting to continue the letter. And yet even here, Fanny adds two quick, pointed, musical parting shots: 'Adieu. Who sang your *Scena*? Malibran [Maria Malibran, the mezzo-soprano] is in Italy.'

Elsewhere in her letters, a simmering anxiety is palpable, as when Fanny was asked by Felix to provide something for a Christmas album for his fiancée, Cécile. She asks her brother to let her know 'soon exactly what you would like, for there's always much to do before Christmas. Can I use paper, as I'd prefer, or am I to write directly into the album?' Her domestic and practical concerns are compounded by her artist's awareness that Felix himself was composing for the album: 'my only hope is that you also didn't choose *Feuchte Schwingen* . . . otherwise I'll kill myself'. She is joking, of course, but despite or because of the joke, one senses the strain. Years later, the domestic and musical would continue to entwine, with the events of the winter of 1844 revealing yet again the interplay of music and domestic responsibility. The Hensels had been receiving worrying reports from Florence. Rebecka, Fanny's sister, and her husband, the mathematician Gustav Dirichlet, who had so admired her sixties years earlier, had not returned to Berlin, first because of Rebecka's jaundice, then Gustav's typhoid fever. Now, against doctor's orders, Rebecka was pregnant. The Hensels rushed to Florence, as far as one could rush anywhere in winter in January 1845, where Fanny nursed Rebecka; Wilhelm, reluctant to leave his wife, nevertheless continued on to Rome in order to find the models necessary for his own work. Rebecka's baby was due in April, so Fanny ordered clothes to be sent from Berlin, but on 13 February Rebecka went into labour. Apparently, the doctor arrived at the same time as a baby daughter, called, fittingly, Florentina. For the following month, Fanny simply kept things going, managing Rebecka's household and correspondence, and helping care for her baby girl. Even in the midst of domestic crisis, Fanny (at least in her letters to Felix) never stops being a musician, as a description of her new niece's crying is used to take a witty swipe at Berlioz, the composer:

> I intend to lead art, which has strayed much too far from nature, back to its original path, and to this end am studying with great enthusiasm the utterances of my youngest niece as the mood strikes me. A certain degree of confusion and bad craftsmanship predominates, a *mezzoforte* muttering that promises very interesting effects in its transferral to the orchestra. When Berlioz will have placed the 50 pianos that he considers necessary, I would advise him to place a wet nurse with a nursing child who hasn't been fed for a few hours next to each. I'm convinced that the public, especially the mothers of the children, would be very moved.

In the autumn of 1835, as the months passed, Hensel composed less and less. Then, in November, she stopped writing her diary, possibly prompted to do so by the death of her father that month. For three and a half years, this personal record, such as it is, falls silent. Although Fanny herself, disgusted with her own 'musical apathy', would not have concurred, she had achieved a great deal already by this stage of her life, despite the inextricable intertwining of her music with her family relationships and responsibilities. Her own mother could perceive what Fanny could not, that her rigorous rehearsal techniques, her conducting and her accompanying made her daughter 'truly a rare phenomenon among women'.

Her achievements depended, however, on remaining within the gilded cage of Leipzigerstrasse 3. Only in such a privileged setting could Fanny Hensel create, for example, the magnificent *Sonntagsmusiken*, the 'Sunday musical events' that took place in her very own *Gartensaal* (Garden Room), the most significant, indeed the only significant, arena for Hensel as composer, conductor and performer. These 'Sunday musical events' have been described as Hensel's 'salon' but were actually something rather different, indeed much more ambitious. Predictably, however, the composer's own accounts of the *Sonntagsmusiken* are tagged on to a letter to Felix, which proudly announces that she looks after Sebastian herself, having decided not to employ anyone to care for him, and that she walks with him everywhere on errands and visits, during which he delights his mother with his talking. Fanny adds, in a self-deprecating coda to this vision of maternal activity, that she has been 'making a great deal of music this winter', that she is 'extremely happy with it' and that her 'Sunday musicales are still brilliant, except for the last one, which had a brilliant lack of cohesiveness'.

Hensel is being modest, possibly disingenuous. From around 1831, she built up the *Sonntagsmusiken* into 'much-admired musical events exceeding the scope of the usual forms of sociable gatherings of the time'.* On 21 January 1839, to give just one example, an audience would crowd into the *Gartensaal* (spilling over into a bedroom in the main residence) to hear a reading of Mozart's opera

---

* The *Sonntagsmusiken* continued something of a tradition in Fanny's mother's family. Her great-aunt Cäcilie was instrumental in the founding of a Viennese concert society, the significant Gesellschaft der Musikfreunde, but it was great-aunt Fanny von Arnstein who presided over an illustrious salon. During the Congress of Vienna, her guests included Wellington and Talleyrand, as well as literary and artistic celebrities. When Fanny von Arnstein, resolutely Prussian despite living in Vienna, died in 1818, her niece Lea remembered her as 'the most interesting woman in Europe, a miraculous phenomenon in our stupid, egoistic times'.

La Clemenza di Tito, given by Hensel's usual soloists, but supplemented by the English star soprano, Clara Novello, newly arrived in Berlin. No wonder that, if a musician or composer came to Berlin, they sought an invitation, not least because Hensel set high standards for audience behaviour, insisting for example on silence during the performance, which was not always a given at the time. Gradually, the concerts edged closer to becoming public events; refreshments began to be served; for a performance of Felix Mendelssohn's *Paulus*, a libretto was printed and set out for the three hundred guests; programmes were printed; guests beyond the Mendelssohns' immediate circle were permitted to attend. Strangers were coming to Leipzigerstrasse 3.

There they witnessed Fanny Hensel, musician, composer and conductor:

> She seized upon the spirit of the composition and its innermost fibres, which then radiated out most forcefully into the souls of the singers and audience. A *sforzando* from her small finger affected us like an electric shock, transporting us much further than the wooden tapping of a baton on a music stand. When one saw Fanny Hensel perform a masterpiece, she seemed larger. Her forehead shone, her features were ennobled, and one believed in seeing the most lovely shapes . . . No common feeling could have possessed her; she must have been contemplating and breathing in the realm of the sublime and beautiful. Even her sharp critical judgements shared with close acquaintances were founded on ideals she demanded from art and human character alike – not in impure motives of exclusion, arrogance and resentment. Whoever knew her was convinced that she was as ungrudging as she was unpretentious.

These glowing words come from a fellow musician and composer, Johanna Kinke (she who would fall to her death in London in 1858), who understands and appreciates Hensel's professionalism, her insistence on rehearsals, her preference for working with only expert singers and musicians. Perhaps, as musical celebrities such as Franz Liszt clamoured to attend, 'this semi-public space, shared with exclusive audiences drawn from the elite of Berlin society', was indeed the place where 'Hensel found her own voice as pianist, conductor and composer'. Perhaps.

Her composer's voice was determined, in content and scope, by the predominantly private nature of her life, which meant that Hensel always composes for private spaces, even when she occasionally writes larger-scale works. She focuses primarily on the solo song and the character piece for piano, the latter undoubtedly the central form of Romantic piano music but, for Fanny Hensel, a central form intended for a circle of family and friends, rather than for the public concert hall. This is not to diminish her achievement. Far from it. In her chosen genres, even when 'chosen' implies chosen *for* her, she is a superb composer and very much her own woman. Her piano works can be, and often are, described as *Lied ohne Worte* (Songs without Words), a genre popularized in part by her brother who had published six sets of songs without words between 1832 and 1845. Hensel herself, insists that *her* works are 'piano lieder', and she uses the form to probe dark harmonies, to explore complex key relationships, to apply chromaticism with startling intensity and to blur generic boundaries. Her songwriting is equally impressive. Hensel's setting of a powerful poem by Lenau has been described as the culmination of her lieder making. *Dein ist mein herz* [Thine is my heart] shows all the 'subtle craft of her late style – the major minor exchange, the expressive opening up of traditional tonality to new chromatic combinations and relationships, and the delicate interweaving and mirroring of piano and voice, all designed to heighten our appreciation of Lenau's moving poem':

> Thine is my heart, my pain, thine own and all the joys that burst forth . . . The dearest thing I may acquire in songs that abduct my heart is a word to me that they please you, a silent glance that they touch you.

The lyrics seem to speak for Fanny's own desire for acceptance, her offering of her music on the altar of the men in her life.

But once again, through the winter of 1837–38, she found she could not compose. Then even the concerts faltered, this time because of the devastating effect of an outbreak of measles. Rebecka's new baby, Felix, died. Fanny's sister was so distraught that she had to be physically restrained in bed. Wilhelm tried to help, sketching images of the dead baby in an attempt to comfort the grieving mother. Fanny took a more practical approach, travelling with her sister in June 1839 to the Pomeranian sea resort of Heringsdorf on the island of Usedom. Rebecka began to recover, whether by the 'cure' provided by several weeks of sea bathing or the fact that the sisters spent the days singing Fanny's *a cappella* duets.

The emotional trauma of this period galvanized Hensel in some way. Only a month after her nephew Felix's death, she was composing again, the first of a series of works demonstrating greater and greater ambition, particularly in her writing for piano. There was more to come, for, on 27 August 1839, the Hensel family (together with their cook) set off for a long-desired trip to Italy. Their destination was Rome, but the journey south itself seemed to bring to the surface Fanny's exuberant, almost fierce, engagement with life and with music. Whether critiquing a performance of Allegri's legendary *Miserere* (Fanny's perfect pitch revealed that the choir 'began in A minor and progressively lost its pitch in a gradual, unauthorized descent to somewhere between F and G minor') or throwing herself into the carnival, wearing a veil rather than a mask because of her glasses, she was in her element. She gained an admirer, a young Charles Gounod, thirteen years her junior, who became almost fixated on her, willing and able to learn at her feet about the German musical tradition, and to celebrate and applaud Fanny's own compositional activity. As Fanny acknowledged, with her usual deadpan irony, she was living in 'an atmosphere of admiration and homage'. Even in her youth, she writes, 'I never was made so much of as I have been here, and that this is very pleasant nobody can deny.'

When, where, how and for whom she could compose had been determined for Fanny Mendelssohn Hensel since her early childhood. She had accommodated herself again and again, showing both perseverance and creativity. Now, in Italy, Fanny Hensel found a new freedom, responding directly to the sights of Rome, creating musically demanding works such as *Villa Medici* or *Ponte Molle*. Hensel remained careful, however, when writing to others, to maintain the image of the amateur, domestic, feminine, composer:

> Composing a good deal lately, and have called my piano pieces after the names of my favourite haunts, partly because they really came into my mind at these spots, partly because our pleasant excursions were in my mind while I was writing them. They will form a delightful souvenir, a kind of second diary. But do not imagine that I give these names when playing them in society, they are for home use entirely.

And she still composed the kinds of pieces that she had done since she was a girl, and for the same reasons. In early 1840, she was writing something for her mother's upcoming birthday on a 'played-out rattletrap of a piano'. But in a letter to Lea, Fanny knows that something has changed: 'Do you recognize your daughter, dear mother?' she asks.

The transformation continued back in Berlin, where Hensel composed a miniature cycle of three interconnected songs that 'hint at her aspirations to composition on a large scale' in a year that marked the high point in her career as a writer of song. She also completed *Das Jahr*, for solo piano, 'arguably her most impressive accomplishment', 'more forward-looking and original than' her brother Felix's work, one of the 'greatest of the unheralded piano suites of the nineteenth century', writes Hensel's biographer, and I would wholeheartedly agree. *Das Jahr* is a powerful, compelling, at times sumptuous, at others pellucid, piece of music, nearly an hour in length. The twelve movements/months, and the austere '*Epilog*', are 'interlocked by related musical and extramusical elements and by an overarching key plan', which Todd compares to the great piano cycles of Robert Schumann. Two of the most striking elements are the use of chorales, testimony to Hensel's passionate commitment to the music of Bach, and the use of a unifying motif, derived from the haunting, muffled, descending bass octaves with which January starts.

And yet, even with *Das Jahr*, Hensel deprecated her own talent, minimized her achievement and set it, unthreateningly, within a domestic sphere:

> Now I'm engaged in another small work [*kleine Arbeit*] that's giving me much fun, namely a series of 12 piano pieces meant to depict the months; I've already progressed more than half way. When I finish, I'll make clean copies of the pieces, and they will be provided with vignettes. And so we try to ornament and prettify our

lives – that is the advantage of artists, that they can strew such beautifications about, for those nearby to take an interest in.

Fanny is rearticulating the creed asserted by her father some twenty years earlier: 'Music will perhaps become his profession, whilst for *you* it can and must only be an ornament [*Zierde*], never the root [*Grundbass*] of your being and doing'; remain 'true to these sentiments and to this line of conduct; they are feminine, and only what is truly feminine is an ornament to your sex.'

This creed meant that *Das Jahr*, like so many of Hensel's compositions, was created for a particular person and occasion (in this case, Wilhelm Hensel's birthday); that it would be performed, as ever, in the private setting of the *Gartensaal*; and that it would only be circulated amongst friends and family. It made an exquisite manuscript: a visitor to Berlin, Sarah Austin, saw a copy in 1842 and was delighted with the 'series of beautiful pieces for the pianoforte, called after the months', not least for the accompanying illustrations by Wilhelm:

> These were written in an album, and at the head of each month was a charming drawing illustrative of it by Professor Hensel. And all this was simple, dignified, free from the ostentation and sensibleries which sometimes throw doubt or discredit on such manifestations. One had always the fullest assurance that Madame Hensel said less rather than more than she felt.

The title page of this beautiful score reads '*Das Jahr. Zwölf Charakterstücke für Fortepiano von Fanny Hensel*' (The Year. Twelve Character Pieces for Piano by Fanny Hensel). The formality suggests that Fanny may have wished to have her masterpiece published. It did not happen.* Instead, her portrait was taken by Moritz Daniel Oppenheim, German-Jewish painter to the rich, famous and cultured, and Fanny Hensel appears as a lady of the leisured classes. What is more, Fanny, who was not conventionally beautiful (she had one shoulder higher than the other, needed to wear glasses at all times and may have been, as a distant relation by marriage wrote, unkindly, 'indescribably plain'), becomes conventionally pretty. There are no references to music. The portrait does not even show her hands.

Composition as feminine ornament, as domestic virtue, as private pleasure: one has to look hard for the moments when Fanny Hensel appears, momentarily, to stray beyond these boundaries, even in her own psyche. And yet, from time to time she does, although almost always followed by an immediate withdrawal from the field. In 1825, for example, approaching her twentieth birthday, the young Fanny Mendelssohn drafted a proposal for a new amateur music society to promote instrumental music lest it 'disappear in the bad taste of the time, egotism of the organizer, and pandering to the public'. She took the trouble to work it all out, down to the details of fees and lending libraries, but then quickly backed away from controversy in her assertion that the society would need to be run by men because 'women of private backgrounds shy away from appearing before an audience'. Later, she became closely involved with the Berlin Singakademie's performance of Felix's oratorio *Paulus*, and wrote to her brother:

> I thought to myself 'If you were only up there, everything would be fine.' Lichtenstein sat next to me and heard my

* The work was unearthed by scholars in 1993, with a full-colour facsimile appearing in 2000.

sighs. They started 'Mache dich auf' at half the right tempo, and then I instinctively called out, 'My God, it must go twice as fast.' Lichtenstein invited me to show them the way but told me that Schneider, the music director, had assured them that one cannot be ruled by a metronome marking. Then I assured them that they could be ruled by my word, and they had better do it, for God's sake.

As this anecdote suggests, when Fanny's acute musical sensibility was in play, then very little would stop her, but these impromptu moments of self-assertion were rare and short-lived. However, in 1836 when she was thirty-one Fanny took a first, if tentative, step towards getting her music printed. She wrote to a family friend, Karl Klingemann, who was interested in publishing her compositions in London:

> I enclose two pianoforte pieces which I have written since I came home from Dusseldorf.* I leave it to you to say whether they are worth presenting to my unknown young friend, but I must add that it is a pleasure to me to find a public for my little pieces in London, for here I have none at all. Once a year, perhaps, some one will copy a piece of mine, or ask me to play something special – certainly not oftener; and now that Rebecka has left off singing, my songs lie unheeded and unknown. If nobody ever offers an opinion, or takes the slightest interest in one's productions, one loses in time not only all pleasure in them, but all power of judging their value.

* It has been suggested that the two pieces being offered to Klingemann, to be shown to a publisher in London, were Hensel's scintillating Prestissimo in C major and a passionate Allegro agitato in G minor.

Typically, Fanny backtracks from this somewhat bleak assessment of her life as a composer ('unheeded', 'unknown', without a 'public'), and offers a more positive analysis, emphasizing the importance of the family circle. Felix, she reassures Klingemann, was a 'sufficient public' for her, even though he is rarely in Berlin:

> Moreover my own delight in music and Hensel's sympathy keep me awake still, and I cannot help considering it a sign of talent that I do not give it up, though I can get nobody to take an interest in my efforts. But enough of this uninteresting topic.

Felix, Fanny's 'sufficient public' (if only he were around more), has a complex role at this crucial moment in her life. Her composition remained inextricably entwined with her brother's very existence, reliant on his stimulation, his approval and his response as a fellow composer. The affection of brother and sister, the musical intimacy that so disconcerted Wilhelm Hensel, is articulated in a famous letter in which Fanny seeks to explain to Felix his power over her:

> I don't know exactly what Goethe means by the demonic influence [she uses the word *Wesen*, a presence neither good, nor bad, but powerful] but this much is clear: if it does exist, you exert it over me. I believe that if you seriously suggested that I become a good mathematician, I wouldn't have any particularly difficulty in doing so, and I could just as easily cease being a musician tomorrow if you thought I wasn't good at that any longer. Therefore treat me with great care.

Knowing full well Felix's opposition to her publishing, in 1835 Fanny attempted to gain his approval by emphasizing her passive role in the proceedings: 'In the recent past, I've been frequently asked, once again, about publishing something; should I do it?' Fanny compares herself to the donkey who starved to death because unable to choose between two bales of hay: Felix on the one side, and Wilhelm, who had always supported her desire to publish, on the other. And yet at the same time she describes herself, to Felix, as 'rather neutral about it'. Her brother, in response, two months later, is unstinting in his praise for her compositions, but writes that he still has his 'old reservations' about publishing. Felix was the only voice that counted. Wilhelm Hensel, as ever, was keen for Fanny to publish her work, but as Fanny wrote to Felix, she would 'comply totally' with her husband's wishes in 'any other matter, yet on this issue alone it's crucial to have your consent, for without it I might not undertake anything of the kind'. Two years on, even Fanny's mother Lea supported her, and wrote to Felix to say so, in June 1837:

> On this occasion permit me to pose a question and request. Shouldn't she publish a selection of her lieder and piano pieces? For about a year she has written, especially in the latter genre, many really excellent examples, perhaps not without having in mind some ideas from your first few *Lieder ohne Worte*. All that holds her back is that you have not called upon or encouraged her to do so. Wouldn't it be reasonable for you to cheer her on and take the opportunity to secure a publisher?

Lea's plea may reflect her concern for her daughter that summer. Fanny had fallen pregnant again in the spring of 1837, as had her sister Rebecka, resulting in both sisters missing Felix's marriage to Cécile Jeanrenaud on 27 March in Frankfurt, his bride's home. In Berlin, a day after the wedding, Fanny was confined to bed and ordered to rest although, characteristically, she still managed to complete a piano prelude the same day. Bed rest did not prevent the loss of a second baby. No one thinks to record how far advanced the pregnancy was this time, although a letter from Fanny on 23 December reveals that she knew she was pregnant at that time. She jokes that she would like the wedding to be moved to Leipzig for 'certain reasons, which modesty prevents my mentioning', knowing full well that it would take place in Frankfurt. By the end of March, she would therefore have been at least five months into the pregnancy. On 14 April 1837, Felix, well into his honeymoon travels, received news of his sister's 'unpleasant accident'. Both he and Cécile acknowledged that the experience must have been 'very disagreeable for her', admired the fact that she was 'well and cheerful' and hoped that the weather would be kind to her. The entire episode reveals a world in which a miscarriage is 'unpleasant' or 'disagreeable', and in which Fanny's modesty and cheerfulness is a given.

If Felix and Cécile believed that better weather, and a bit of sea bathing, would help Fanny, then her mother Lea may have hoped that Fanny would be supported through the miscarriage if she could take her compositions to a wider audience. Felix did not see things in the same way. He wrote privately to his mother, insisting that she keep the contents of the letter secret from Fanny and Wilhelm. He acknowledges that if Fanny decided to publish, then he would support her:

> But to *encourage* her to publish I cannot do, since it runs counter to my views and convictions . . . I regard publishing as something serious (it should at least be that) and believe one should do it only if one is willing to appear and remain an author for one's life. That means a series of works, one after the other; to come forward with just one or two is only to annoy the public . . . Fanny, as I know her,

has neither enthusiasm nor calling for authorship; then, too, she is too much a *Frau*, as is proper, raises Sebastian and cares for her home, and thinks neither of the public nor the musical world, nor even of music, except when she has filled her primary occupation. Allowing her music to appear in print would just stir her up in that, and I can't get used to the idea even once. Therefore I will not encourage her, please excuse me. But show these words neither to Fanny nor Hensel, who would think ill of me or misunderstand – rather, say nothing about it. If Fanny's own drive or desire to please Hensel leads her to publish, I'm prepared, as I said, to help her as much as I am able, but to encourage her to do something that I don't think is right, I cannot do.

Even if the explicit contents of this letter were never communicated to Fanny or Wilhelm, it achieved its effect. Although by the end of 1837, Fanny had completed eleven piano pieces, nothing appeared in print. It was during that winter that she found it so hard to compose.

Five years passed, and there was still no movement. Lea's death in 1842 not only deprived Fanny of her mother, but also of a supporter of her tentative steps towards a public identity. The following year, 1843, Fanny recovered enough to revive the *Sonntagsmusiken* in the autumn. She also arranged to have an album of her piano music prepared by a copyist, as a gift for Felix. It bears the title: 'Twelve piano pieces by Fanny Hensel, *née* Mendelssohn-Bartholdy. For Felix 1843.' Fanny looked through the copyist's work before sending the album to her brother, adding handwritten corrections such as accidentals, performance indications, dynamics and missing notes. She always did care how her work appeared. She continued to compose, and in new genres; 1843 was the year in which she wrote her only piano sonata, 'a genre largely off-limits to earlier female composers in northern Germany', and, in Hensel's hands, one that makes immense demands upon the performer. In the 1840s, the sonata existed at the boundary of public and private, amateur and professional music making, and was increasingly seen as a testing ground for serious composers and, therefore, simply to write a sonata put Fanny Hensel closer to the border between public and private, amateur and professional, than she had ever been before.

A letter from this time expresses all Fanny's ambivalence about her own status. The figure of the dilettante continues to haunt her:

> A dilettante is already an alarming being, a female author even more so, but when the two entities are combined in a single person, she becomes the most frightening creature imaginable.

This may be irony (Fanny Hensel's reputation put her far above the female dilettantes she herself despised), but it hints at very real fears on the composer's part. After all, she knew only too well how her work was judged, even when not in print. A fellow composer such as Niels Gade might sing her praises as a performer (she is 'utterly excellent') and as composer (he was 'completely transported' by her music, and even acknowledges that Fanny might well have influenced her famous brother, if only because she was the elder of the two), but he is compelled to add a caveat: Hensel's compositions were 'for a lady . . . really very pretty'.

Still nothing was done. Fanny continued to compose, continued to send delightful letters to her brother, continued to relish her son's antics. She noted, with dismay, a worsening of the political situation in 1844: the 'daily prohibitions, the scribbling and grinding of the government and police from all sides'. Prussia must be in a bad way, she wrote:

If it is really in danger the moment three students form themselves into a union, or three professors publish a periodical! The never-ending prohibitions, the meddling with everything, the constant espionage, carried on in the midst of peace and in spite of the quiet disposition of the nation, has now reached a climax which is perfectly intolerable.

Berlin's fault lines were only too visible. In the Hensels' part of the city the wide streets were lined with impressive mansions, and the spacious squares housed the buildings that announced Prussia's power. Yet, from these streets and squares, the Berlin *haute* bourgeois could see, and smell, the smoke from the furnaces of the iron foundries in Oranienburg, the 'land of fire' that would transform Prussia's, and then Germany's, economy and landscape. Beyond the city, the harvests failed in 1845 and 1846. The year the engineering company Siemens was founded, 1847, began with food riots: the people were starving. Felix at least could escape: a combination of the generally worsening political situation in Prussia, and the composer's utter frustration with the nation's king as a patron, drove Fanny's brother away from Berlin again.

The spring of 1846 at last brought change, when Fanny Hensel made a new friend, Robert von Keudall, a talented pianist and philosophy student, and a future amanuensis and confidante of Otto von Bismarck. Fanny was delighted with Robert, who was nine years her junior, a 'lively and charming man', with 'such an ear for music as I have not met with since Gounod and Dugasseau'. Soon Robert was visiting every day, exploring actively the huge array of compositions that Fanny had produced over the years. For him, she started to work on a collection of fifty-one works, some old, some new divided precisely into three genres: piano pieces, lieder and part-songs. Todd, Hensel biographer describes this 'methodology concentration' as almost 'Schumannesque'. As Fanny wrote in July 1846: 'Keudell keeps my music alive and in constant activity, as Gounod did once. He takes an intense interest in everything that I write, and calls my attention to any shortcomings, being generally in the right too.'

Suddenly, Fanny had the confidence to assert herself and, on 9 July 1846, she wrote a remarkable letter to Felix:

Actually I wouldn't expect you to read this rubbish now, busy as you are, if I didn't have to tell you something. But since I know right from the start that you won't approve, it's a bit awkward to get under way. So laugh at me or not, as you wish: I'm afraid of my brothers at age 40, as I was of Father at age 14 or more aptly expressed, desirous of pleasing you and everyone I've loved throughout my life. And when I know now in advance that it won't be the case, I thus feel RATHER uncomfortable. In a word, I'm beginning to publish. I have Herr Bock's sincere offer for my lieder and have finally turned a receptive ear to his favourable terms. And if I've done it of my own free will and cannot blame anyone in my family if aggravation results from it (friends and acquaintances have indeed been urging me for a long time), then I can console myself, on the other hand with the knowledge that I in no way sought out or induced the type of musical reputation that might have elicited such offers. I hope I won't disgrace all of you through my publishing, as I'm no *femme libre* and unfortunately not even an adherent of the *Young Germany* movement. I trust *you* will in no way be bothered by it, since, as you can see, I've proceeded completely on my own in order to spare you any possible unpleasant moments, and I hope you won't think badly of me. If it succeeds – that is, if the pieces are well liked and I receive additional offers – I know it will be a great stimulus to me, something I've always needed in order to create. If not, I'll be as indifferent as I've always been and not be upset, and then if I work less or stop completely, nothing will have been lost by that either.

What is particularly compelling about Fanny's words here is her consciousness, barely articulated but nevertheless present, that she remains, on one level, the fearful fourteen-year-old girl who had been forbidden to have a professional career.

Felix did not reply at once, which 'somewhat hurt' Fanny. In the meantime, she received further offers from publishers, noting with her usual irony that they were offers 'that no female dilettante has probably yet received'. And still Felix did not respond. At last, four weeks later, he wrote to his 'dearest Fenchel', apologizing for his silence. His letter is short, and to the point. He offers his sister his 'professional blessing [Handwerkssegen] on your decision to join our guild', and hopes that she will experience only the joys of public life: 'may the public pelt you only with roses and never with sand.' Felix signs off: 'The fellow journeyman tailor, FMB.' There is a conscious echo of the moment back in 1824 when Felix had been symbolically welcomed, with the full blessing of his family, into the brotherhood of Mozart, Haydn and 'old father' Bach. He had been fifteen years old, suggesting that, just as Fanny was haunted by her teenage self, so perhaps was Felix. Only now could the siblings acknowledge, obliquely, the legacy of the decisions made for them decades earlier. Felix's response was not ideal, but it would do: 'At last Felix has written, and given me his professional blessing in his kindest manner. I know that he is not quite satisfied in his heart of hearts, but I am glad he has said a kind word to me about it.'

Now, the floodgates opened after those decades of containment: 1846 was 'a creatively explosive, prolific year for Fanny – arguably her *annus mirabilis*', writes her biographer. She 'committed to composing on a regular basis and all that it entailed – to winnowing, revising, and polishing works, and for the first time began to see her music through the press on a sustained, regular schedule'. Keudall provided her with critical advice throughout. To a family friend, she was careful to emphasize her passive role in the business and her willingness to let it drop if needs be:

> In addition, I can truthfully say that I let it happen more than made it happen, and it is this in particular that cheers me . . . If they want more from me, it should act as a stimulus to achieve, if possible, more. If the matter comes to an end then, I also won't grieve, for I'm not ambitious, and so I haven't yet had the occasion to regret my decision.

She was equally careful in her handling of Felix, and with good reason. According to his wife, Cécile, his response to Fanny's opus 1 was somewhat melodramatic. He sang all the songs, 'and continually swore in between that he wanted to avenge himself'. Cécile goes on, probably tongue-in-cheek, to describe Felix as 'egotistical', and suggests that his previous opposition was driven by his desire 'to begrudge the world something so beautiful'. Although Fanny had apparently been happy to communicate with her brother directly about the publication of works that he knew well (his 'old friends'), her opus 1 and opus 2, she took care to write to Cécile about opus 3, which contained new material, and admitted to a 'guilty conscience' that she was making public works with which Felix had not been directly involved.

Fanny's 'conscience' did not, however, prevent her compiling, when asked by publishers, a list of her compositions that were still 'floating around the world concealed'. Three more collections headed for the presses. The year ended with the writing of a piano trio, conceived (as so many previous works had been) as a birthday present for a family member, in this case, Rebecka. The *Piano Trio*'s first movement begins in suppressed tension, and builds to a powerful close. The second movement runs seamlessly into the third, which is marked *Lied*, linking it clearly with her earlier *Songs for piano*. The writing for the piano is fascinating, giving great freedom to the performer whose part, in the final movement, is marked *ad libitum*. As an album note puts it, the music 'drives to a grand climax as the strings, once again set two octaves apart, soar high above the *tremolandi* piano, and the trio powers its way to a resounding close in D major'. In her diary, in May 1846, Fanny Hensel wrote 'I feel as if newly born.'

She was only too well aware how long this moment had taken to arrive:

> I cannot deny that the joy in publishing my music has also elevated my positive mood. So far, touch wood, I have not had unpleasant experiences, and it is truly stimulating to experience this type of success first at an age by which it has usually ended for women, if indeed they ever experience it.

The wonder is heightened by a sense of the time that has passed: 'To be sure, when I consider that 10 years ago I thought it too late and now is the latest possible time, the situation seems rather ridiculous, as does my long-standing outrage at the idea of starting op. 1 in my old age.' Fanny is, of course, being ironic about her 'old age'. She was only forty, and feeling good on it, noting in August 1846 that 'the indescribable feeling of well-being, which I have had this entire summer, still continues'.

Fanny understood that her belated public emergence had come late. What she did not know is that it would be so short-lived. By the spring of 1847, she was once again unsure of her way as a composer, and it seemed that the world around her was also in crisis. The political situation in Prussia was becoming increasingly tense, with the desperate and hungry protesting on the streets in Berlin in April. Fanny expressed sympathy with the plight of her poor countrymen, but also noted, wearily, 'now politics will dominate the next time period; everything else will be impossible'. She herself was 'having a dreadful time; nothing musical is succeeding for me – since my trio I have not written a single usable bar'. The trio did, however, have its first performance towards the end of April.

Hensel would in fact write a song over the next couple of weeks, completing it on Friday 13 May, seventeen days after writing that 'nothing musical' was succeeding for her. On Saturday, she was working with her chorus on rehearsals for the following day's *Sonntagsmusiken*, and she lost sensation in her hands. This was not a new experience. In the months after her mother's death, in December 1842, Fanny had noticed certain worrying physical symptoms, including a lack of sensation in her arms, but by the autumn of 1843 she believed that she was managing the symptoms with a cure very much of her time:

> The numbness has almost disappeared, and the weakness comes and goes by fits. Galvanism did not suit me, and I am now trying bathing them in a decoction of brandy, which prescription has acquainted me with the interesting fact that in Berlin, where every third shop sells schnapps, there is no distillery, and I shall have to see where I can get the stuff. I played very well here the other day, but the next, at Mme Decker's, worse than any night-watchman – in a word, I can no more depend upon myself now than I could at fourteen, and it is hard to become incapable before I have reversed those figures.

Again, for Fanny, that age, fourteen, becomes the symbol of her own fragility and fear, the young girl inside the mature woman. And yet although she could not 'depend upon' herself, she continued to work, composing, directing, seeing her work into publication, her schnapps at the ready. When she experienced her symptoms again on 14 May, she told the chorus to continue ('May is Laughing'), and went into the next room to treat her hands. Someone heard her say 'How beautiful it sounds.' Another believed she said 'just like mother's' as she collapsed. Fanny had always believed that she would die like Lea, and she was right, for the tell-tale symptoms of the previous years had finally coalesced into a major stroke. By the time her brother Paul arrived some forty-five minutes later, she was unconscious. Fanny Hensel died before 11pm that evening.

Felix, when told, screams, falls to the floor, faints and ruptures a cranial vessel. Wilhelm sketches his beloved wife on her death bed ('one of his best likenesses' but 'the hardest task he ever fulfilled') and then retreats into grief, never fully recovering. He cannot find words to express his loss, only drawings, and not many of those. He can only say: 'Her life was truth; her end, blessed.' Fanny is buried in the cemetery of the Lutheran Holy Trinity Church where two lines of music, a phrase from her final song, *Bergeslust*, are inscribed on her tombstone, honoured, in death, as a composer first and foremost by this most loyal of husbands. Felix dies six months later on 4 November, also of a stroke. Thousands follow his coffin, first in Leipzig, and then in Berlin, where he is buried next to his sister. The tombstones of Abraham and Lea stand only a few metres away.

In the days following her mother's death, as she sorted through Lea's papers, Fanny had pondered her own mortality in her diary:

> Who of my beloved will one day read these lines? May
> they read everything, and may I, as the eldest, also be the

first, and may my dear husband and Sebastian stand by me
when I depart this life, though I still would like to have a
bit more time.

Her request for a 'bit more time' is heartbreaking in the light of her
death at forty-one. Yet it is not only her own death that she is
considering here, but her posterity. Fanny Hensel's question as to
who 'will one day read these lines' can be asked of her compositions. Who would hear them? Not many people, is the short
answer. Fanny Hensel's work would quickly disappear from public
view. Only now is the painstaking work of scholars, in the archives
in Germany and elsewhere, unearthing the sheer scale and quality
of her achievement as a composer. Only now can Fanny Hensel's
music, silenced for so long, be heard by those with ears to listen.

Berlin today shows little interest in commemorating Fanny
Hensel. She can still be seen, however, in an unlikely place (the
British Royal Collection) and in a surprising guise (as the prophetess Miriam, sister of Moses). It was Wilhelm Hensel, of course,
who allows us to see his wife as a musician. He was the man who
encouraged Fanny every step of the way in her quest to compose,
who wanted her to publish, and who could not bear her loss.
Wilhelm used Fanny as his model for Miriam in his large canvas
called *Song of Praise*, which he proudly took to London to show the
newly crowned Queen Victoria. She in turn was delighted with the
picture, but did not wish to offend British artists by buying a
Prussian's work. Wilhelm bided his time, and a few years later
presented the work as a gift to the queen. In return, Victoria gave
him jewels for his own real-life 'Miriam'. Fanny, back in Berlin, was
somewhat embarrassed: when would she wear the things? She may
also, somewhere, have been uncomfortable with her representation as Jewish Miriam, the older sister of Aaron and Moses. After
all, she was only recently assimilated, still the sister of 'jewboy'

Felix. To me, there is something fitting about Fanny being memorialized as Miriam, whose song, 'Sing unto G-d, for He has triumphed greatly; horse and rider He cast into the sea', noted in Exodus 15:20, is an archetypal moment when a woman emerges from the shadows, shakes her timbrel and, for a moment, leads the music.

The forgetting of Fanny Hensel sometimes had very little to do with gender. Revolution came to Prussia in 1848, and the previous decades were lost to sight in the political struggles that followed. A handful of Hensel's works, including the *Piano Trio*, opus 11, were published in 1850, but Fanny's moment had well and truly passed. In the twentieth century, even if anyone had shown interest in Felix's sister, the Nazis sought to wipe the Jew Mendelssohns off the German cultural map.

On the other hand, the forgetting of Fanny Hensel had everything to do with her gender. At the time of her death, reviewers, faced with her posthumous publications, kept their comments short, dwelling primarily upon Fanny's stylistic dependence upon Felix, and unable to look past their own ideas of what a woman was capable of composing. Hensel's lieder may not 'betray a woman's hand', they may even suggest an 'artistic study of masculine seriousness' but nevertheless, all but one 'lack either a commanding individual idea, or else clear phrasing'. Another critic admired 'all the outward aspect; yet we are not gripped by the inner aspect, for we miss that feeling which originates in the depths of the soul and which, when sincere, penetrates the listener's mind and becomes a conviction'. And yet another, praising the 'gracious, pleasant element' still felt a lack of 'powerful feeling drawn from deep conviction'.

These kinds of comments mark a subtle, but devastating, shift in the way in which the work of women composers was understood between the era of Martines and that of Hensel. The compositions of Martines and her predecessors were certainly understood in terms of the composer's sex, but it was deemed remarkable, exceptional, sometimes even admirable and useful to the powers that be, for a woman to produce such fine music. A woman composer would have to take care that she was properly feminine, according to the values of her society, but the music she composed was not *in itself* deemed feminine.

By the 1840s, if not before, and fuelled by the increasing institutional and academic study of music, beliefs about 'masculine' and 'feminine' music changed the way in which a woman's composition was heard. If a woman attempted to compose in a masculine way, all that happened is that she betrayed herself as a woman even more clearly. The understanding and evaluation of the male body and mind as stronger than, and more intellectual than, that of woman generated a hierarchy of musical structures and forms, with large-scale instrumental compositions at the top and small-scale songs at the bottom. Women were expected to write, and did write, in genres with which they were associated, particularly songs and piano pieces, genres that reflected the stereotypical ideals of femininity, pieces that were gentle, undemanding and simple, directly emotional rather than complex and intellectual. It was not just the critics who believed they could detect the sex of the composer in his, or her, music. Clara Schumann, a late addition to the Hensel circle, and the recipient of Fanny's kindness, subscribed to the view as well, admiring Fanny Hensel as a person, despite her 'rather brusque manner', but doubting her ability as a composer because women 'always betray themselves in their compositions'.*

---

* Fanny, meanwhile, did not think much of Clara's husband's work, writing that she could not 'acquire a taste for this Schumann', but she did not ascribe her dislike to his gender.

Fanny Hensel spent her life as a composer working within a musical establishment that believed in, and policed increasingly effectively, the boundaries of masculine and feminine music, dictating which forms could and should be approached by women (songs, yes; symphonies, no) and her achievement as a composer would be judged by its standards for centuries after. For it was Fanny Hensel's misfortune to be living in, indeed assimilated into, a Protestant, German haute bourgeoisie whose values would come to dominate the Western classical music tradition in the nineteenth century, from Central Europe to North America. At first sight, previous eras' insistence on silence, or the equation of composition with prostitution, seem long gone, replaced by a more benign vision of the female musician as a domestic goddess, her creativity confined to the home – an accompaniment, literally and metaphorically, to family life. The idea would prove to be a poisoned chalice. Just as women composers began to escape the shadow of the courtesan, the new challenge would be to gain access to the great, new and, crucially, public arenas for classical music, the opera houses and concert halls of Europe and North America. For Hensel's successors, even now, this remains the final frontier.

'May Robert always create; that must always
make me happy' Clara Schumann

Chapter Six

SCHUMANN

Clara Schumann's part in what has been described as the 'greatest musical love story of the nineteenth century' and her status as one of the great performers of that century, the child prodigy who sustained a career as a pianist and teacher over six decades, make her the most familiar name in this book.

What follows, however, is the more troubled story of Clara Schumann, composer. It begins, as it did for Francesca Caccini and Barbara Strozzi, with a father's ambition. Friedrick Wieck, piano seller and music teacher of Leipzig, turned his daughter, Clara, into a performing phenomenon. He did so single-mindedly and single-handedly: Clara's mother, Marianne, left Friedrick for another man when her daughter was only four and a half. Under Leipzig's Saxon law, she knew she could only keep Clara with her until the girl's fifth birthday because Friedrick 'had the legal right to take possession of me beginning in my fifth year'. These words are in the child Clara's voice, and they appear in her diary, but it is her father who wrote them, yet another mark of the degree of control he exerted over his daughter's life.

Friedrick took 'possession' of a child who for the first four years of her life was apparently deaf, and certainly mute, and transformed her into the prodigy of prodigies. A letter to his ex-wife, written when Clara visited her mother for a short time at age six, lays bare his potent mix of care and ferocity. Friedrick is concerned that

Marianne should say nothing about what has happened between the two of them, and furthermore, 'you will give the child little pastry and make sure you do not condone any naughtiness . . . When she practices, do not allow her to rush. I expect the most rigorous adherence to my wishes; if not my anger will be incurred.' Friedrick saw Clara as 'his work', and however much he was tempted to give up on her during what was, at times, a tempestuous adolescence (she was 'lazy, careless, untidy, pig-headed and disobedient', again words from 'her' diary, but penned by him) he wanted to finish that work. In the closing years of the 1820s, Friedrick showed himself to be both psychologically canny and almost obsessively driven in the pursuit of 'his work', a pursuit conducted in terms of a military campaign, with enemies, battles and, most importantly, 'triumph, triumph' to be had. His skills came into play on the day of Clara's first official Leipzig Gewandhaus concert, at the age of nine, when the carriage that picked her up from the family home took her in completely the wrong direction. Clara arrived at the Gewandhaus in tears, unaware that a beautiful glass coach should have collected her. Friedrick saved the day: 'I quite forgot to tell you, Clarchen, that people are usually taken to the wrong place when they perform in public for the first time.' And Clara played.

Friedrick taught Clara everything she knew. (He then followed that up by teaching her half-sister, Marie, everything *she* knew.) He taught Clara from an early age about life as a professional musician, and about the music business itself. She witnessed Friedrick urge his second wife to ensure that her stepdaughter's performances appeared in the Leipzig newspaper. She noted him request a young student, Robert Schumann, who was involved in journalism, to do what he could about publicity. Friedrick introduced Clara to the rigours of touring, and she learned to take in her stride the challenges of life on the road, including the spiders at the 'pigsty guesthouse' in Weimar, which damaged her expensive silk dress because it was 'hung the wrong way out'. When Clara's half-brother, Clemenz, (her 'dearest darling') died suddenly at the age of three, Friedrick took her away the very next day, to Dresden, cancelling two planned Leipzig concerts but thrusting her into performances in a new, and very different, city. And Clara played.

This was how she was taught to live. No wonder that she comforts herself, in the face of musical enemies, by writing 'I am a girl within my own armour.' Her psychological armour also served to protect her from her father's more violent behaviour. Robert Schumann, when he was new to the Wieck household, was shocked by Friedrick's treatment of Clara's younger brother, Alwin. The boy fumbled a performance. Friedrick threw 'his prey down'. The 'boy begged and implored' to continue playing, whilst being assaulted by his father. Clara, meanwhile, 'smiled and calmly sat herself down at the piano with a Weber sonata'. Robert makes no comment on Clara's smile, but her ability to continue a performance in the midst of chaos, illness, even violence, hard-won though it may have been, would sustain her throughout her life. Over the years, Clara Wieck would record acute physical symptoms just before, or even during, a concert, or note circumstances that would have put most performers completely off their stride. And yet she played on.

For, above all else, Clara was Friedrick Wieck's best pupil, a walking advertisement for his abilities as a creative and inspirational teacher. Clara, at five, played by ear; she was encouraged to transpose little pieces; she improvised on her own or given themes; and all this before she could even read music. At age ten, the formal harmony, counterpoint and composition classes began. She learned about orchestration, she had singing and violin lessons and attended concerts every week. And from the moment she started her public performing career, at age nine, audiences loved her. Clara Wieck was 'no hot-house flower, there is nothing forced

about her; her extraordinary virtuosity is rather an early manifesta-
tion of her innate music genius'. Her remarkable 'depth of understanding and feeling in her playing' went with a certain sadness, a
seriousness about the young girl, but that was all part of the Clara
Wieck romantic mystique:

> She has a look of unhappiness and of suffering, which
> distresses me; but she owes perhaps a part of her fine
> talent to this inclination to melancholy; in examining
> closely the attributes of the Muses, one could almost
> always find there some traces of tears.

Friedrick understood that, as a young girl performer, Clara needed
to combine brilliance with innocence. A dash of melancholy
merely added a further frisson to her identity on the platform.
There were, however, class issues in play as well. Clara was raised in
Leipzig, the music and publishing capital of the German-speaking
world, then and now businesslike but not thrusting, respectable
and fair-minded, a city whose bourgeois values Friedrick both
espoused and exploited. For a relatively small city, as it was in
Wieck's time and is again now, Leipzig punches way above its musical weight. Its citizens come out in force, every week, to hear music,
and the city takes care to celebrate its own composers, as well as
those that came to the city (Felix Mendelssohn) or left to go elsewhere (Richard Wagner). Could Clara, however, make the transition to the completely different world of Dresden, with its coun-
tesses and princes, palaces and pomp? She could and did, in part by
not competing with the great ladies of the Dresden court, by
remaining the simple girl from Leipzig. Friedrick reported back to
his second wife, on 19 March 1830, that his daughter was feted by
Dresden's elite, but that it 'seems to have only the best effect on
Clara because she is playing with a self-assurance that she has never

shown before and she is, and remains, the Clara of old'. Friedrick is concerned that aristocratic Dresden might turn his daughter's head: 'If I notice anything the least bit damaging, I will leave immediately, so that she can be in proper middle-class surroundings.' Friedrick both wants and needs his daughter to remain unspoilt, since that is part of her charm.

Felix Mendelssohn was one of the few who saw Clara's feistiness, believing she was the best interpreter of one of his own works, his *Capriccio*, because she played 'like a little devil'. The little devil is more in evidence than the concert-platform melancholic in Clara's own letters from her teenage years. She delighted in her party for her sixteenth birthday, when a whole host of young men, including Robert Schumann, bought her a gold watch. They all ate together, Mendelssohn was there, there was dancing, then a late-night walk. 'It was marvellous', she wrote to her best friend. It was after that party that Robert Schumann kissed her: 'When you gave me that first kiss, I thought I would faint.' More than anything, however, perhaps even more than Robert's kisses, Clara Wieck loved performing. At eighteen, and in Prague, she gloats over her thirteen curtain calls, and then, a couple of weeks later, it gets even better: 'four curtain calls after *every* piece (which is against the law)'.

But did she love composing? Wieck was certainly trained well, and with two specific ends in mind. In order to improvise brilliantly, as she was expected to do and did, she needed to understand musical harmonies and forms. Secondly, and even more significantly, it was customary in the 1830s for performers to play their own compositions at recitals. Because Clara Wieck was a child prodigy on the piano, she became a child-prodigy *composer* for the piano.

Her early compositions are therefore designed to show off her particular skills as a pianist, such as her ability to play tenths due to her big reach (Goethe noted that 'the girl has more power than six boys put together'), a reach that is crucial to the successful performance of one of Wieck's favourites amongst her own works, the *Scherzo*, opus 10. More generally, her surviving adolescent compositions tend to be 'big virtuoso works designed to show off her technical prowess', in the words of one musicologist – crowd-pleasers to suit the tastes of the new middle-class audiences that paid for an evening of musical entertainment. Works such as *Romance variée* opus 3, *Souvenir de Vienne* opus 9 or her opus 8, which pieced together variations on opera themes, had a clear purpose and impact for audiences, but that was not all there was to them. Wieck, even at age eleven, had a gift for harmonic surprise. Her adventurous modulations, rhythmic freedom and the genres she chose reflected the advanced tendencies of their day and resemble the works of other young, emerging composers of the new Romantic school such as Robert Schumann, Felix Mendelssohn and Frederic Chopin. Outstanding among the works of Wieck's adolescence is her *Piano Concerto*, opus 7, which she began at the age of thirteen and first performed three years later, soon after the thrilling sixteenth birthday party, on 11 November 1835, at the Leipzig Gewandhaus where Felix Mendelssohn had just taken up his post. (Mendelssohn got to know Clara quite well during this time, playing Bach with her, and writing 'You know I am *always* ready to do this and am *always* thinking of playing something with you whenever you want to give me that pleasure.')

The *Piano Concerto* is a dramatic and innovative work, a record of the composer's virtuosity and independent musical thinking in her mid-teens. Like all Wieck's compositions, it was a vehicle for display, full of what have been called 'performance-oriented gestures' but it also powerfully infuses a sense of improvisation within a structured, large-scale work. Indeed, it confused one reviewer at the time: 'If the name of the female composer were not on the title one would never think it were written by a woman.' A Viennese critic was less impressed, particularly by the profoundly unconventional key changes between movements, with the first movement in A minor, the second in A flat major, and then a third movement that returns to A minor. He could only explain it with the suggestion that 'women are moody', and goes on to make a larger, social point about deviant women: 'If in their cherished domestic and matrimonial circumstance the daughters of Eve would make no other, larger leaps, deviations or evasions than such a teensy half-step, then everything would be just fine.'

These comments, and others like them, help to explain Clara Wieck's recurrent anxiety about the value of her own compositions. Nevertheless, despite the anxiety and whether inspired or bullied to do so by her father, she continued to compose on a regular basis through her teenage years, if only to provide material to display her own talents. A portrait of her, aged fifteen, shows a sweet, placid girl, with one hand on the keyboard and her own music, the *Piano Concerto*, at the ready. It was all part of the picture of the unspoilt virtuosa with the sorrowful eyes, which Friedrick had worked so hard to create.

It was, however, during precisely these years that Friedrick Wieck's influence over his daughter began to wane. His place in Clara's life was filled by Robert Schumann. The 'most feted romantic love story in the history of Western music' (to quote the *Cambridge Companion to Schumann* – Robert Schumann, of course) is well-known. Friedrick Wieck, for all his admiration for Robert Schumann, profoundly opposed his relationship with his daughter. Yet Wieck's opposition merely fanned the flames of desire, inciting a secret correspondence between Robert and Clara, which is indeed the stuff of romance. Their eventual marriage, a day before Clara's twenty-first birthday, was a final victory for the lovers – and for love – in what had become over the years a vicious and protracted legal battle with Friedrick, and a denouement worthy of a novel. There were, however, other less elevated elements to this love story. The eighteen-year-old Robert Schumann joined the Wieck household in 1828, when Clara was only eight years old, 'an odd little child with a stubborn streak, beautiful eyes, and you liked cherries more than anything', Robert remembered later. He became friends with the little girl over the following years, and then romantically interested in her when she was about thirteen or fourteen. Previously, and at the same time as his early involvement with Clara, Robert was close to, indeed engaged to, a young woman called Ernestine von Fricken. He was intimate with another woman, known only as 'Christel' or 'Charitas', in the early 1830s when he contracted syphilis which eventually destroyed his mind and his body. Robert's painfully candid letters about his experience of mental illness reveal that during a period in which he was terrified that he was losing his mind, he went to the doctor who told him: 'Medicine won't help at all; find a woman; she will cure you at once.' Ernestine was Robert's first woman-as-cure. Clara was his second, and last. Later, he wrote gratefully to Clara that 'You have brought me back to life again, and I want your heart to lead me to ever greater purity. I was a poor, beaten man who could no longer pray or cry for 18 months; my eyes and my heart were cold and as hard as iron. And now? How different everything is, like being reborn through your love and your *faithfulness*.'

What did the relationship with Robert mean for Clara Wieck? From his first surviving letter to the twelve-year-old girl, dated 11 January 1832, Robert was engaged with her as a composer. He asks, 'Have you been composing a lot? And if so, what? Sometimes I hear music in my dreams – what a composer you are!' or, later, asks her to send along some variations that she has written. She did more than that. It was to Robert that she dedicated, with appropriate expressions of modesty concerning her own skill, and appropriate expressions of admiration of his, the *Romance variée*, opus 3:

> Much as I regret having dedicated the enclosed trifle to you, and much as I wished that these variations not be printed, the evil has already come to pass and cannot be altered. Therefore, I ask your forgiveness for the enclosed. Your ingenious setting of this little musical thought will redeem the errors in mine. I would like to request yours; I can hardly wait to make a close acquaintance with it.

Clara Wieck was already a seasoned professional musician by the time she and Robert became intimate, but when it came to composition, she was as eager to please him as she was to please her audiences in the concert hall. She reports on her progress to her mentor with some pride:

> You are probably smiling, but it is true. 1. I finished my score; 2. I wrote out all the parts myself, and that in two days; 3. I've made the clear copy of my *Variations in F* to send to the printer, also my '*Danse de Fantomes*' (Doppelganger chorale) and the '*Une nuit de Sabbat*' (witches' chorale). I've begun to orchestrate the concerto, but I haven't copied it over yet. I've changed the tutti slightly.

Whilst Clara's father saw her composition as intrinsic to her success as a public performer, Robert was much more attracted by the idea of a creative involvement with a fellow composer who would help him in his own ongoing struggle to write music. By February 1838, Clara, if she remains 'faithful' to him, has become essential to Robert's own compositional success:

I'm writing more easily and clearly by far now and, I think, more gracefully; I used to patch smaller passages together, and the result was many strange things, but little that was beautiful . . . I've done almost nothing but compose for four weeks, as I already wrote you; it just flowed; I always sang along while composing – and most of the time I was successful. I'm playing with forms. For the most part I've felt for the last year and a half as if I had the secret; that sounds strange. There's still a lot in me. If you remain faithful to me, everything will come to light; it will remain buried if you don't. I'll write three violin quartets next . . . You have to write something for my journal; otherwise I'll divorce you – do you hear?

The final sentence, asking Clara for a new composition, is both a joke (the couple are a long way from being married in the first place) and, crucially, merely a postscript to the main focus of the letter, which remains Robert's own creative journey. In turn, Wieck wrote of her own struggles to compose:

I played the piano too much yesterday and today. I composed for three hours yesterday without a break, and it didn't agree with me . . . But can I really write something? You wouldn't believe how confused I am now. I sit in front of the piano for hours, but I'm having the same problem with the keyboard as you often have with the letters of the alphabet. Today I finally finished something, but I think it would be a little too long for the supplement.

Clara Wieck's final sentence, far from being a postscript, instead reveals her main concern: publication. Robert wanted to publish something by Clara in a supplement to his 'journal'. She, tactfully, makes clear that she has already promised the hard-won new composition to the publisher Härtel 'for the book which is coming out at Christmas'. Wieck is quick to reassure Schumann that she is composing for him as well ('I started a romance for you a long time ago, and it's really rolling around in my head, but I can't get it down on paper. And the piano here doesn't have a very good tone. But I'll work on it soon') but, then, returns to her canny command of the music business qua business. She wonders whether Robert has asked 'Chopin and Liszt for something for the supplement? I already had Emilie ask Chopin for something on your behalf; you are not mad that I meddled in your affairs, are you?' Then, she switches back again, positioning herself as a composer for Schumann, and only Schumann: 'I would love to ingratiate myself to my husband-to-be with a nocturne or a romance. Perhaps I'll have an inspired idea.' In the meantime, Wieck sent Schumann her *Souvenir de Vienne*, which she composed in Vienna earlier in the year.

The Viennese tour, which took place over the winter of 1837–38, was Clara Wieck's apotheosis as a concert performer. She was so popular that the police had to be called to control the crowds. She was so popular she had a cake named after her. *Torte à la Wieck* notwithstanding, Clara, at least to Robert, takes care to belittle her compositional offering. Robert, for his part, is 'very happy' with her *Souvenir de Vienne* but it is not enough: 'so compose something for me', he writes, and preferably by the beginning of September, because he needs to have two supplements completed by November. Instead, over the summer of 1838, Clara, not yet nineteen, did manage to write a piece for Härtel's Christmas collection, her *Scherzo*, opus 10. Robert offered tempered praise: 'I like the nature and structure of the scherzo very much, but then it becomes too unstructured for me.' Wieck had a higher opinion of the work than Robert, based, as ever, on her understanding of audience tastes. As she notes in Paris, the *Scherzo* 'caused a real sensation yesterday', it is 'so well-liked here; I always have to repeat it.' It would be the only piece from her youth that Wieck published in a collection some forty years later.

Clara Wieck remained, throughout her life, absolutely certain of what it took to please an audience. Very little would shake that. But this certainty was complicated and compromised by her belief (justified, many would argue) in Robert's genius, and her appreciation that he could see past musical fashion in a way that she could not. Robert became the best and final judge of her own work. When he asks her to show him a new composition, she writes: 'I have a strange fear of showing you a composition of mine; I am always ashamed. The *Scherzo* that everyone likes is the one in the commemorative book by Härtel that you didn't like.' Clara's knowledge of what 'everyone likes' (except Robert) allows her to advise Robert, the genius, about audiences:

> Listen, Robert, would you compose something brilliant, easy to understand, something that has no titles, but is a complete, continuing piece, not too long and not too short? I would like so much to have something of yours to play at concerts that is suited to a general audience. It's humiliating for a genius, of course, but expedience demands it. Once you provide an audience with something they can understand, you can show them something

* Some months later, with Clara in Berlin, and with real hope that their marriage might take place, Robert is more positive about at least the performance potential for the *Scherzo*: 'I'm looking forward to news about your concert. I can hardly wait for the museum to open so I can read the Berlin newspapers. You chose rather well. Don't forget to play your *Scherzo* now and again; it's something nobody will play the way you do.'

more difficult – but first you have to win the audience over.

Robert, in sharp contrast, believed that the only way one could develop a serious musical culture was apart from the tastes of the public. The public sought out virtuoso performances and did not care what was being played, so long as it was brilliant. Robert, and his like-minded friends, were not populists: 'Everyone knows that full artistic genius is not always found in dazzling artistic soirees and concerts, by the light of a thousand candles.' According to this criteria, Clara Wieck, queen of the dazzling artistic soiree and concert, was not a full artistic genius. Paradoxically, the more successful a work, the less worthy it appeared to Robert.

As Fanny Hensel had discovered to her cost, both nature and culture were being used to authorize opposition to women's composition. With each passing year, attitudes became more entrenched and, by the time Clara Schumann was attempting to sustain her compositional activity, music written primarily for performance (rather than for being listened to in rapt awe) now came under ever more severe censure, with such music regarded as 'degenerate and equated with the figures of woman and the dilettante or amateur', in the words of one music historian. As the same writer points out, to 'trivialise female artistic activity was hardly new. What is distinctive is the regulative role assumed by sex, which functions in a disciplinary way.'

This conflict of values between Clara and Robert, representative as it was of a wider cultural shift, simmered throughout her teenage years. The concerto that Clara refers to in her proud letter to Robert, quoted above, is her *Piano Concerto*, the outstanding work from her mid-teens, written between the age of thirteen and fifteen, and premiered in Leipzig under the baton of Felix Mendelssohn. Clara, her father's daughter, was furious that Robert had commissioned a review in his own journal from a colleague, rather than reviewing it himself. Not only that, the review was less than generous. Clara fights back according to her own, performance-based, criteria: 'I wouldn't play it as often if I hadn't pleased the experts and the average concert goers with it so much, here and in public recitals in Prague.' In reply to Robert's hint that it is her father who insists on her playing the *Piano Concerto*, Clara responds that she is in charge of her repertoire, 'of course', and recounts another triumphant performance: 'Of the many pieces I played, my concerto was received the best.' She knows the audience and the connoisseurs love it, and is aware of the work's faults, thanks in no small measure to Robert's critique, but is amazed that Robert believes she is ignorant of them: 'Do you think I am so unaware that I don't know the faults of the concerto?' Clara knows them 'precisely, but the audience does not, and furthermore does not need to know'. She ends by asserting that 'there is no better feeling than having satisfied an entire audience'. Satisfying an entire audience is what Wieck lives for. She has done so in her *Piano Concerto*: what more did she need to do as a composer?

It was not only on this topic that Robert and Clara clashed during their courtship. His views about women and music were not exactly consistent. At times, Schumann envisaged their marriage as a musical union: 'We will also publish a certain amount in both of our names; posterity should regard us as one heart and soul, and be unable to tell what is by you and what is by me. How happy I am.' On another occasion, he reassured Clara that she would not need to sacrifice her talent to his because, being an artist himself, he understood her needs:

> I think we will continue to improvise for one another, as we used to, and compose the most wonderful operas together, and I'll often listen to the music coming from

your room and think 'Why the one who's playing is your
Clara!'

But, when Robert informs Clara that she 'will want to remain an
artist', his definition of what that means is a narrow one: 'you will
want to be supportive, work with me, share joy and sorry with me.
Write to me about that.'

Her success in this supportive role, as inspiration and interpreter, is acknowledged by musicologists to this day, who write
that Clara's 'influence over Schumann's piano music cannot be
overestimated, either as creative muse or as performer'. Indeed, at
times, Robert used Wieck's music within his own, as when,
amongst other composers' mottos, he quotes Clara's first in his
Davidsbündlertänze, opus 6, and then returns to her again in the
penultimate movement '*Wie aus der ferne*' [as from afar].

Wieck was far from sure about Robert's vision of her artistic
future, writing that she would be unhappy if she could not be fully
immersed in her work: 'Must I bury my art now? Love is all very
beautiful, but, but . . .' Robert, in turn, responded by recounting a
dream in which he threw her ring into the river, and 'was filled with
a passionate longing to plunge in after it'. The message is clear and
powerful: assert yourself against me, and I will kill myself. At other
times, Schumann wrote with painful eloquence about his struggles, and begged for Clara's understanding:

> I want to confide in you a few things about myself and my
> character, given how difficult it is to figure me out, how I
> often respond to the most tender signs of love with cold-
> ness and rejection and how I insult and ignore especially
> those who mean it so well with me. So many times have I
> asked myself why this is and have blamed myself, for in my
> most inner self I am grateful for the smallest gift. I

understand every move of the eye, every slightest movement in the heart of others. And yet I still so often fail in
words and gestures in response. But you will know how to
take me, and you will surely forgive me. Because I am not
bad at heart; and I love from the depth of my soul all which
is good and beautiful.

Robert Schumann loved and needed Clara's energy and strength. It
had been so for years. At his most charming, and writing to an
adolescent Clara, he tells her that her letter was 'you. You stood
before me, talking, laughing, jumping as usual from serious matters
to humorous things, playing with veils, as diplomats do – in short,
the letter was Clara.' As the two became intimate, Robert would
write passionately, 'Just love me a lot, do you hear – I ask a lot
because I give a lot . . . Your radiant image, however, shines through
all the darkness, and I can bear things more easily.'

Clara, for her part, invested wholeheartedly in the idea of
herself as Robert's saviour, appearing to relish the idea of being
subsumed by him. Complete happiness, she wrote, would be
when she can throw herself into his arms and say, 'Now I am yours
forever – my music and I.' Clara's physical and psychological
symptoms during the months she spent in Berlin with her mother,
having finally made the break from her father (whose antipathy to
the marriage only hardened with each passing month) seemed to
confirm her decision. Through the winter of 1839–40 she experienced blackouts in the middle of public performances, suffered
from chest pains and a series of debilitating illnesses. However,
when she played Robert's music in private concerts her symptoms
disappeared. To Clara, these were all intimations of her destiny.
The defeat of her father in a court of law allowed her to fulfil that
destiny. At 10am on 12 September 1840, Clara married Robert. It
was 'the most beautiful and the most important' day of her life. It

remained to be seen which of Robert's Claras would emerge in married life: the opera composer and collaborator, or the wifely supporter.

One day after their wedding, the couple moved into a large, almost new, apartment in Leipzig's Inselstrasse. In doing so, the new Frau Schumann moved from the centre of her home city to its then periphery. Between Inselstrasse and the old centre lay the 'Graphics District', packed with the printers and publishers who constituted her new husband's professional world. The beautifully proportioned rooms in Inselstrasse are the epitome of bourgeois good taste, and it is easy to imagine musical gatherings in the elegant and spacious reception room. Today, one can visit the Schumannhaus and see the room in which Robert composed, a piano with Friedrick Wieck's name on it and a series of images of Clara in traditional feminine roles, whether created in her lifetime or today. There is even a Clara Schumann cookbook.

The visitor in search of Clara Schumann, the working mother, is less rewarded. She gave birth to two babies in the apartment, Marie in September 1841, then Elise in April 1843. Where did the children sleep? Where did the servants sleep? And the Schumannhaus remains silent as to where Clara composed. That she did continue to do so is attested by *The New Grove Dictionary of Music*, which takes up her story once married:

> Her compositional style changed; she herself was maturing as an artist and the daily involvement with Robert and their joint studies influenced her work. She wrote fewer character-pieces and turned, as Robert Schumann had, to songs; three (*Am Strande*, *Volkslied* and *Ich stand in dunkeln Träumen*) were presented to her husband on their first Christmas together.

It is true that the newlyweds studied counterpoint together and that Robert was delighted with the three Christmas songs, composed in the odd hours when he was out and Clara thus could use the piano freely. Her husband thought that, in these songs, Clara 'gushes here like a young girl', whilst a modern critic writes, 'seldom has such happy breathless excitement been portrayed in music, with such intensity from the very first note'. It is also true that the songs were incorporated into a joint collection, and were published on 1 September 1841, soon after the birth of the couple's first child, Marie. Could the seductive, creative mutuality that Robert had offered Clara in the earliest days of their life together become reality? 'I see that we have to be man and wife. You complement me as a composer, just as I do you. Each of your ideas comes from my soul, just as I owe of my music to you', he would write.

But Robert Schumann's pre-marital visions of collaboration were hard to sustain, undermined from within by his beliefs about women, and from without by the practical realities of married life, both working in conjunction with Clara's own assessment of her ability. She wrote of the three songs: 'I have no talent at all for composition!'

Clara's parents could provide only limited support for her. Friedrick Wieck, now living in Dresden and desperate for a reconciliation with his daughter, encouraged her to make the journey from Leipzig by reminding her that she could bring her new baby and not even pay for her, and she duly travelled on the first German long-distance railway line to see her father, a journey that still captures the transition from Leipzig's bourgeois respectability to the courtly splendour of Dresden as the traveller glimpses the latter's elegant spires. Robert, meanwhile, was equally keen for Clara to see her mother, and, in 1843, organized a surprise visit to Marianne in Berlin. Clara took her eldest daughter, Marie, still only a toddler, and her account of the journey will be familiar to many parents: 'It was fortunate that we travelled first class because Marie didn't sit still *for five minutes* on the whole trip.' On arrival, of course, Marie was not tired at all. Her mother was exhausted, but then Marie 'would only get in *my* bed. I didn't sleep all night, for there was hardly enough room for one person, let alone two.'

Robert was capable of compassion for his wife when he witnessed just how difficult it was for her to focus on anything, let alone composition. He wrote in their joint diary on 28 June, by which time their daughters, Marie and Elise, were twenty-two months and just two months old:

> Clara is now setting her songs and several piano pieces in order. She wants always to move forward but Marie is grasping her dress on the one side, Elise also creates much to do, and the husband sits deep in thoughts of *Peri* [his oratorio]. So, forward, always forward through joy and sorrow, my Clara, and love me always as you have always loved me.

For all Robert's compassion, his own attitudes served to make it almost impossible for Clara Schumann to 'move forward'. By his own admission, Robert's 'dearest wish' was that Clara would have 'no further appearances in public', because an artist 'with a bonnet on her head and a bunch of keys at her waist' was what he wished for his wife. The raw emotion of Clara's letters home when she was making precisely those 'further appearances in public' (her first tour after becoming a mother) did not help:

> Man of my heart, I have an inexpressible longing for you and also for my little angel, the very image of you . . . Oh don't be angry with me, my beloved Robert! Heaven knows I had the best intentions when I left you. I wanted

to help you; I wanted to make taking care of the family at least a little easier for you by making a small contribution – if I am unable to do that, take the good intention for the deed; you will still be fond of me, won't you? . . . Give the baby a thousand kisses; I hope you found her quite well; talk to her about Mama sometimes – so I'm there too . . . Write and tell me lots, everything about the baby, and let me know what you are doing, most importantly how you are doing.

Clara's emotion now became too much for Robert: 'Calm down, my fiery bride, too much happiness achieves nothing. Marriage is different. Then there is cooking to be done.' The rules were different for Robert, the creative, rather than the merely performing, artist. As he had written in 1837: 'You know the nature of my work; you know it's creative work and can't be done at any time of day like the work of a craftsman and so forth.'

Once married, Robert's compositional activity took precedence not only over his wife's composition but even over her piano practice. She wrote, desperation lurking close to the surface:

> My piano playing is falling behind. This always happens when Robert is composing. There is not even one little hour to be found in the whole day for myself! If only I don't fall too far behind! Score reading has also been given up once again, but I hope it won't be for long this time.

As a wife, Clara's role was now to 'stimulate' and 'encourage' her husband, a role justified by some simple, but powerful, formulae. 'Men stand higher than women', wrote Robert. Composition is more important than performance. Indeed, when six years into their marriage a plaster relief was made of the couple, Robert insisted on being portrayed in the foreground, since the 'creative artist' had higher status than the 'performer'. (His *amour propre* also suffered when the couple went walking, because Robert did not appreciate that his wife walked more quickly than he did, since, as he put it to a friend, 'a man is not happy to be 20 paces behind a woman'.)

And yet, the day-to-day reality of her life with Robert (relentless work schedules, equally relentless pregnancies, recurring anxieties about money, Robert's frequent breakdowns and the demotion of her own work) would never dent Clara Schumann's image of her marriage. She was one player in a great Romantic, in both senses of the word, drama. Her part in the narrative was to be the ideal feminine artist. Clara Schumann, composer, is a casualty of that narrative.

What is telling is that Clara Schumann, performer, is not. For, whilst she accepted that she would be 'both artist and housewife' she nevertheless insisted 'I cannot abandon my art, or I should reproach myself ever afterwards!' By 'art', she means performing. For all her boldness, this is not really a surprise, given her personal history and the values of her time. And so, it is possible that precisely *because* of the difficulty of working in the marital home, Schumann continued to tour as a performer, even fitting in an extended trip to Copenhagen between the birth of Marie and Elise. Robert, meanwhile, was unhappy when Clara was away. In response to a request for news about the children, he starkly informs his absent wife: 'I feel dead without you.' He returned to gambling and drinking when Clara persisted in completing the Copenhagen tour, from which he had had to withdraw. Then again, Robert was not much happier if he travelled with Clara. She eventually persuaded him to come with her on a tour to Russia, leaving toddler Marie and baby Elise with Robert's brother and wife, but the four-month tour, from January to May 1844, was, as ever, punishing. In Riga, Clara gave five concerts in five days, with four different programmes, and without another musician to take any of the strain. The 'mental strains of this tour would clearly have repercussions' (writes one of Clara Schumann's biographers), but the repercussions were for Robert, not his wife. *She* had been trained up by Friedrich Wieck. It was Robert who had a major breakdown in the summer of 1844.

It has been suggested that this breakdown precipitated the couple's departure from musical Leipzig, and their move to court-dominated Dresden in December of that year. For a time, Robert's health improved and Clara, for her part, composed what for the *New Grove Dictionary of Music* at least is her greatest achievement, her *Piano Trio*, opus 17. Its final movement has a 'contrapuntal cunning of which Mendelssohn would not have been ashamed even if a little too academic for Schumann', writes one critic (meaning Robert, of course), and is a product of the counterpoint studies that the couple had undertaken in the early months of their marriage and resumed again after the move to Dresden. Years later, one of Clara's friends recounted an anecdote about Mendelssohn's own response to the *Piano Trio*: he 'had a big laugh because I would not believe that a woman could have composed something so sound and serious'. It is a delightful reminder that Fanny Hensel had helped liberate her brother from his era's beliefs about women's capabilities, if not his beliefs about the appropriate stage for those abilities. Other contemporaries were equally surprised, since women 'rarely attempt the more mature forms because such works assume a certain abstract strength that is overwhelmingly given to men'. However, Clara Schumann 'is truly one of the few women who has mastered this strength'. Even now, the *New Grove Dictionary of Music* turns to the vocabulary of mastery to describe her achievement: 'written in 1846, at a time of great stress', the *Piano Trio* 'has an autumnal, melancholy quality, and demonstrates a mastery of sonata form and polyphonic techniques'.

A 'time of great stress' is something of an understatement. Clara had arrived in Dresden heavily pregnant with her third child, Julie. Only eleven months after Julie's birth, in February 1846, Emil was born, the couple's first son. There was no sustained improvement in Robert's health in Dresden, so the family spent the summer in Nordeney, only for Clara to suffer a miscarriage there. These were the months during which, remarkably, Clara wrote her masterpiece. She would publish the *Piano Trio* the following year under even more challenging circumstances. In June she was pregnant again, having spent the winter/spring of 1846–47 touring, accompanied by Robert, Marie and Elise. She left Julie and Emil back in Dresden, but in June Emil died, aged only sixteen months.

Clara's own words about the *Piano Trio* attest to her pleasure in composition, despite or because of the crises surrounding her: 'There is nothing better than the pleasure of composing something oneself, than hearing it played. There are some nice sections in the *Trio*, and I believe that its form is also rather well executed.' It is a fleeting moment of satisfaction. Significantly, once Robert had written his own *Piano Trio*, the familiar doubts crept back in. 'Of course', she wrote, the *Piano Trio* 'remains the work of a woman.' Women's work always lacks 'force' and sometimes 'invention'. But to demean her own achievement is not enough. She must praise Robert: 'How wonderful is such an incessantly creative, powerful spirit: how I glory in the fortune that heaven has granted me sufficient intellect and feeling to comprehend this heart and soul so completely.'

Is it any surprise that Clara could not sustain her joy in composition, when she had a husband who, on a regular basis, reminded her of his superior status as artist? At his most pompous, Robert is a patronizing boor:

> We fought once about your conception of my compositions. But you are wrong, little Clara. The composer, and

only the composer, knows how to present his compositions. If you think you could do it better, that would be as
if a painter, for example, wanted to make a tree better than
God had done.

Is it any surprise that Clara did not pursue her composition when
her husband Robert recognized the obstacles in her way, but
complacently dismissed them as unimportant?

> Clara has composed a series of small pieces, which show a
> musical and tender ingenuity such as she has never
> attained before. But to have children, and a husband who
> is always living in the realm of imagination, does not go
> together with composing. She cannot work at it regularly,
> and I am often disturbed to think how many profound
> ideas are lost because she cannot work them out. But
> Clara herself knows her main occupation is as a mother
> and I believe she is happy in the circumstances and would
> not want them changed.*

Is it any surprise that Clara did not pursue her composition given
that she often found composing challenging even before marriage
and motherhood? 'I would really like to compose a fantasy on a
theme (something brilliant for the French), but I can't do it, and
can't find a theme, either', the young Clara had written from Paris,

---

* A contemporary commented on Robert's relationship, or lack of it, with
his children: 'he did not possess the gift to occupy himself with them either
continuously or deeply. If he coincidentally met them on the street, he
certainly stopped, took out his lorgnette, and looked at them for a moment,
while amicably remarking, in pursing his lips: "Well, well, you darlings?"
Then his previous facial expression took back over and he carried on, as if
nothing had happened.'

exasperated with herself: 'It's a sin how long I haven't composed anything.'

Is it any surprise that Clara did not pursue her composition given her beliefs about women's capabilities, beliefs that haunt every page of this book? She writes:

> I once believed I had creative talent, but I have given up this idea; a woman must not wish to compose – there never was one able to do it. Am I intended to be the one? It would be arrogant to believe that. That was something with which only my father tempted me in former days. But I soon gave up believing this. May Robert always create; that must always make me happy.

In the light of all this, it is impressive that she composed at all after her marriage.

The irony, of course, is that Clara Schumann achieved what she did, including the concert tours (which Robert opposed), because she believed that by continuing in her professional activity she was making it possible for *Robert* to compose. Nothing would be allowed to interfere with his 'lovely life as an artist'. Clara's determination to support her husband as composer underlies one of the iconic stories about her. The Dresden Uprising of May 1849 was one of a series of revolutionary events occurring in the German lands during the final years of the decade. According to one version, Clara escaped from their Dresden house with her eldest daughter, Marie, and Robert, in an attempt to save her husband from being brought into the conflict. Once settled at a friend's estate, gradually 'she fetched all the children and their belongings from Dresden, returning in the middle of the night with another woman, and leading them to safety while Robert remained behind composing.' At the time, Clara Schumann was seven months pregnant with her sixth child. Another account suggests that because Robert was in no condition to fight, Clara hid him as long as she could, then decided to escape with him and Marie, while the other children, aged eighteen months to six years, were left behind with the servants. She returned when she could to retrieve the younger children. What is clear is that the Schumann family found safety with friends. What is also clear is that despite the encroachments of mental illness, and the sense of great frustration and unhappiness experienced in Dresden, Robert was at this time highly productive. He wrote in April 1849 that 'this has been my most fruitful year', because, at last, he was able to focus almost exclusively on composition.

As Robert wrote more and more, so Clara wrote less and less. She was never, however, going to stop performing. She lived for performance, the encores, the exclusive command performances, any chance to satisfy an audience in the way only she knew how. Pregnancy and childbirth did not stop her. She gave her first concert as Clara Schumann when she was three months pregnant with her first child. Seven further pregnancies, at least two miscarriages, the death of Emil and the institutionalization of her second son, Ludwig, did not stop her. A relentless life that was measured out minute by minute did not stop her,* and her national and international performing schedule is exhausting to read about let alone achieve.

How did she do it? It helped that servants were cheap, three taler for three months of work (as an indication, two bottles of champagne cost four). It also helped that one of her favourite piano students, Emilie Steffens, seemed happy to fulfil the role of 'wife',

---

* In Dresden she taught for two to three hours a day; played for one hour; arranged music for the piano, for students or for Robert; spent an hour each day walking with Robert; handled the family's correspondence; oversaw publications of music, learned English with a young woman from Plymouth; and found time to edit Chopin's works.

running the household and supervising the childcare through the Dresden years. Clara's letters to Emilie display some very modern signs of the absent, workaholic parent, who seeks to retain control over all aspects of her home life without actually being there, such as her request to Emilie to suggest what presents her younger children would like. A letter from Dresden, back to Robert in Leipzig, is equally revealing. Clara wants news of her daughters: 'What are my dear little Marie and Elise doing? Does Marie whine a lot? Oh, how I'd like to have a good look at all of you every morning – then I could work easily the rest of the day.' Clara Schumann wanted to know that her children were alright, to see them every morning, but she then wanted to get on with her work.

Letters such as these complicate the enduring image of Clara Schumann as domestic goddess, and suggest another way of understanding these years of pregnancy, childbirth and performing. As the scholar Paula Gilletts argues, then, and even now, women's participation in music:

> Took place in a context pervaded – and sometimes dominated – by non-musical criteria: will performance on this instrument detract from female beauty? What degree of expressiveness is appropriate for a girl destined for a life that requires restraint and self-effacement? Does the self-display of public performance unfit a woman for marriage and motherhood? du Pré's cello between legs

The very choice of instrument made by Friedrick Wieck was gendered, since the piano was deemed one of the few instruments acceptable for women, because the player remained seated, and therefore modest. To play involved no facial distortions but, instead, the pianist 'touched her instrument only with the extremities of fingers and toes, with the actual sound mechanism masked from view'. The violin, by contrast, was unsuitable for a woman as she would have to bend her head and use rapid arm movements, neither of which were deemed appropriate to her sex. As Schumann's century progressed, these views changed. So long as the woman remained properly feminine, so long as she did not become expert, then she could play the violin, but these concessions actually reveal the deeper taboo at work, one that goes to the heart of understanding women and music.

The violin was itself (*herself*) understood as female, with its softly curving shape, its belly, back, waist and neck. The violinist plays the instrument-woman with a bow (or stick). No wonder, then, that the male violinist was often understood as a masterful lover of his delicate, exquisitely responsive and beloved instrument, a perception heightened by the soloist's caressing arm movements and facial expressions, sometimes accompanied by closed eyes, suggestive of inward joy or ecstasy. In the late nineteenth century the performer Sarasate 'weds his violin each time he plays' with a 'spirit of ardent love'. Well into the twentieth century, Yehudi Menuhin, one of the great and, fortunately for him, male, violinists of his era, said that the violin's shape is 'inspired by and symbolic of the most beautiful human object, the woman's body' and therefore must be played by a 'master'. Menuhin (and he was not alone) was genuinely worried about what happens when a woman plays upon her own body:

> Does the woman violinist consider the violin more as her own voice than the voice of one she loves? Is there an element of narcissism in the woman's relation to the violin, and is she, in fact, in a curious way, better matched for the cello? The handling and playing of a violin is a process of caress and evocation, of drawing out a sound which awaits the hands of the master.

Quite how putting a cello between one's legs is an antidote to women's dangerous 'narcissism' remains unclear, but the fundamental message is a powerful and silencing one: female production of music must not only be conducted with propriety, according to what is deemed feminine, but must also include and defer to the male and the masculine.

Female piano playing fitted these criteria perfectly. Indeed, as the nineteenth century progressed, the piano was viewed, increasingly, as 'the very altar of homes'; its function was to control passion, to provide comfort for the female player and, vitally, for her family. Clara's recurring references to music as solace, whilst undoubtedly powerfully true for her personally, were also absolutely of her time.

Being of her time, year after year, Clara Schumann had to justify and mitigate her public, professional excellence with a lifelong display of exemplary womanhood. And so she sustained her career on a knife edge between assertion and placidity, between passion and innocence, between the masculine and the feminine. A review of a performance in 1865, when she was in her mid-forties, shows just how successful she was in treading this fine line – she does not choose to play 'extremely forceful pieces; but in what she does play she rather shames the brilliant virtuosos of our time, by the masculinity of her playing. There is nothing effeminate or retiring, nor any over-abundance of emotion. Everything is distinct, clear, sharp as a pencil sketch.' On the other hand, she is feminine but not too feminine, using small accents to establish an emotional imprint, rather than the stresses of other female players. Even 'in this typically feminine realm of emotion', the reviewer states, 'I observed more profound understanding than profound feeling.' If the Google doodle that celebrates her achievement in our time (as a pianist rather than composer) is anything to go by, she traversed that knife edge with success because she continues to be identified as an exemplary wife and mother. If the shadow of the courtesan still hovers over the nineteenth-century woman composer, then one way of understanding Clara Schumann's relentless pregnancies is to see her as attempting to place herself utterly within the camp of mother, not whore because, although it was not discussed openly, some forms of contraception were available, whilst abstinence was always a possibility. What, one wonders, was going through Clara's mind when Robert had his first serious breakdown of their marriage when she was pregnant with their third child? Many women would have used his illness as a reason, if only on grounds of financial uncertainty, to attempt, or indeed to ensure, that no more children were born to the marriage. Yet, she fell pregnant with a frequency that is truly exceptional (and relied, physiologically, on not feeding her own babies so that she could become fertile again quickly). Robert and Clara conceived Felix, their last child, in October 1853. He would be born a day after his father's birthday, on 11 June 1854. By that date, Robert had already been over three months in the mental asylum of Endenich.

Clara Schumann sustained two powerful kinds of performance, in the concert hall and in the home. What of Clara Schumann the composer? She would have one final creative period, during the summer of 1853. In January of that year, the family had moved into a large apartment on Bilkerstrasse in Düsseldorf. For the first time in their married life, the Schumanns had enough space to accommodate both their pianos and their six surviving children and it may simply have been this practical consideration that allowed Clara Schumann to compose three works that year. She wrote at the time: 'When I can work regularly I feel once more really in my element. A quite different feeling comes over me, lighter and freer and everything seems to become brighter and cheerful. Music is a large part of my life, and when I must do without it, it is as if I were deprived of bodily and mental vigour.' Work, in this letter, does not necessarily mean only composition, but it presumably includes it, for at this time she wrote her best work in the eyes of some critics: *Variations* on a theme by Robert, given to him on his birthday, 10 June. To Clara, this, her opus 20, was a 'weak attempt'.

It would be the last of Robert's birthdays that the couple would spend together. Clara had known of, but interpreted in her own way, her husband's mental health problems since the earliest days of their relationship. She either minimized the issue, or saw it as part and parcel of his genius. When Robert heard voices ('eternally torturing music', demons 'hurling him into hell', making it impossible to sleep), Clara focused on the creative nature of those voices:

> Friday 17, shortly after going to bed, Robert got up again and wrote down a theme which, as he insisted, had been sung to him by angels; once it was written down, he lay down again and phantasized all night, with his eyes open and looking at the sky. He firmly believed himself to be surrounded by angels who offered him the most magnificent revelations, all in the form of wonderful music.

She viewed Robert's illness as being of a religious nature, an interpretation that, as one biographer has pointed out, placed her husband in the role of the 'artist who remains forever beyond reach, beyond reproach and, notably, beyond human vulnerability or failure'. As the illness worsened, and impacted not only on his domestic but his professional life, she tried, without much success, to cover for him professionally. When, in 1851, the couple had moved to Dusseldorf, Robert was unable to conduct so Clara, at the piano, attempted to compensate with hand signals and body language.

The final crisis came on 27 February 1854, when Robert threw himself into the Rhine. Rescued, he asked to be taken to Endenich, an asylum run on enlightened lines for the time. Clara Schumann's response, as composer and performer, embodied Robert's vision of her moving 'forward, always forward'. In collaboration with Johannes Brahms, whom she had met just five months earlier, but who, on hearing of Robert's crisis, had immediately moved to Dusseldorf to provide support to Clara (pregnant with her eighth child), she went ahead with the publication of her opus 20.*

The work was merely the first of a flurry of publications. Through 1855, Clara, working now with the twenty-two-year-old Johannes rather than Robert, courted her publisher ever more assiduously. She would, however, write only two more works (sets of three 'Romances', opuses 21 and 22), dedicated respectively to Brahms and another young musician friend, Joseph Joachim, the two men who would be her closest male friends during these years and beyond. Joachim, like Brahms some ten years younger than Schumann, would perform with her well over two hundred times, and, although Clara never used the intimate form 'du' with Joseph Joachim (as she did with Johannes Brahms) he was, she wrote, 'as dear a friend as Brahms, and in him, too, I have the utmost confidence'. The fact that she was still writing music, and still writing music for and in response to the men in her life, does not, however, conceal the fact that, by the summer of 1853, Clara Schumann, composer, was finally in retreat.

In the months, and then years, during which Robert endured his tragic decline at Endenich, Clara Schumann, performer, would

---

* The creative interplay between Clara and Johannes Brahms echoed that between Clara and Robert. Brahms wrote a set of variations on one of Robert's themes, but also incorporated a theme from Clara's early *Romance Varié*, opus 3. The original manuscript has the note: 'Little variations on a theme of his, dedicated to her'. Robert had responded to the same theme back in 1833. Meanwhile, Clara's own final major work, presented to Robert on his last birthday at home, was her opus 20, also *Variations* on one of Robert's themes, and also including a quotation from her own opus 3.

come, overwhelmingly, to the fore. Her son, Felix, was born in June 1854. Only four months later, in October, she embarked on a concert tour until December; then another between January and July 1855; then another, again from October to December; the following year, exactly the same; and then, in the third year, she toured from January to March, ending up in England in April 1856.

She toured with a heart 'full of worries and longing' but with a powerful sense of purpose. She would now provide for the family, and this she certainly did, for the tours were successful. It did no harm to Clara as performer that she was viewed, understandably, as a tragic figure, her suffering viewed in deeply romantic terms by, amongst others, Franz Liszt: 'To the moist, youthful lustre of her eyes, there has succeeded a fixed and anxious look. The flower crown, once so loosely woven in her hair, now scarcely hides the burning scars which the holy circlet has impressed so deeply on her brow.' Others believed they had seen the sadness all along: 'She never had a childhood. Her father was determined to make a virtuoso of her, and she never knew the joyousness of youth. Even then her countenance showed her secret sorrow.' The British novelist, George Eliot, was more prosaic, not to mention more realistic, writing that Clara Schumann was a 'melancholy, interesting creature. Her husband went mad a year ago and she has to support eight children' (although in fact it was only seven, due to the death of Emil).

Through these years, the doctors at Endenich would not allow Clara to visit Robert, since they believed that any visit would worsen his condition. Friends who were permitted to visit, including Joseph Joachim and Johannes Brahms, either gave falsely optimistic reports or saw Robert on one of his better days, which meant that Clara apparently had little sense of just how bad things were for her husband. The *New Grove Dictionary of Music* provides the final moments of this great love story. When Clara finally learned from Brahms in June 1856 that Robert had not left his bed for several weeks:

> She decided to investigate for herself. Twice prevented from seeing him by Richarz [Schumann's doctor] and Brahms (during visits to Endenich on 14 and 23 July), she was finally admitted to his sickroom on 27 July. Now in the throes of pneumonia and barely conscious, Schumann mustered the strength to embrace her and mumble a few words of recognition. At 4 p.m. on 29 July, he died, quietly and alone; Clara had gone to the railway station to meet Joachim. Two days later he was buried in a cemetery near the Sternentor in Bonn. Among the mourners at the simple service were Brahms, Joachim, Dietrich, Wasielewski and Hiller. According to Klaus Groth, the small cortège attracted a crowd of onlookers, who came 'flooding from every street and lane as if to watch a prince pass by'.

Clara, standing by the corpse of her 'ardently beloved husband' experienced a moment of 'quiet'. Years earlier, she had understood the voices Robert heard as a spiritual phenomenon, but now 'all my thoughts went up to God with thanks that he was finally free. And as I knelt at his bed . . . it seemed as if a magnificent spirit was hovering over me – ah, if only he had taken me along.'

Rather than joining him in death, Clara would continue performing until 1891, including nineteen tours of the British Isles. All her previous motivations were now intensified by her desire to establish her husband's legacy as a composer. Her great, and abiding, need for music sustained her through yet further losses, as when Clara's daughter Julie died at the age of twenty-six in November 1872, only six months after the death of Clara's mother, Marianne; Clara wrote to an old friend that 'It often seemed to me *emotion*

– and still does – that when I played, my overburdened soul was relieved, as if I had truly cried myself out.' Work, as it always had been, from the moment her father whisked her off to Dresden when little Clemenz died, was 'the best distraction from pain'. With the death of Robert, however, Clara Schumann's life as a composer was effectively over. Her life as the guardian of the legacy of Robert Schumann, composer, began in earnest.

There have been various suggestions as to why Clara Schumann stopped composing when Robert died. It 'can best be explained in the context of the astonishing number of her responsibilities as mother and musician', or perhaps it was that without the stimulus of birthdays or Christmas for which to write a piece of music, Clara Schumann did not have a reason to write. Neither suggestions are completely convincing because being a mother didn't seem to stand in Schumann's way as a performer. With regard to composi- *essay* tion, Clara did write one piece in the aftermath of Robert's death, *Romance in B minor*, as a Christmas present in 1856. While the musical approach remains the same, the cast list changed with Brahms replacing Robert Schumann: Clara echoes one of Johannes's own themes from the 'Intermezzo' to his *Piano Sonata No. 3*, opus 5. This was an isolated event, however, merely high-lighting the fact that although Clara could have continued to compose in the ways in which she had done for the previous twenty-five years, that is, for the men in her life, negotiating crea-tively with their music, she chose not to do so.

Instead, Clara's retreat from composition goes to the heart of her own self-understanding. On a pragmatic level, to stop composing would do no harm to her career in widowhood since, unlike the era in which she had made her name as a child virtuoso, performers *Note* were not now, in the 1850s and beyond, expected to play their own compositions. The same went for improvisation. The nature of concerts had changed, in part precisely because of the efforts of women like Clara Schumann and Fanny Hensel. With each passing year, Schumann established herself more firmly as an interpreter of the new classical canon, and worked ever harder to make sure that her husband would become part of that canon.

On a more profound level, something more powerful was at work. When Clara wrote, tellingly, to Joseph Joachim: 'I may not be a creative artist, but still I am re-creating', she reveals that she sees herself as an interpreter, not a maker. This self-understanding is, of course, in one respect, simply Clara Schumann's internalization of the entrenched values of her time, values that were at first challenged by her father's ambition for her, but then validated by Robert Schumann's reservations about her compositional ability, which were, in themselves, rooted in his own assumptions about gender. A review of her opus 15 refers to the old adage 'that the female sex is more suited to imitation than to original creativity in the artistic realm', whilst nevertheless acknowledging that, within those limits, her work is really quite good. Views such as these impacted on Clara Schumann almost every day of her life, and it appears that very little could and did shift her beliefs about women and composition, even meeting Fanny Hensel. Schumann esteemed Hensel highly, and even considered moving to Berlin to be near 'undoubtedly the most distinguished [woman] musician of her time and a very important person for musical life in Berlin – one heard only the best at her place. I had dedicated my trio, which I am awaiting from the printer daily, to her and now she is dead!' But, to Clara, Hensel's weak point was her composition, because she believed that women 'give themselves away' in their music. This may explain why Schumann rarely played her own work after her husband's death, only giving a performance of her *Variations*, opus 20, for some her best work, in 1886 at the age of sixty-seven.

Clara Schumann's biographers have celebrated, rightly, her 'great talent, struggle and survival'. This humble daughter of Friedrick

Wieck, piano teacher and seller, triumphed not only in the bourgeois music worlds of Leipzig and London, but in the courtly worlds of Dresden, Vienna and St Petersburg. Unlike most of the women in this book, she never completely faded from public consciousness and, because of that, more than any other woman in this book, her music is now heard. And yet the story of Clara Schumann, composer, is a far from straightforward one. She may have been, as is claimed, a 'creative partner' to the men in her life, whether her father, husband or even Johannes Brahms, but these were creative partnerships in which some were more equal than others. Clara Schumann's drive, determination and sheer energy were not, however, focused on equality. She had other goals: she sustained her relationship with Robert Schumann, not only in defiance of her powerful father, but in defiance of Robert's death; and she sustained her performing career, overcoming obstacles that would have blocked the path of a lesser woman. Powerful internal and external forces ensured that composition came a poor third to these great goals. To continue as a composer was simply one battle too many, a bridge too far, even if Clara had been determined to do so. In a life lived moving 'forward, always forward through joy and sorrow' it seems something of a miracle that Clara Schumann, composer, existed at all. The woman who wrote, in a burst of pleasure of an afternoon of composition, that there 'is nothing that surpasses the joy of creative activity, even if only for those hours of self-forgetfulness in which one breathes solely in the realm of tones', can sometimes be hard to see. Her words are enough to suggest what had been lost to Clara Schumann, and to us.

Daniel Barenboim after a hard day set back & listen to music to forget "nothing wrong with that, but that was not the intention of composers"

'Everything must be finished before 1 January. It MUST!!! Will I be able to do it?' Lili Boulanger

Chapter Seven

BOULANGER

Maurice Ravel at the piano; dinner with Gabriel Fauré; a note of encouragement from Charles Widor: it is hard to over-estimate just how privileged was the Parisian musical world into which Lili Boulanger was born on 21 August 1893. Her grandmother, Marie-Julie Hallinger, born nearly one hundred years earlier, had been one of the most celebrated singers of her era. Her father, Ernest, winner of the most prestigious accolade in French music, the Prix de Rome, back in 1835, was a successful opera composer and taught at the Paris Conservatoire. Lili's mother, Raïssa, was a Russian princess, someone with the connections and the charm to sustain a musical coterie within which her two daughters could shine, for there was also big sister, Nadia: precociously talented, driven, a musician who, as a teenager, would reach heights never before achieved by a woman at the Paris Conservatoire and beyond. And all this in the 9th *arrondissement*, the hub of musical Paris, in the elegant and newly built townhouses that stretched up the hill towards Montmartre, north of the Opéra.

Any cracks in this family portrait were carefully, and successfully, papered over. When Lili lost her father at the age of six, by which time Ernest was seventy-seven, her mother, Princess Raïssa Mychetsky, merely stepped up her game. No matter that she may well have been plain Rosa Miller, the daughter of a German governess working in Russia; that she was more likely twenty-three rather than nineteen when she had married sixty-two-year-old Ernest, until then a confirmed bachelor.* No matter, even, that one biographer finds it impossible to believe that Ernest was the father of the four daughters that Raïssa bore between 1885 and 1898. (Whether the biographer is suggesting that Ernest was gay, asexual or impotent remains unclear, but he kindly suggests fathers, taken from the musical coterie in the 9th *arrondissement*, for the two surviving daughters, Nadia and Lili, whilst remaining less interested in the parentage of the two other little girls born to Raïssa, one dead at eighteen months, one at five months.) Yet none of this mattered because the day-to-day reality for Raïssa's daughters was that they had a mother who operated as Princess Mychetsky/Madame Boulanger, and whose husband accepted Lili and Nadia as his own. Raïssa herself may have been no Pauline Viardot, the singer and composer who presided over one of the most celebrated artistic meeting places in Paris, just down the road from the Boulangers, but, in widowhood, she did not merely continue but enhanced the circle of connections so important to her daughters' futures. When Raïssa, Nadia and Lili moved into 36 rue Ballu in 1904, how convenient that in the very same building lived Paul Vidal, a leading composition teacher at the Paris Conservatoire! How pleasant that Gabriel Fauré should send a note to Nadia in August 1905, the same year he became Director of the Paris Conservatoire: 'give me news of your sister, of your mother, of your sonata'.

Nadia's experience of, and enjoyment of, this privileged world was, however, compromised by her status as both the eldest and the

---

* There have been many questions asked about Lili's mother, some more absurd than others. Had she been married already, perhaps to one Chuvalov? Did Ernest meet her in Russia, or was she one of his students at the conservatoire? Was she Orthodox or Roman Catholic? Was she even an illegitimate daughter of the tsar?

healthiest Boulanger daughter. It fell to big sister Nadia (rather than Princess Raïssa, with her 'hypothetical aristocratic background', in the words of one cynical biographer) to provide the income that would sustain the Boulanger lifestyle in the rue Ballu. By all accounts a workaholic throughout her long life, Nadia developed her taste for a punishing schedule in these years. Her motivation was never in doubt. She had promised to look after her little sister Lili, and she took that promise seriously. At Lili's birth, she remembered, 'I walked into my mother's room a carefree child: I left it an adult.' She was six.

For a time, it seemed that Lili Boulanger seemed content to sit back and enjoy the social ride created by her parents, sustained by her mother and financed by her sister. The most frequent phrase in Lili's earliest surviving diary for 1908 (she would be fifteen in August of that year) is *'monde fou'* – 'an amazing crowd.' The year in which Lili reached her eighteenth birthday, 1911, is filled with visits to the theatre, concerts and opera; with charades and dinners; and four spring-time weeks with her mother in the south of France, at Saint Raphael. It was also the year in which Lili learned to ride a bicycle, helped no doubt by the inexorable rise in women's skirt lengths, now daringly reaching just above the ankle.* Lili's eighteenth-birthday celebration, on 21 August 1911, was a joyous occasion. The very end of this intensely lived year brought more concerts, more plays and a party on 27 December: *'Me couche a 4 h 35'* she writes, and she does not mean the afternoon.

Earlier, when Lili was eleven, this already privileged world became even more so, when her seventeen-year-old sister entered

---

* Her first cycling lesson was on 27 July, at Gargenville fifty kilometres west of Paris. Two weeks later, she made an expedition to a hamlet some six kilometres away, then the following day, sixteen kilometres, there and back, to Mantes. A day off the bicycle was followed by an impressive expedition to Houdan, just over thirty kilometres away. *Chapeau*, Lili!

into an intimate relationship with one of their father's friends, Raoul Pugno. Over the coming years, Nadia would perform, collaborate, travel, eat and, it would seem, sleep with Pugno, a celebrated pianist, teacher and composer, renowned for his musical partnership with Eugène Ysaÿe, the 'king of the violin', and very well placed at the conservatoire. That Pugno was known as a womanizer, was obese, was married (in practice if not in law) to Marie Fischer and had a daughter by her, Renée, who was two years older than Nadia, did not seem to matter. From the summer of 1904, Raoul Pugno, along with Marie and Renée, became a significant element in the lives of all the Boulanger women, who began spending weeks and months in Hannecourt, a hamlet close to the large village of Gargenville, some fifty kilometres west of the 9th *arrondissement*, where Pugno had a house. Gargenville functioned as an extension of the 9th *arrondissement*, easily reachable by train from the Gare St Lazare, a place where men such as the writer Gabrielle d'Annunzio, the librettist for Raoul and Nadia's opera, would visit with his mistress of the moment. D'Annunzio may have written, somewhat waspishly, of his old friend's collaboration with the teenage Nadia ('it's truly the first time that a virgin fertilized an old impotent') but the professional and personal intimacy shared by Raoul Pugno and Nadia Boulanger was accepted without comment by both his and her family in an era dubbed the 'golden age of male adultery'. By 1908, Raïssa had bought Les Maisonettes in Hannecourt, three adjoining houses, just two minutes' walk from the Pugno household.* The charades of 1911, and the visit to Saint-Raphael, were both *chez* Pugno.

---

* The latter has gone, but Les Maisonettes survive and at the time of writing are being lovingly restored to their former condition, complete with Boulanger furniture, artwork and memorabilia, but with the addition of a new auditorium so that music can be still be heard.

An aspiring composer could not fail to thrive in this environment, even with only a fraction of Lili Boulanger's talent. There was only one thing in her way: her body. It was female and, since the age of two and a severe case of bronchial pneumonia, it had been ill. Being female every day of her life, and being a sick female on so many of those days, not only shaped what Lili Boulanger was physically able to do, but it also shaped what it was believed she *could* and *should* do. She may have been born into an era in which female composers would achieve unprecedented prominence as composers of large-scale works, not to mention an era in which the first wave of modern feminists would articulate their challenge to political and social establishment, but she was also born into an era in which musical genius remained understood as an exclusively male preserve. More importantly, day by day, Parisian socialite and bicyclist extraordinaire Lili Boulanger's pleasures were always snatched from the jaws of pain, exhaustion and frustration, if not despair.

And yet, from 1909, the year in which Boulanger first talked about applying herself passionately and seriously to composition, she found ways to overcome or to work round the limitations presented by her sick, female body. By 1911, she was hitting her stride as a composer, developing a recognizable musical style, characterized by 'beguiling sidestepping' modulations and the incorporation of 'modal elements within a basically tonal musical language'. The creative influence of Gabriel Fauré, in the modal touches and the frequent enharmonic modulations, is visible and understandable given his intimacy with the Boulanger family, but it also points to a difference between the two sisters. For Nadia, the presence of a figure such as Fauré in her life worked to diminish her. In response to his encouragement, she replied, dismally: 'If there is one thing of which I am certain, it is that my music is worthless.' In contrast, Lili, it seems, was influenced by the established composer, not silenced by him.

Boulanger's inside track into the Paris music world, evident in her casual dedication of an early piece, *Renouveau*, to Paul Vidal, her 'dear friend and teacher', meant that, to fulfil her ambition she did not *need* to attend the conservatoire, because the conservatoire came to her in the form of Georges Caussade, only in his late thirties but already in post for five years as professor of counterpoint, and the man with whom Boulanger would follow an intensive programme of private composition classes, sometimes even three hours on a Sunday.

Nevertheless, the semi-public sphere of 36 rue Ballu had its limits. No matter that Lili Boulanger studied with Vidal, Fauré and Caussade, or that she took the occasional conservatoire class. If she wanted to succeed as a composer in a world beyond rue Ballu and Gargenville, and it seems she did, then she needed to engage fully with the Paris Conservatoire, an organization for whom the term institutional sexism could have been invented. It was not that women were not accepted as students. It was simply that the nature of their studies there were determined by long-standing ideas about both the capabilities of women (how could they excel in the masculine disciplines of counterpoint and fugue?) and their imagined future roles as dilettante, bourgeois performers. Reforms had been made, notably by none other than Gabriel Fauré, family friend, teacher of Ravel and Director of the Paris Conservatoire since 1905, but the reality remained that while women could attend and even achieve great success at the conservatoire, there was a limit to how far a woman could actually go there. Lili knew this only too well, because she had witnessed Nadia's attempts to win the most important competition in French music, the prestigious, coveted Prix de Rome.

That Nadia was able to enter in the first place was hailed as a 'great victory of feminism'. However, when in 1903 the reformist government decreed that 'women artists, of French nationality and unmarried, more than fifteen years of age and less than thirty, can from now on take part in the competitions for the Grand Prix de Rome', it was a decision imposed upon L'Académie des Beaux-Arts, who, for their part, were not going to make it easy for any woman who did dare to take part. The very rules and regulations of the competition were deterrents, with age, for example, significant for women in ways not applicable to men. If a woman were in her mid-twenties, and, God forbid, won, then she would be thirty or more when she had completed her 'prize', a four-year stint at the Villa Medici in Rome. Unmarried out of necessity at the time of the competition in order to enter, she might remain, also God forbid, unmarried by the end of it. For women of a certain class – or, more importantly, their families – the absence of female servants, the ban on family members as chaperones the requirement to eat communally when candidates were secluded at the Palace of Compiègne during the final round of the competition, and then in Rome as the winner, were all pause for thought. This was one of the main reasons that the very first female entrant withdrew from the Prix de Rome: how could propriety be maintained?

None of these concerns appeared to trouble Nadia Boulanger, however, who first entered the competition in 1906, and then made it through to the final round at Compiègne in 1907. She had every right to feel confident, since she had won almost every competition possible at the Paris Conservatoire and, in her own mind at least, her sex, not to mention feminism, were irrelevant. 'Forget that I am a woman, and let's talk about the music!' ('*Oublions que je suis une femme, et parlons musique!*') she would say later.

In 1907, Nadia Boulanger would discover that her music was not enough. She did not win. There was an immediate review, followed by an immediate decision to enter the following year. Her teacher Charles Widor, casting around for reasons, could only point to problems with the performance of her work since Nadia's technique, he believed, as a composer was 'superior to that of all the competitors' (he reassures Nadia that he and Raoul Pugno had discussed this fully), and 'as for the fundamentals, you have nothing more to learn.' Widor proposed that they would work on the 'external and decorative side of things in the coming year' but first, though, Pugno would take Nadia for a consolatory break in the south of France.

Nadia failed to win in 1908, however, and then again in 1909, even though it was generally acknowledged that she had written the best work. It seems that the judges could not, or would not, forget that she was a woman.* Ironically, Nadia's compositions themselves represented little threat to established notions of femininity. As musicologist Caroline Potter observes, her only significant large-scale pieces (other than works composed for Paris Conservatoire competitions) are a *Rapsodie variée* for piano and orchestra, written for and premiered *by* Pugno, and the opera *La ville morte*, composed in collaboration *with* Pugno. It was not *what* Nadia Boulanger wrote that was threatening, it was simply that she, as a woman, wrote it.

Lili watched, learned from and was motivated by her sister's experiences. Later, Nadia remembered Raïssa Boulanger asking the sixteen-year-old Lili what she intended to do with her life. She answered that she wanted to win the Prix de Rome as her father had done, and to bring back to the family the prize that had just eluded her sister. Lili Boulanger's actions from 1910 onwards

---

* L'Académie des Beaux-Arts remained cruel to Nadia Boulanger throughout her life. Even on the occasion of her ninetieth birthday, although she was given a gold medal, and made a *Grand Officier* of the *Légion d'Honneur*, she was still not elected because it was feared that the nomination of a female musician would create a dangerous precedent, encouraging members of all the other sections to then present their own female candidates. Only in 1980 was the novelist Marguerite Yourcenar admitted, too late for Nadia Boulanger, who had died two years earlier.

suggest that (whether she did actually say these words or not, and whether family honour was her sole motivation) she was focused on doing just that. However, it was only in 1911 that the composer concentrated her entire attention on the Prix de Rome, with her composition lessons with Caussade throughout that year being directed to that goal. So too was her formal enrolment, supported by Gabriel Fauré, into the Paris Conservatoire on 10 January 1912. Two months later, it was agreed: she would enter the Prix de Rome that very year. As the Boulanger expert and pianist, Fiorella Sassanelli, argues, the sheer speed at which Lili turned herself into a composer is breathtaking for it was less than two years since she had decided on the path, and just over a year since she had dedicated herself – heart, soul and (fragile) body – to the cause.

As winter turned to spring in 1912, Lili Boulanger's excitement is palpable. A celebratory dinner for twenty-one people will stay in her memory for ever: even the weather is delightful, like June, not March; 'Jacques comes into my bedroom' (he is never mentioned again); she goes to a ball dressed as the medieval Isabeau de Bavière, and says that the outfit was 'very successful – even too much so'; when snow comes in April, it too is welcomed, as exciting and splendid as the sun in March. Throughout, Boulanger's lessons with Caussade continue every couple of days because, even if she is in Gargenville, she can simply take an *aller-retour* to Gare St Lazare. Teacher and pupil focus on developing her fugue technique, and on her writing for voices, but they also share a love for anagrams and word games. No wonder that Boulanger makes good progress on *Les sirènes*, for the unusual combination of a solo mezzo-soprano and chorus of soprano, alto and tenor voices and piano, and that she completes *Pour les funérailles d'un soldat* (For a Soldier Burial), a military-style work in which male voices predominate, but in which the dominant tonal context is complicated by the presence of modal inflections. In what would become a characteristic move, she includes fragments of medieval plainchant, after the words 'Let the prayer of the dead be said before us' in *Pour les funérailles d'un soldat*, and, in an equally characteristic move, the work is dedicated '*a mon cher Maître et ami Georges Caussade en profonde reconnaissance et sincère attachement*' (for my dear Master [teacher] and friend Georges Caussade in profound gratitude and sincere attachment). Caussade for his part sends Lili a photograph of himself, signed '*A ma charmante et si distinguée élève Mademoiselle Lily* [sic] *Boulanger*' (To my charming and most distinguished student Miss Lily Boulanger). It shows a gentle-faced young man trying, and failing, to grow a beard in an era of substantial beards. (Boulanger's rather obvious crush on her 'Master and friend' is noted by most biographers, although only one suggests that they became lovers.)

It was all coming together. Lili was particularly thrilled by the first performance of her own work in her own home. On one level it was just another evening at the Boulanger household in rue Ballu. Raoul Pugno and Nadia Boulanger played piano duets; Maurice Ravel performed his own music, and stayed to dinner; and, in Lili's own words: 'For the first time, things by me were played.' One of her works was 'encored – everyone was very kind – Caussade came – completely overwhelmed'. The hard work continued into April. The exhilaration is still there, but so too is the sense of imminent collapse. She notes, delightedly, a telegram from Caussade, but then: 'I am working a lot, progressing more. In the night Monday–Tuesday I copy the fugue until I go to sleep and do the orchestration. I feel very ill.' The next day: 'Return from Gargenville. I cry and am ill. I am nearly finished. Haven't slept since Monday morning. 6pm: lesson with Caussade.' (Just as Boulanger notes the precise time and date of the completion of pieces of music, or the date and destination of a cycle ride, or the number of people who came to dinner, she here notes that this is her eighty-first lesson with Caussade). She ends: 'I am exhausted.' Her life, her world, is encapsulated in her breathless phrases: 'Doctors – Caussade is lovely – go to bed at 4am – I am quite tired – I see Fauré, *très gentil*. I am ill.'

Illness would mean that despite, or because of, all the hard work, Boulanger had to withdraw from the Prix de Rome competition in the summer of 1912. By September, Lili and her mother were heading for Marienbad, then to Berck, Pas-de-Calais, in search of a cure. At Berck, on the north coast of France, Boulanger spent an utterly miserable Christmas period, alone, surrounded by invalids like herself. She was delighted to return to Paris on 29 December, where Georges Caussade met her at the station.

What was wrong with Lili Boulanger? The fraught business of attempting a retrospective diagnosis is complicated further in Boulanger's case by the lack of explicit evidence concerning her treatment. Whilst it is now generally believed that she suffered from Crohn's disease, which, even today, is difficult to differentiate from intestinal (or abdominal) tuberculosis, labelling her illness is, in a sense, the least important aspect of understanding the impact on her life of recurrent bouts of intestinal pain, coupled with high fevers, severe diarrhoea, bloating and understandable exhaustion.[*] The treatments for abdominal tuberculosis could be as dismaying and haphazard as the disease itself, with some doctors advocating starvation, others over-feeding, some lots of exercise, others complete bed rest, but almost all prescribing opium, the drug of choice both for pain and for diarrhoea. Physical symptoms aside, Boulanger's illnesses probably protected her from the pressure that

---

[*] The symptoms of Crohn's disease include recurring diarrhoea, abdominal pain and cramping, extreme tiredness, unintended weight loss, blood and mucus in the faeces and, more rarely, pain in the limbs and high fever. Boulanger's recorded symptoms all appear in this list. The most common clinical features of abdominal tuberculosis include abdominal pain, weight loss, recurrent diarrhoea, low grade fever, a cough and distension of the abdomen.

Nadia experienced (to provide for the family, to care for her little sister), but it also meant her behaviour was policed in ways that Nadia's was not. One day in the summer of 1912, for example, Lili went out with her great friend Miki Piré and her tutor Georges Caussade for a ride in a cabriolet. They returned three hours late because of a thunderstorm, by which time Nadia, waiting with Pugno back at Les Maisonettes, was sick with worry. According to Piré, Lili promised never to come in late again. It is a trivial story, and Piré has a tendency to write about anything associated with the Boulanger sisters in a heightened emotional fashion, but it appears that, despite living in a relatively bohemian milieu, despite the new freedoms for many women, despite being able to ride her bicycle, Lili's movements were curtailed as much by her family's anxiety as by the symptoms themselves.

In her own time, her health, or lack of it, was the primary lens through which the composer was viewed. When a journalist, in 1908, had travelled out to Gargenville to report on Nadia, whose Prix de Rome attempts had made her something of a celebrity, he also noted Lili:

> Very tall, slim, supple, her gestures are delicate and lively, and her distracted and wandering eyes are nonchalant and dreamy. Scarcely recovered from a long illness, she is resting in the country, awaiting a full return to good health, so she can allow her surprising gifts to blossom.

This is just one example of the phenomenon whereby Boulanger's 'surprising gifts' are acknowledged, but it is her illness, allied to a particular type of femininity, that remains the focus. This view of the woman seeps into understanding her music, and not only in Boulanger's lifetime. Her *Hymne au soleil* (Hymn to the Sun), one of the works she wrote in preparation for the Prix de Rome, is described in the *Musical Times* of 1968 as exhibiting 'for the first time a streak of sturdy masculinity, inexplicably at variance with the composer's character and temperament'. Sturdy masculinity? Impossible to imagine such a thing from a sickly girl with dreamy eyes.

As she grew older, and more ill, there was less and less expectation that she could, or should, have a conventional woman's life of marriage and motherhood. According to some, however, Lili's loss was music's gain, since celibacy would allow her to devote herself, entirely, and with virginal, rather than maternal, femininity, to her art. The composer's own sister subscribed to these views about women and music, arguing that since artists 'think only of their art', then art is 'totally incompatible with the joys of family life'. Nadia continues: 'From the day a woman wants to play her one true role – that of mother and wife – it is impossible for her to be an artist as well.' Nadia Boulanger would, through choice or fate, reject or miss her 'one true role'. Lili Boulanger's illness made 'her one true role' impossible, at least in the minds of her contemporaries. In the void created, the artist – despite, or because, she was a *femme fragile* – might be allowed to flourish.

The dreamy invalid is, however, nowhere to be seen in a letter from Boulanger to Fernand Bourgeat, a significant figure in Parisian music circles, written in the run-up to her second attempt on the Prix de Rome, and demonstrating that Boulanger was quite capable of ruthlessly calling in favours and assiduously courting powerful men, whilst remaining, on the surface at least, an ingénue:

> I don't often get on your nerves, admit it – so let me do it for once and ask you to do your utmost to oblige your old Lili. I will present at the exam one chorus and one vocal quartet – intervene with those members of the jury whom you particularly honour with your friendship in order to persuade them to have these two pieces performed, and

ask them to award the prix Lepaulle to me if they find my
work as good as people say, and to have my compositions
played in the orchestra class.

Others did their bit. Raoul Pugno sent a series of ingratiating letters
to the members of the jury of the Prix Lepaulle, praising Lili, the
daughter of his much-missed friend, Ernest. It all helped. Lili duly
received that prize on 30 January 1913, giving her the right to
a performance of her work by the orchestra at the Paris
Conservatoire. This was how the music world worked, and
Boulanger knew it. On another occasion, the elderly and influential composer Vincent d'Indy was surprised and delighted to
receive an intensely worded letter of flattery from the young Lili
Boulanger, and one has to assume that neither of these Boulanger
letters were one-offs, despite the best attempts of those who have
sought to edit her ambition out of the records.

And so 1913 soon turned into a rerun of the previous year, but
this time, if it were possible, even more focused on the prize.
Boulanger would work with Caussade almost every day, including
Sundays, and returned to Paul Vidal's composition classes at the
Paris Conservatoire. By February, she was already exhausted, so
Lili, with her mother, Nadia and Raoul Pugno, headed south to
stay with Miki Piré on the French Riviera, where they celebrated
Miki's twentieth birthday. Caussade joined them: the composition
lessons must go on, the preparations must continue. (Fiorella
Sassanelli sees Caussade as almost the fourth member of the
Boulanger family by 1913, particularly following the death of his
own mother in the January of that year.) Motivated by his admira-
tion of Lili's 'belle vaillance' and 'energie exceptionelle', Caussade was
being remarkably selfless, since if Boulanger did win the Prix de
Rome, she would do so as an official student of Paul Vidal and
Caussade himself would gain no public glory.

May came and, as in the previous year, Boulanger was chosen as a finalist. Would her health allow her at least to complete the competition this time? Exhaustion and pain, the inability to eat normally (not to mention the diarrhoea) all made it that much more difficult to negotiate that very public rite of passage, the Prix de Rome. As a composer, however, Boulanger knew what she had to do. All the finalists did, because it was a very tired formula requiring each composer to create a fifteen- to twenty-minute cantata from a text, invariably mediocre in quality, containing three characters involved in a love triangle of some kind. In preparation, Boulanger had spent her time with Caussade writing cantatas such as *Maia* (with a 'nonsense' libretto set in Africa, says one critic, a description that does not even begin to cover the plot's racist, sexist clichés) or *Frédégonde*, yet another love triangle, this time in a medieval setting. Now, at Compiègne, she had the story of Faust and Hélène to set. As one critic puts it: 'any composer who could create convincing characters and real drama and emotion from this sorry text surely deserves a prize'.*

At the Palace of Compiègne, Boulanger entered her studio and got to work, meeting her fellow competitors only for meals and recreation periods, and the authorities turning a blind eye to Raïssa's occasional appearance with 'little treats' for her daughter. As ever, Lili noted on the score the moment she completed her cantata: 'finished on Sunday, June 15, 1913 at 7pm'. So far, so good: her body had not let her down this year.

The five finalists' works were duly deposited with the judges, who would rank them ahead of the final stage of the competition,

---

* The triangle in *Faust et Hélène* comprises Méphistophélès (a baritone), Faust (a tenor), and the beautiful Hélène (a mezzo-soprano). The libretto's characterization is wooden in the extreme with Hélène, for example, 'merely an irritating nag who is constantly asking Faust if he still loves her', according to one critic. It all ends badly: Hélène is spirited away, and Faust is left broken-hearted.

the performance of the cantatas. A delighted Boulanger notes the ranking in her diary:

> 1st: Dupré
> 2nd: me
> 3rd: Delmas
> 4th: Mignan
> 5th: Delvincourt

She also notes that Pugno stayed to dine, and that 'Maman teases me so much that I cry about it.' These naive expressions, sincere no doubt, sat alongside an assiduous professionalism. Boulanger knew that she had to convert that second place into ultimate victory, and she knew how to go about it. Her task, during the few weeks she had ahead of the semi-public performance of her cantata at the L'Académie des Beaux-Arts, was to choose her singers and pianist, and rehearse them thoroughly. She immediately contacted her singer friends, desperate to know what would work, what would not. She could rely on Nadia to be her pianist. She put in hours and hours with George Caussade. But perhaps most importantly, she understood, whether consciously or unconsciously, that, on the day, her own behaviour and appearance would be the keys to success in a society that was still profoundly uncomfortable with the sight of a woman in visible authority. Nadia's desire for people to forget that she was a woman was an impossibility in the context of the final round of the Prix de Rome, when composers not only rehearsed and performed but, crucially, conducted their own work. Even now, the sight of a woman conducting an orchestra remains troubling to a significant, and powerful, minority; how much greater the discomfort then.

Lili Boulanger pitched it perfectly. She conducted but she did not conduct. As one observer noted, 'her modest and simple bearing, her gaze cast down on the score, her immobility during the performance, her absolute abandonment to the will of her excellent interpreters – she did not allow herself even once to beat time or indicate a nuance – all this contributed to her cause'. Add to this the presence of Nadia on the platform, and Lili's frail physique, and contemporaries were falling over themselves to offer the most sentimental description: 'The frail grace of Mademoiselle Lili Boulanger [moved] the audience, softened by the sight of the touching group formed by the contestant and her sister united at the piano in an attentive and affectionate collaboration.' Boulanger, 'standing near the piano, a slim shadow in a white dress, so simple, calm, serious and smiling, such an unforgettable image', forced all observers to recognize 'the superiority of the eternal feminine'. So it was, that in her white dress, with eyes downcast, Lili, 'the eternal feminine', did what her sister Nadia did not: she won the Prix de Rome, becoming the first woman to win the first prize for composition.

Her femininity was crucial to success. As one journalist put it, 'Though she is a winner of the Prix de Rome, she is no less of a woman.' The fear that lay behind these relentless reassurances of Boulanger's femininity was, then as now, a very powerful one. Give women the chance to succeed and they will take over. Give women access to male institutions, and they would abandon their traditional roles. What would happen to society then? And what would happen to women? In post-Revolutionary France, there was even a word for the nightmare. If women renounced their assigned role of 'republican motherhood', they would become sterile *hommesses*.

One of the journalists who applauded Boulanger's victory attempted to use it to show up the foolishness of these fears, arguing that it was ridiculous to think that 'mixed' classes at the conservatoire would lead to the dominance of women in those classes, even more ridiculous to imagine a conservatoire in which Nadia Boulanger would replace Gabriel Fauré as director. There was no 'pink peril' to be feared, in fact, quite the opposite since allowing women to compete for the Prix de Rome had not threatened men's proper power, but had brought all-important feminine qualities to the world of music: 'woman', with her 'personal and delicious form of sensitivity' was to be welcomed, not excluded. Paradoxically, this defence of woman ends up keeping 'woman', and by extension Boulanger, firmly in her box, a box labelled sensitive, modest and passive.

This was, however, the landscape of belief within which Lili Boulanger worked – and she made it work for her. Brilliantly. When she was interviewed after her success, she was asked how she came to compose a particular theme, and her response, a double act with Raïssa, is almost painfully disingenuous, given the sheer hard work that had gone into her victory:

'Oh yes, indeed. I dreamed that – didn't I, Mother?' 'That what?' 'Well, that I was a little child and was teaching my little doll to play the piano.' 'You see', said her mother, smiling, 'she is still only a child.'

This dreamy child, '*petite* Lili' (as she was invariably addressed, despite her height of five foot nine inches), could pose no threat to the musical establishment, even if her success was hailed in some quarters as 'the first serious victory for feminism'.

Almost drowned out is any discussion of the music itself. Few, if any, thought to comment on Boulanger's striking combination of the tenor and contralto voices, exploiting the large crossover in register between the highest male voice and lowest female voice, or the way in which, at the end of the duet at the heart of *Faust et Hélène*, the two voices imitate each other at pitch, symbolizing the union of the two lovers. At the time, Claude Debussy was one of the few to offer a musical analysis, noting approvingly that the entry of Hélène 'on otherworldly pulsations of divided violins, sways gracefully', but, on the other hand, insisting that the Prix de Rome was something of a farce, and hardly a proper representation of a composer's ability. He had a point, and it is a view that colours responses to Boulanger's music today, including influential musicologist Richard Taruskin's dismissal of *Faust et Hélène* as a 'salad of near quotations from *Parsifal* and *Siegfried*', the work of a 'harried contestant' working to a deadline.

The fact remained that the Prix de Rome was of vital importance to a composer's success, and it launched the winner onto a well-trodden path. First, performance: on Sunday 16 November 1913, *Faust et Hélène* had its premier, sharing a programme with Franck's *Symphony in D minor*, and music by Debussy, Berlioz and Bruneau. Boulanger had joined the French musical establishment. Second, publication: Ricordi, then as now one of the most important music publishers in the world, gave Boulanger a contract, providing a regular income, the regular publication of her works and all the publicity that a large publisher could provide. The Gothic/modernist cover to Ricordi's *Faust et Hélène* is a vivid reminder that Boulanger was coming of age in a brave new world. Even more importantly, the Ricordi contract sanctioned Boulanger to enter the traditionally male-dominated territory of opera, stipulating that, within eight years, she would write 'two operas, each of them forming a complete stage-spectacle'. Third: the gifts of time and a very special place in which to create her music because, like all other Prix de Rome winners, Boulanger would spend four years at the Villa Medici in Rome, devoting herself to her art.

Almost immediately, however, Boulanger strayed from that well-trodden path by failing to travel to Italy with her fellow prize-winners on the conventional departure date of 1 December. There was and remains much speculation as to her reasons. Had she been 'frightened away in advance' for some reason? Was her health the problem? Was it that her mother disapproved of the set-up in Rome? The records, such as they are, provide inconsistent answers. Georges Caussade is strangely absent: was Boulanger now working independently or is this just a coincidence? With regard to illness, on 6 December, Boulanger wrote in a feeble hand, in pencil, to her friend Miki, enclosing two pressed Parma violets, her favourite flower. She seems a very sick woman, but four days later she is attending a banquet and soiree. Christmas came and went, and still Boulanger remained in Paris.

Lili's unexplained, but continued, presence in Paris would turn out to be fortuitous. On 3 January, a telegram came to rue Ballu with the news that Pugno was dead. He and Nadia had been touring in Russia, and now Lili's sister had to make the long journey back alone, arriving into Paris at midnight on 9 January. Friends gave her what comfort they could, Ysaÿe writing '*Courage amie pleurez mais vivez pour son oeuvre qui est vôtre*' ('Courage, my friend: cry, but live for his work which is yours too'), and Nadia took her place alongside Marie and Renée in the front row of the funeral. Everyone noted her ravaged face. Everyone congratulated Lili on the good fortune that she was not yet in Rome.

Behind the scenes, negotiations were taking place about the unprecedented delay in Boulanger's arrival at the Villa Medici, and it was agreed that the composer would join her fellow prizewinners on 20 February 1914. However, in yet another sign that Boulanger, or perhaps her mother, was determined to do things her own way, Lili and Raïssa in fact only left Paris on that very day, and found time to stop off in Nice for a stay with Miki Piré. Miki's 'entire devotion' to Lili, indeed her 'tender love' for the composer, fills her letters. Lili's responses are less ardent, but show a love for, and dependence upon, Miki, particularly during periods of illness. (Earlier, Miki had written even more passionately to Nadia, who did not respond in kind.) Nice seems to have been a place where the composer could work. Boulanger began the song cycle based on poems by Francis Jammes (a gift from Miki), which would become her longest surviving work, *Clairières dans le ciel* (Clearings in the Sky), thirteen songs recounting a lover's response to the disappearance of a mysterious young woman.*

From Nice to Florence, and from Florence to Rome. At last, on 12 March 1914, Lili Boulanger arrived at the Villa Medici. Raïssa came along too, much to the dismay of the villa authorities who insisted upon no 'familial intervention' because it would spoil the artistic camaraderie. The director had a point. Did Raïssa expect to chaperone her daughter for the full four years? In the event, she moved into a Rome hotel after a few days. After yet another bout of illness, necessitating nine days in bed, Lili finally entered into the social and creative world of the villa and, with fervour, dining at the best restaurants, enjoying late-night ice cream and even going to the cinema. And she composed.

Her task, on paper, in her first year of residence was to compose a substantial piece of chamber music, preferably a string quartet, and also six short songs, with orchestral accompaniment, together with a separate reduction for voice and piano. Typically, Boulanger bends the rules. Her song cycle *Clairières dans le ciel* goes way beyond the six-song requirement, yet there was no attempt to write a quartet. There were, however, tensions at the Villa Medici. Albert Besnard, the director, had been hostile to Boulanger even before he met her, perhaps unsurprisingly given the catalogue of delays, miscommunications and downright lies that preceded her arrival in

---

* The work has been mined from these poems, *Clairières dans le ciel*, has been mined for its alleged secret messages concerning Lili Boulanger's erotic life. One interpretation, noting that it was Miki who gave Lili the poems in the first place, and that Miki expressed 'love' for Lili, argues that the voice of the 'Poet' is Lili and the absent woman is Miki.

Rome. Moreover, he believed Lili's illness was feigned, a belief merely fostered by her rejection of his offer to supply a doctor and her inability to join her fellow *pensionnaires* for communal meals, and yet her penchant for taking them all out to dinner at a restaurant – with her mother. Boulanger's behaviour went against both the spirit and the law of the Villa Medici.

Things came to a head in May of this glorious Rome springtime of 1914. An exhibition opened at the villa; Lili played in the orchestra, before going out for the evening at 10pm, with several friends, including Nadia who was visiting. Boulanger's diary takes up the story:

> We come back, have supper, sort out the exhibition, go to Dupas' studio, stayed there . . . *faisons blague* [literally, telling jokes] then at 5am, we go to *le Janicule* by car [the Janiculum hill, in the west of Rome, across the river in Trastevere] . . . then breakfast in a *une crèmerie* at 6:30 in the via del Tritone.

Even by the standards of the Villa Medici it was a particularly good night out. The director, Besnard, did not see it that way, and hauled Boulanger into his office for a dressing down. Boulanger in turn was furious with Besnard and, in a deeply characteristic move (at least to those who really knew her), sent a fierce telegram to Paris, denouncing the director to the authorities, and insisting on an opportunity to give her side of the story: 'Situation with director becoming impossible. I ask to come to Paris to explain myself. I will leave immediately. Respects. Lili Boulanger.'

This telegram, with the evidence of her active social life and her demanding programme of composition, speaks of a woman of self-confidence, possibly even arrogance, rather than the *femme fragile* represented in, and to, the press. Does it also suggest that Boulanger truly did want out of the Villa Medici? If so, her fury with Besnard apparently blinded her to the fact that not only was she having a rather marvellous time in Rome, experiencing freedom unknown to her in Paris or Gargenville (let alone Marienbad or Berck), but she was also in an environment in which she was able to concentrate on composition.

Her next step seems to suggest she did indeed want out. Once again going over Besnard's head, she requested permission from, and was granted permission by, the Paris authorities to travel during July in northern Italy for research purposes, so long as she did not return to France. Boulanger spent the last few days of June in a round of parties and farewells. On 30 June, as planned, she left Rome, but she was not heading for northern Italy. Instead, she arrived into Paris on the night train late on 1 July, having spent only 113 days at the Villa Medici.

If these events had unfolded over any previous summer, it is possible that, with a bit of give-and-take from both sides, Boulanger might have returned to the Villa Medici, completed her four years there, and thus remained on the well-trodden path. This was, however, no ordinary summer. On 28 June 1914, whilst Lili said her farewells in Rome, Arch-Duke Ferdinand and his wife were assassinated in Sarajevo. Exactly one month after her return to Paris, the French mobilized for war. The day after the German occupation of Brussels, Lili celebrated a subdued twenty-first birthday in Gargenville. She wore her trademark white: everyone else was in black, in honour of Raoul Pugno.

By the end of August, Paris itself was threatened. The French government relocated, 'temporarily', to Bordeaux whilst, famously, troops were rushed to the defensive lines via a stream of Parisian taxi cabs. The city did not fall, the German advance was checked, but 250,000 Frenchmen would lose their lives at the Battle of the Marne. At Gargenville, meanwhile, Lili had an 'important conversation' in her 'office' with a young man, Jean Bouwens on 30 August.

She says nothing more about this conversation, but it seems probable that she and Jean, two years her junior and the son of the Boulanger family's most loyal friends, the architect Richard Bouwens and his wife Marthe, became engaged. It was the Bouwens' wealth and generosity that, for the next four years, would protect the Boulanger women from the worst privations of wartime Paris. Then, as the first trenches were dug, and it seemed less and less likely that it would all be over by Christmas, L'Académie des Beaux-Arts ruled that all those who had not been mobilized should return to the Villa Medici. However, even though she went on record to say she would return to Rome, in a letter to Besnard with whom she had had an inexplicably amicable meeting in Paris in November 1914, Boulanger did not leave France.

Boulanger's delayed arrival at, and then her relatively speedy departure from, the Villa Medici, coupled with her failure to return there in late 1914, might suggest that it was enough for her to have won the Prix de Rome. The honour of the Boulanger family had been restored. Yet, despite war, despite the recurrent bouts of illness, despite even the 'important conversation' with Jean, Boulanger remained committed to a career as a composer, but not necessarily the Villa Medici way. The Boulanger way was, as ever, a privileged one. She could, for example, travel to Nice in September 1914, far from the encroaching battlefields, and complete her song cycle, *Clairières dans le ciel*. Back in Paris in the winter of 1914, Boulanger took the first steps towards writing an opera, finding a libretto. All the composer's ambition and confidence are evident in her approach to the literary giant, Maeterlinck, king of the symbolists, the writer who had provided the text for Claude Debussy's *Pelléas et Mélisande*, premiered in April 1902, and something of a 'cult opera for modern French composers'. So popular was Maeterlinck's work with composers that only one of his plays remained untouched, a play 'surrounded by the aura of being the first symbolist masterpiece for the theatre', a grotesque and violent fairy tale that would influence writers from Strindberg to Oscar Wilde: *La princesse Maleine*.

Other composers, including Debussy, had asked to set it but Maeterlinck had always said no. Then, in January 1915, the music publisher Ricordi wrote to Boulanger:

> Monsieur Maeterlinck is all ready to entrust you with *La Princesse Maleine*, and he doesn't oppose modifications, cuts, etc., etc. So it is for you to decide if you still want to set this poem to music: if the answer is yes – which I hope – it would be very easy to arrange Maeterlinck's play as an opera libretto – and if you agree, I would do this task myself.

What a coup! *La princesse Maleine* would be Boulanger's opera.

For all Ricordi's enthusiasm, there was then a hiatus. Boulanger had other things to occupy her in the spring and summer of 1915. In April, she talked 'seriously' with Jean Bouwen's father about 'our decision'.* The meeting is recorded in red ink in Lili's diary, rather than her usual pencil, along with a cryptic series of numbers and dates: '268+281=549 (*550 jours le 7 avril – 79 semaines le 4 avril*)', then, the next day, '*18 mois. Encore!* 549.'† One of Boulanger's biographers, Spycket, has worked out that the number 549 corresponds to the date 8 October 1916, when Jean Bouwens would turn

---

* Without offering any material evidence, Jerome Spycket suggests that Richard Bouwens, Jean's father, was also the father of Nadia, and, moreover, that Raoul Pugno was actually Lili's father.

† I find Boulanger's diary entries touching in their characteristic use of numbers and codes to give shape to her life, dominated as it was by illness: '544 – I still suffer, stay always in bed. Jean comes back from Bourges, brings me a piece of pottery' or '16 April: (4 months f. [sic] – J.B.L.B)' or '30 April – 527 – 9 months since the conversation in Gargenville in my office.'

twenty-one. Perhaps the couple were waiting until then to make known their engagement, begun in the first weeks and continued through the first year of war, but in the meantime, Jean left for Bourges to train to be an aviator. Lili spent May and June of 1915 very sick.

When the war, now being fought with poison gas and Zeppelins, closed in again on Paris, Nadia and Lili Boulanger responded in inimitable style. Whilst other women, including Miki, turned to nursing, the sisters set up a communication network, offering material and moral support to all those conservatoire composition students who were now in action. They were ideally placed (not to mention well-versed) in getting support from influential, wealthy men and duly brought in figures such as the Americans Whitney Warren and Blair Fairchild to create the Comité Franco-Américain du Conservatoire National. As, day by day, news came of family friends – men such as Maurice Ravel glimpsed in his new role as a military driver, a change the letter writer finds unbearable (everything is *bizarre, anormal, inutile . . .*') – the much-valued initiative grew rapidly, taking more and more of the sisters' time.

The war was changing the musical climate in ways that, paradoxically, would help Lili Boulanger to achieve her goal of public recognition because, with each passing month, positions were hardening with regard to music and national identity. In 1915, Debussy, for example, claimed that his country was weak because it had not remained true to a purely French tradition of music, with everything going wrong from the time of Rameau's death some 150 years earlier. This kind of musical nationalism created a space for the female composer, who was otherwise excluded from producing great music, now understood as masculine in its 'force and energy, concision and clarity' in the words of the composer Vincent d'Indy, the author of the influential *Cours de composition musicale* (Musical Composition Course). D'Indy was also sure he knew what feminine music was: 'verbosity and modulatory vagueness' and 'ornamented melody' – all very nice . . . but. With France under threat, however, d'Indy finds it possible to praise Boulanger, the female (and therefore necessarily feminine) composer, both praising her work with the committee, which constitutes a 'material defence of our country under attack', and her music that is serving to rid 'our Latin art from the pernicious influence of fake German culture'. Boulanger's 'feminine' art can have a place within the larger project of restoring French greatness, a step towards the 'victory' in which 'our Music' will burn again with 'the flame of our traditional French qualities: clarity, precision, and a sense of proportion'.

In this world of heightened nationalism it was, for once, a secondary issue that Boulanger was female. Indeed, the accident of her sex protected her from the fate of the six million Frenchmen who were casualties of what would become known as the First World War. Boulanger never saw the mud of the trenches, was never gassed or shell-shocked, never forced to bury her friends. Instead, she 'directed' a performance of *Faust et Hélène* on 28 March 1915 at the Trocadéro. Just possibly, as a French patriot, she could actually conduct this time? Georges Caussade, on active service, wrote the same day with passionate enthusiasm for the work and its composer: '*Encore Bravo! Bravo!! Bravo!!! Avez été vraiment extraordinaire, tout simplement. Il faut à présent penser à vous soigner, et sérieusement*' (You have, quite simply, been truly extraordinary. We must now seriously think about your care [possibly your treatment, or possibly making sure you are looked after]).Later in the year came the first performance of her prescient *Pour les funérailles d'un soldat*. Ironically, the war enabled Boulinger's music to be heard.

The war was also influencing the way that Boulanger thought about her opera. How could it not, when she was only able to meet with Ricordi's representative in Paris, Paul Gentien, when he had a week's leave from the battlefields? Boulanger told Gentien that she wanted 'to write a work related to current events which would not be precisely that'. Her words, relayed by Gentien in the letter to Boulanger that he wrote a day after their lunch, and already back with his unit, are ambiguous but provocative. Gentien warned the composer that her vision would be 'excessively difficult to realize dramatically' and gave the example of a recent play that had told 'the story of the current invasion' and succeeded in possessing only 'the offensive and banal appearance of *faits divers*' (an idiom for trivia/local news). He suggests that 'the solution would be to write a sort of very simple fairy-tale with only a few protagonists, the general subject of which would be a war', and proposes Claudel's *L'annonce faite à Marie* (The Tidings Brought to Mary) as a suitable and patriotic opera subject. Maeterlinck seems to be forgotten for the moment.

Months pass. On 20 January 1916, Boulanger notes in her diary that Zeppelins flew overhead at 10am. The same day, she lunches with the Bouwens in Paris. They discuss Maeterlinck. Suddenly, his libretto is back on the table. Had Boulanger worked out a way in which her opera could be more than *faits divers*, since, after all, *La princesse Maleine* has a war at its heart? Or had she given up the idea of writing a war opera as a futile gesture? (Later, in the early 1930s, there is mention of a 'now lost *Poème Symphonique*' in which Boulanger had tried 'to put into music the impression evoked by plains devastated through battles: the night, the wounded, the colour and the solitude', but nothing more is known about this work, allegedly composed in 1915–16.)

Whatever her reasons, events moved quickly. So did Boulanger. On 13 February 1916, Boulanger leaves Paris for Rome and the Villa Medici. She travels with her mother, and with the only previous female Prix de Rome winner, the sculptor Lucienne Heuvelmans. As ever, they break the journey in Nice. There,

Boulanger meets Maeterlinck. Two days later, he writes to her to confirm their arrangement. Boulanger is delighted, and travels on to Milan where she meets with Ricordi, who, it is confirmed, will prepare the libretto. She reaches the almost deserted Villa Medici at midnight on 21 February 1916. The same day, eight hundred miles to the north, the Battle of Verdun starts, Germany's attempt to sap France of men and resources. The battle lasts ten months, with over a million casualties: 'I am extremely troubled by this German offensive against Verdun – how much more sadness – I think of everyone who will not come home and my heart aches', writes Lili in her diary. Later, in June: 'naval battle in the North Sea between the English and the Germans – how dreadful! – with no other result than countless abominations and suffering – ah! it's too painful'.

Physically, if not emotionally, far removed from the battlefields, Boulanger started work on her *Maleine*. As a Prix de Rome winner she was expected to write an opera – she had a contract to produce an opera, and everything suggests that she was determined to do just that in Rome. For a few days, all went well. Heuvelmans started working on a bust of Boulanger; the composer herself re-engaged with the pleasures of the city, whether the cinema or ancient ruins; she even had an Italian admirer, one Emmanuel Oldoprandi. There is no more mention of Jean Bouwens. But soon, too soon, Boulanger's health collapsed (bronchitis this time) and she was forced to spend six weeks in bed, only able to walk to the window. Her letters to her friend Miki are, unsurprisingly, full of frustration:

> I feel discouraged . . . not because of the suffering, not because of boredom, but because I understand that I would never be able to have in me the feeling that I have done what I would like to do, but what I have to do, since

I cannot follow whatever it is with being interrupted for a
long time so that my efforts cannot be sustained!

Weeks, then months, passed at the villa. May brought slightly
better health, and Boulanger focused on creating motifs for her
opera's central characters, noting on 5 May, 'Perhaps I have
Hjalmar's theme in what I did today', returning to *Clairières*, orches-
trating the song cycle, and beginning new works: 'went to the
piano and found the beginnings of a sonata for piano and violin';
'work a bit on the psalm – which I'm getting back to'.

In fact, the composer was working on at least two psalm
settings, the longest of which would be a setting of Psalm 130 (*De
Profundis*). Boulanger's composition sketchbook shows that she
was toying with different section titles: Death knell with *Dies Irae*;
Bell pealing for a baptism; Song of personal feeling; or Song of all-
enveloping peace. Caroline Potter sees these headings as hints
that, privately, Boulanger was considering the work as a requiem
for her dead father. In public, however, the work would be entitled
Du fond de l'abîme (From the Depths of the Abyss), using the text's
first line, and it makes compelling listening, Boulanger using tenor
and contralto soloists, one of her favourite combinations, with a
mixed chorus and a large orchestra, deployed to underline 'the
dark text by emphasizing the lower instruments'. Earlier, in *Faust
et Hélène*, Boulanger had explored the interplay between contralto
and tenor, with the male voice rising above the female voice. Now,
in *Du fond de l'abîme* the two solo voices end section eight on a
unison.

In her marked turn to religious works, at the expense of her
opera, Boulanger is yet again straying from the conventional path,
in this case the values of secular, anti-clerical France, a country in
which church and state had been formally separated just ten years
earlier. Perhaps, by 1916, witnessing war, and experiencing illness,

Boulanger, so assiduous in catering to the tastes and values of her Parisian world, had begun not to care what that world thought of her.

Boulanger's next step has a hint of this, but also suggests she had not lost sight of her professional goals, as she left Rome, for the second time, in June, after only four months at the Villa Medici. Yet again, she broke her journey home in Nice, met with Maeterlinck and Ricordi, this time to discuss the final shape of her opera's libretto. In Nice, Boulanger received a signed photograph from the great man ('To my dear little collaborator Lili Boulanger who, by order of the gods of music and destiny, is to give to the Princess Maleine the soul for which she has been waiting') and then, on her return to Paris, a letter:

> All my thoughts are with you in your pain and your anxi-
> ety. But I have a confidence which comes to me from I
> don't know where and which I would like to share with
> you. I feel – I would nearly say, I know – that the child-
> genius who must give a voice to La princesse Maleine
> cannot pass away before having accomplished her work,
> which seems fused with her destiny. Maeterlinck.

'Pass away'? Had it come to that? It is Miki Piré who remembered, many years later, that Lili had been told by a doctor in Rome that she only had two years to live, but Miki also said that no one knew this but her. If Caroline Potter is right, that Boulanger originally envisaged her *Du fond de l'abîme* as a requiem, if she is consciously echoing the famous '*Libera me*' section of Fauré's *Requiem* in her own 'heartbeat' accompaniment, then is it too much to suggest that the composer was, consciously or unconsciously, writing her *own* requiem whilst in Rome for the second time? The truth will never be known, but a terminal diagnosis might further explain

Boulanger's decision to leave the Villa Medici. It also makes all the more remarkable her apparent determination that the show would go on.

Back in Paris, and knocked out by a gruelling return journey, the composer made another swerve in artistic direction, turning away (again) from her opera, and completing a much smaller work, the song 'Dans l'immense tristesse' (In Immense Sadness), three days after her twenty-third birthday. It is an 'extraordinarily dark' setting of a poem on the death of a child by the deaf, blind and mute Madame Galéron de Calone, a song with 'few parallels in the solo vocal literature as a study of despair'. If Boulanger was contemplating her own mortality, then, in a tragic irony, the song setting would actually be prescient of another death. A few days after the completion of 'Dans l'immense tristesse', on 3 September 1916, Lili's goddaughter Madeleine died, the daughter of Renée and George Delaquys, granddaughter of Raoul Pugno. She was only five years old. Somehow, Boulanger struggled through the autumn. In October, Nadia recorded in her diary an 'indescribable crisis' in Lili's health: 'the motionless body asked us to warm it up by rubbing it. There is something awful in the blistering of this dying being, but for us she wants to live and this fight is tragic, she, happy to end so much suffering but still resisting while understanding our despair.'* Nadia did not want the world to see this diary entry, sealing her words about Lili's desire to 'end so much suffering' in a suitcase that was deposited in the Bibliothèque Nationale with strict instructions that it should not be opened until many years after her

---

* 'Après une crise que rien ne peut décrire, après avoir eu les yeux vitreux, le corps immobile nous a demandé de la réchauffer par des frictions. Il y a quelque [chose] d'atroce à ce boursouflage de cet être mourant, mais pour nous elle veut vivre et cette lutte est tragique, elle heureuse devant la fin de tant de souffrances et pourtant résistant en comprenant notre désespoir. Agenda 1916, 21 octobre', transcribed by Fiorella Sassanelli, privately communicated.

death. It was long thought that the suitcase might contain lost compositions, or reveal erotic secrets, but the documents that have been found are both more banal and more tragic, for they contain the truth of Lili's suffering.

At the same time, other events and compositions from the final months of 1916 complicate any simplistic mapping of life upon art, and challenge the lurking, and reductive, trope of the *femme fragile* who simply pours her overpowering emotions into her music. Boulanger's *Marche gaie*, from 1916, is about as different to '*Dans l'immense tristesse*' as two works can possibly be. It was registered with the Société des auteurs, compositeurs, et éditeurs de musique, but was long thought lost until it surfaced in an American attic. With its 'stomping common-chord texture and harmony of the second section', and its use of a musical pun (an echo of a theme in Mendelssohn's famous 'Wedding March'), the work is spirited and joyful. The Mendelssohn reference, together with the manuscript's dedication to 'my lovely little friend, Jeanne Leygues' may explain its purpose. Leygues was a wealthy young Parisian who, like so many others, had started nursing during the war. The American Paul Rockwell was one of her patients. Rockwell, and his aviator brother Kiffin, had been amongst the very first Americans to sign up to fight in Europe's war, years before America itself joined the fight in August 1917. Kiffin would be killed in September 1916. Paul and Jeanne would marry on 4 December in Paris and it seems likely that Boulanger's 'stomping' *Marche gaie* was composed for the wedding ceremony.

Marche gaie has, understandably, been seen as a measure of Boulanger's spirit. As Caroline Potter argues, the 'fact that she continued composing despite everything is testament to her extraordinary determination and strength of character'. But it is also a reminder of her professionalism, and the extent to which she continued to operate according to her publisher's expectation, that individual works be arranged for different instrumental ensembles (in this case, piano reduction and chamber orchestra) so as to ensure as wide a market as possible. This kind of assiduous professionalism is equally visible in Lili's letter to Nadia, written around the time of '*Dans l'immense tristesse*', in which she asks her big sister for advice in her dealings with Ricordi and Maeterlinck:

> My little Nadia, This letter for Ricordi seems fine to me. The other one too. [Lili encloses two draft letters.] But, I don't know why, I can't bring myself to send them without you having seen them. The one for Maeterlinck has strange writing – the ink wouldn't mark the paper – and I started it too low down the page – I would have redone it, but I couldn't find more paper like that. On the other hand, read it carefully, and let me know if you think that Ricordi, having it for one reason or another in his hands, wouldn't be a little annoyed by it, because after all, the publishing house is him, isn't it – nothing can be done without his say-so – but on the other hand . . . what do you think??? Do whatever you think best. If you don't think the handwriting of the letter for Maeterlinck is good enough, but the content is, don't send it – I'll redo it tomorrow when you come back, and [you should] send him a telegram more or less like this: Would be very grateful to you if you would return the signed contract to Ricordi. Letter follows – thank you, compliments, sincerely yours . . . or something along those lines. Another thing – bring me, if you can, a little bottle of cucumber milk from Roberts. My deepest love for you and my best kiss, In haste, Bébé

Boulanger's assiduity paid off and on 30 November 1916 the contract for *Maleine* was finally signed. For the feminist musicologist, Annegret Fauser, Boulanger used *Maleine* 'to create a woman's text about war and its horrors, leaving all glorious and militaristic aspects aside', and if this is the case, then *Maleine* was the work that Boulanger wanted to write some sixteen months earlier, a work with war at its heart, 'a work related to current events which would be not precisely that'. Fauser also suggests that Ricordi, prompted by Boulanger, made significant cuts to Maeterlinck's original text, with the intention not only of providing a coherent libretto (which he did), but also to focus all the attention on the struggle between the two female protagonists, Princess Maleine and the evil Queen Anne. Another critic goes further, to argue that Boulanger's libretto 'portrays women in important political positions, rather than as mothers, nurses, or other types of caregivers', in a direct response to the experience of 'women's wartime roles'. If these interpretations are accepted, then they serve to complicate still further the image of Boulanger as the *femme fragile*, as does a photograph from 1917 showing Boulanger with Fachoun, possibly a Pyrenean Mountain Dog, stretching up to lay his paws on Lili's arm, his head reaching up to his five-foot-nine-inch mistress's chin. Boulanger clearly had no time for ladylike lap-dogs.

Nadia Boulanger offered a very different, and much less consciously feminist, understanding of her sister's commitment to *La princesse Maleine*, and one that meshes much more easily with the enduring image of the *femme fragile*. Nadia believed that Lili identified personally with the character of Princess Maleine. The conflation of composer and character is the harder to resist because Lili/Maleine embody so beautifully French symbolist ideas about 'woman' and death: since women are 'the closest relatives of the infinite which surrounds us'; since only women 'know how to smile at' the infinite ('with the familiar grace of the child which is not afraid of its father'); since only women 'preserve here on earth, like a celestial and functionless jewel, the pure salt of our souls'; since only women are 'ideal yet futile recipients of the eternal' (because of 'their lack of intellect'); and since only women live in a 'realm of instinct', then it follows that a woman 'does not die as we [sic] do: she dies like animals or little children'. French symbolist thinking makes the Maleine/Lili identification seem horribly plausible, although without the benign gloss given by Nadia. The child-woman Lili Boulanger, the 'ideal yet futile recipient of the eternal' is writing her own death.* In the libretto, Maleine dies, animal-like, accompanied by Pluto, her black dog who 'whimpers and howls in the face of approaching danger, while Maleine utters incoherent phrases, expressing her fear in child-like exclamations'. If this is a glimpse into Lili Boulanger's psyche it does not make comfortable reading.

Nor does her diary from December 1916. On Christmas morning, she is 'like the smallest of babies, I wake at 6 o'clock to find packages of all sorts. A nativity scene.' She cannot help but cry: 'I calm myself quickly, because for the first time, I am going out in the car with Nadia, towards the woods. Mother has prepared a wonderful lunch – is kind as always.' Lili attempts to take a drink of chocolate, but fails and has to return to bed. 'The fever climbs each day – when will I recover a little health?' On 29 December she writes: 'I feel so tired that I can't manage to get up – I knit, lying down – I read a little – when will I be finally *cured* – I can hardly eat, I feel so dreadful.' The following day: 'I'm

---

* Maleine's theme begins with a minor second and a minor third, a combination of intervals, which in melodic and harmonic terms is a characteristic feature of Boulanger's music. The motive continues with a chromatic upward movement that contains the nucleus of the Wagnerian 'Tristan motive', widely used in French music as a musical sign of love and desire.

shivering all over – my blood leaps and bounds in my veins like a motorbike starting up.'

Cured? If Boulanger still hoped for a cure in December 1916, what of the 'dying being' recorded by Nadia in her diary? What of the terminal diagnosis Lili had apparently received at the start of the year in Rome? Did she no longer believe in it? Was she in denial? Or perhaps, since there is only the evidence of (the notoriously sensationalist) Miki Piré to suggest that Boulanger had been told she had two years to live, that conversation had never taken place, and Maeterlinck's comments about her passing away were merely a natural, if tactless, response to seeing a very sick young woman. Would a composer knowing she was dying have signed that contract with Ricordi? And would a composer knowing she was dying have made a long and arduous winter wartime journey to Arcachon, near Bordeaux, unless she still had some hope of recovery?

For this is what Boulanger did, in February 1917. For a few weeks, the sea air seemed to bring an improvement and the composer made some gestures towards returning to her opera. Most of her limited energy went into her vocal religious works. Indeed, Boulanger even began a new work, a *Pie Jesu*, a choice that not only demonstrates her debt to Fauré, the composer of one of the most well-loved settings of this text, but also her preference for a more modern, modal vocal line than that of the older composer. In the words of one admiring musicologist, the accompaniment is 'progressively purged of its Wagnerian chromaticism' in its journey towards 'diatonic purity'.

Boulanger's time in Arcachon revealed that it would not, in the end, be her opera that would represent most fully the composer's response to war. Instead, it would be her *Vieille prière bouddhique: prière quotidienne pour tout l'univers* (An Old Buddhist Prayer: A Daily Prayer for Peace for Humanity), begun in 1914, completed in Arcachon, and a work, unlike others from these years, that 'does not specifically reflect ideas of Catholicism and French Catholic identity', but instead prays for the end of suffering for all human beings, no matter their beliefs. Above all, it offers a vision of a world at peace.

Lili's world is getting smaller. Raïssa comes: Nadia tries to resolve the tensions between protective mother and sick daughter. Miki visits, gives Lili a little lead dog, a symbol of fidelity. It is now June and back in Paris Lili undergoes an operation with only local anaesthetic. Laudanum and oxygen tanks keep hope alive, pain at bay. October 1917, and Boulanger is working again, copying a fragment of *Maleine* into her notebook at Gargenville in the days following the Second Battle of Passchendaele, that byword for the futility of war. Perhaps the opera's composition is 'far advanced' by the end of the year (a modern critic certainly wants it to have been so) but November is cruel, December no better. Nadia writes in her diary that the 'awful suffering of last year' is happening all over again, that Lili 'wants to live, her organism is fighting but the illness is stronger. And not being able to do anything!' Boulanger herself writes, desperately, in the manuscript of *Maleine*: 'Copied in December 1917. Everything must be finished before 1 January. It MUST!!! Will I be able to do it?' ('*Il faut tout finir avant le 1er janvier, il FAUT!!! Le pourrai-je?*')*

Boulanger attempts a sketch for *Maleine* on 18 January 1918. Now, though, she can barely write, and dictates her music to Nadia. The last document she signs, on 29 January, is a new contract with

---

* The researcher Anya Holland-Barry suggests that it is no coincidence that these words are written alongside both the motif for Princess Maleine and Boulanger's trademark bells, which may signify both war and the passing of the composer's own life.

Ricordi. Boulanger asks her sister to complete two of her works, her sonata and *La princesse Maleine*. If only she had completed *Maleine*, if only it had been performed, it would have broken boldly into traditionally male territory, and one of its most powerful institutions, the Paris Opéra. She would have joined the great composers. If only.*

Boulanger signs her name for the last time amidst air raids over Paris. In the following six weeks, 295 bombs will fall on the city. She is taken to Mézy-sur-Seine, to the west of Paris, close to Gargenville. Nadia sends a telegram to Miki for she knows the end is at last near. Lili dictates her *Pie Jesu* to Nadia. It is completed, a work that shifts from anguished intensity to calm acceptance of fate, the concluding 'Amen', the 'essence of affirmation', the work a 'triumph' according to later musicologists. Miki arrives: Lili's body is distorted, swollen, the disease has spread to her lungs, she is lost in fever, in pain. On Saturday 9 March, Miki returns to Paris to hear a performance of two songs from *Clairières dans le ciel*, coupled with '*Dans l'immense tristesse*'. That night, a massive air raid on Paris kills thirteen, injures fifty. A German plane is downed. It is an absurd world, of premiers and bombs, of aeroplanes and laudanum. *Pie Jesu* indeed. Miki brings back Parma violets for her friend. Lili is starving to death: for three weeks she has only been able to drink mineral water. Samples are taken from her lungs each day, and tested in Paris. Friends bring ice from the city to calm the fever, reduce the distension. Then, on 15 March, the priest comes, the last rites are given and the composer dies. A funeral at Église de la

---

* Some scholars, most notably Annegret Fauser, believe that Boulanger was close to completing *Maleine*, citing amongst other evidence a 1920 letter from Nadia to Ricordi in which Lili's sister says that the work 'is very advanced' and that she feels compelled to honour what her sister 'so much desired'. Despite this, no manuscript survives.

Trinité, her parish church back in Paris; a gathering at rue Ballu; burial at Montmartre.

Lili Boulanger's life and work, which had been understood in terms of her illness for so long, would now be understood in terms of her death – as, better even than a *femme fragile*, she becomes a doomed saint: 'thin and pale like a young virgin from a Book of Hours', a girl-woman surrounded by the 'halo of eternity'. In hindsight, she is seen to have paid the price for her talent: 'the flame of Lili's talent' was always 'likely to overtax her meagre physical resources'. A tragic celebrity, one of the century's first, she was eulogized as a woman first (her grace, her melancholy, her sensibility), as composer a poor second. Her works remained unrecorded until 1960 when, even then, the critic Marc Blitzstein, writing in *The Saturday Review*, still brings gender to the fore:

> A woman composer of our own century, almost unknown, no longer alive? How good can her music be? It is more than good. It is extraordinary. Make no mistake, here was an original talent.

Blitzstein assures his readers that Boulanger's music is 'masculine in its rugged force, utterly feminine in its purity and lyrical outpouring'.

Nadia Boulanger did her best for her little sister, using her prestige as a teacher and conductor to draw attention to Lili's work, although her influence sometimes served to complicate responses to the music, particularly in that year of revolt, 1968, also the fiftieth anniversary of the composer's death. A journalist from *Le Nouveau Journal* insisted that it was all hype. Lili was a nice girl, but her music did not survive the sentimental myth that had been 'valiantly kept alive for half a century by her sister, Nadia Boulanger, with an obvious sincerity, a will of iron and the tentacular authority which her position as an eminently cosmopolitan teacher of composition gives her'. Nadia, with equal sincerity and authority, worked hard to protect Lili's personal reputation, insisting that 'there was not a shadow of a secret in my sister's life'. No secrets? Even in death, the composer exists in the shadow of the courtesan. No matter that those who speculate about Lili's parentage, or her relationships with men or with women, or the secret messages she may or may not be conveying in her music, have yet to make a convincing case: it does not stop the attempt. Salacious enquiries aside, scholarly assessments of French musical modernism may give Boulanger a mention but she is hardly central, let alone welcomed, into the classical canon.

None of this is surprising, given her sex and her early death, not to mention the fact that she died in 1918 when Paris and the wider world had more important things to think about. What is surprising is the presence in this chapter of two apparently very different Lili Boulangers. The composer signed herself 'Bébé', and represented herself as a child-woman, suggesting that, if her family infantilized her because of her illness, Lili (usually) embraced that identity. This has made it easy for commentators, then and now, to reduce her life to her illness, the composer concealed by the image of the always-dying child-woman 'petite Lili'. At the same time, Boulanger appears to have exploited her status as a *femme fragile* to win the Prix de Rome, to gain Maeterlinck's support and to play the Villa Medici system. She displays toughness, artfulness, *joie de vivre* and, above all, ambition. This determined, professional, adult Boulanger, breaking new ground as a woman and composer, co-existed with *petite* Lili, whether consciously or unconsciously. To be a woman and composer always entails some doubleness, as Boulanger worked assiduously towards her often incompatible goals: to be accepted by the patriarchal musical establishment, and to find her own voice as a composer.

A further irony remains. For all the emphasis on Lili's fragility, and despite the obvious ways in which her illness ensured that major works were lost to pain, and eventually silenced the composer completely, the physical symptoms of a debilitating, then fatal, illness are actually quite well-concealed, and consciously so, in the Boulanger archive. The belatedly revealed contents of the suitcase in the Bibliothèque Nationale show that Nadia's secret was not some scandal of illegitimacy but the quotidian horror of watching her sister die. In Boulanger's own writings (or those not destroyed by Nadia) she rarely gives vent directly to the personal experience of pain. There is one telling exception. Usually a perfectionist, Boulanger is for once musically shambolic, scribbling a monody for voice into one her opera sketchbooks:

> I have pains in the back. I have pains, little pains. I have pains in the back, the whole back, little pains. I have pains . . . in the back, in the whole back. I can't go out because it's raining. Now I'm hot, I'm not cold any more, but I'm too hot. I'm pretty ill, poor little thing. Why am I always in pain? It's not fair, poor little thing, so little. Being too hot, being too cold, that's my lot. It's not fun.

Always, always, there was the pain. Being a 'poor little thing' may paradoxically have enabled Boulanger to achieve some of her short-term goals, but her illness would ensure that she would never pursue those goals to their end. Her commitment to *Maleine* shows that the composer believed she could make further inroads into the traditionally male territory of opera, that she knew herself capable of composing large-scale works for large-scale forces. Boulanger's time, place and family, coupled with her exceptional talent and determination, meant that by the time of her death she had already made the crucial move from the semi-public, bourgeois realm of the salon to the professional, public space exemplified by victory in the Prix de Rome. We cannot know if she would have survived in that space, but Boulanger (if not Bébé) believed she was capable of it, and to listen to her music now suggests that she was right.

'I cannot imagine life without being engaged in composition' Elizabeth Maconchy

Chapter Eight

MACONCHY

It is 1923 and Prokofiev is being premiered in Paris; Bartók in Berlin; Janáček and Martinů in Prague; and Bessie Smith is making her first recordings in New York. Meanwhile, in London, audiences enjoy a diet of Elgar, Holst and Vaughan Williams or, for those with a taste for new music, not to mention an entrée into the Bloomsbury set, perhaps a performance of William Walton's controversial *Façade*, with Edith Sitwell reciting her own poetry through a megaphone, and Walton, her young protégé, conducting the band.

In the same year, a shy sixteen-year-old girl, newly arrived from Dublin, begins her studies at the Royal College of Music (RCM), South Kensington. Only nine months earlier, her father had died of tuberculosis, and now her mother has brought the girl, with her two sisters, to London. The girl will later call her mother 'very brave' in her willingness to pull herself up and make the move to England but, in fact, Violet had done the same thing some six years earlier, moving in the other direction, from Hertfordshire to Ireland, in the desperate hope that the sea breezes of Howth, in Dublin Bay, would keep her husband alive. The journey across the Irish Sea was at least a familiar one for the bereaved girl, because, although born and raised in Hertfordshire, long, happy childhood summers had been spent roaming the Santry Court estate near Dublin, where Violet's father was agent.

Ambitious fathers and talented mothers; prodigy brothers and trailblazing sisters; courts, cities or nations in need of a soundtrack, even if, and sometimes because, it is composed by a woman – these have been the ingredients for success for composers from Francesca Caccini to Lili Boulanger. And then there is Elizabeth 'Betty' Maconchy, with her solicitor father and home-maker mother, growing up in the Home Counties of England and the suburbs of Dublin with no piano-teacher father to provide lessons, no sibling composer with whom to collaborate, no concert halls, no soirees or salons, just an urgent inner compulsion and a lifelong commitment to expressing herself in music.

That commitment would be tested by war, by life-threatening illness, and by the more everyday but nevertheless powerful demands of motherhood. That her music is less well-known and less performed than that of her close contemporary Benjamin Britten does not mean Maconchy failed those tests, or that her commitment faltered. Her passionate determination to pursue her art, the 'rigid self-discipline' she argued was necessary for any composer, was never in doubt. In the event, vast reservoirs of that 'rigid self-discipline' were needed by a woman who set herself the highest of musical standards, and faced a series of challenges that would have led many to abandon the often thankless career of composer. Over the years, there would be what Maconchy called 'moments of silence', but through each 'blank patch' the 'underlying emotion' remained and demanded expression in music, sometimes even if there was no one to hear.

It was in Hertfordshire that Elizabeth 'Betty' Maconchy's parents realized their six-year-old daughter had a special talent, as she picked out the sound of church bells on the family's little-played piano. By the time of the move to Howth, the nature of that talent was becoming clearer. The adolescent Betty was sent to study not only with the best piano teacher in Dublin, one Mrs Boxhill, but for lessons in harmony and counterpoint with a Dr John Larchet.

Betty Maconchy soon outpaced Mrs Boxhill and Dr Larchet. Was it her teachers who recommended the move to London, or was it her newly widowed mother who saw a future for Betty, but only away from Dublin? In Ireland, Betty had never seen a string quartet, only once heard an orchestra perform. In London, she could go to music college, hear as much music as she could wish. But it may not have been only the prospect of a musical education for Betty that made London attractive. The family had only arrived in Howth a year after the Easter Rising of 1916. The 1919–21 armed struggle for Irish independence was followed by a brutal civil war.

Whether pushed from Ireland, or pulled to England, the shy Irish girl with her provincial music education and little or no formal schooling, just a series of good and not-so-good governesses, gained a place at the RCM. Her first year in London was a challenging one, but, once she settled in, Elizabeth Maconchy took the place by storm. The rest should be history. That it is not is one of the driving forces behind this book.

The RCM was a relatively new institution, founded as recently as 1894. By the time of Maconchy's arrival in 1923, it had already improved musical standards in Britain, and was helping to counter the nation's 'unenviable image (both at home and abroad) as *das Land ohne Musik*' (the land without music). For many, however, further steps needed to be taken if British or, more specifically, English music were to emerge as the triumphant successor to the still-dominant German tradition (Brahms, Mendelssohn, Robert Schumann and the rest) or if London were to knock Paris off its pedestal as the city of culture. In the words of one commentator, it was exasperating beyond anything that 'a town like Paris with one tenth of the musical activity of London still looks upon itself as the superior musical centre by right of tradition'.

For some, a nationalist turn to English folk song signalled the way forward. Not everyone agreed. The young composer Elisabeth Lutyens, for example, would come actively to dislike what she saw as the fabrication of a reactionary English folk tradition. For her, the Continent remained the only place where composers could embrace their own nationality *and* still be modern: 'Stravinsky was so Russian, Bartók so Hungarian, Hindemith so German', whilst England seemed to be 'rustically resuscitating songs no one had heard of'. But, as Lutyens recognized ruefully, 'there was no getting away from the fact that I wasn't Russian, Hungarian or German. I was English.'

The English tradition in music had, it was believed, reached its high point during the Elizabethan or Restoration periods, depending on whether you were a champion of Byrd or Purcell. The problem was that these men had come 'too early . . . to take much place in the general repertoire', as the composer Constant Lambert complained in 1935:

> We still devote about 99 percent of our programmes to the 19th and 18th centuries (a ludicrous proportion), and the period in which English music really shines still remains in practical obscurity, in spite of all the work of scholars and editors. Purcell has his followers in Germany, and I once met a Frenchman who had heard of Byrd. But that is about as far as knowledge of the English classics goes.

Which direction would the sixteen-year-old Irish/English Elizabeth Maconchy, arriving with the sketchiest of musical educations and a vast amount of talent, take? At first sight, her enrolment as a student of Ralph Vaughan Williams in the winter of 1925 suggests that she would become one of the 'rustic resuscitators' so despised by Lutyens. After all, Vaughan Williams had been collecting English folk songs since 1902, was the composer of a commanding *Fantasia on a Theme by Tallis*, and had only recently revised his ever-popular, and profoundly pastoral, romance for violin and orchestra, *The Lark Ascending*. Maconchy certainly valued Vaughan Williams's teaching: 'Everything suddenly opened out to me'; it was 'a whole new world when I became a pupil of his'; it was 'like turning on a light'. Did that mean she would follow his musical lead? Absolutely not. To Vaughan Williams's credit, he not only let his student go her own way, he insisted that she do so, because all of his students were expected to think for themselves, 'in their own musical language', however different that language might be to his own. Always independent, Maconchy wanted to, and needed to, find her own path. Unmoved by the German tradition, whether Wagner or Schoenberg, uninterested in English folk song, hardly glancing at Byrd and Tallis, Maconchy instead discovered the music of Bartók. (She and her friends rushed to hear the composer play in London on 4 March 1929. BBC listeners would hear the first half of the concert but it was only the live audience who heard Bartók's *Piano Sonata*, kept for the second half because deemed too difficult for radio listeners.) What appealed to Maconchy was not so much the Hungarian's nationalist fascination with the authentic gypsy music of his own country and his unwillingness to bowdlerize it in the manner of earlier composers such as Brahms and Liszt, but Bartók's ability as a composer to work transformations upon a few basic themes, together with his trademark use of strong motor rhythms.

The world opened up by Bartók and Vaughan Williams was further expanded by the friends Maconchy made at the RCM. Vaughan Williams believed that a composer learned far more from his or her fellow students than from tutors or the 'academy'. His belief would be borne out by Maconchy's experience. A group of aspiring composers, which included Imogen Holst and Grace

Williams, would meet each week to debate and criticize each other's work. Williams became one of Elizabeth Maconchy's closest and most significant friends, their college years providing the foundation for what Maconchy later called 'the life-long habit between Grace and me of mutual consultation and criticism'. No matter that Grace was a zealous Wagnerite. As with the man these young women called 'Uncle Ralph', it was the 'mutual consultation and criticism' that mattered, rather than the sharing of a musical language.

Above all, however, for any young composer, the RCM provided a vital opportunity to have one's music played, for, as Grace Williams put it, remembering her first few months in South Kensington, the 'atmosphere of the place really bowled me over. Here at last was what I had been aching for – real live musical activity.' Maconchy was soon at the forefront of that 'real live musical activity' and, by 1926, not one, but two of her compositions had been chosen for performance by the prestigious Patron's Fund, meaning that for the first time the still only nineteen-year-old composer heard professional musicians perform her music.

That same year, Vaughan Williams was attempting to find a way for his talented student to further her education outside England, and sent off a letter of enquiry:

> Miss Maconchy is just 19 – plays the piano quite well
> and has had a thorough grounding at the hands of Kitson
> and Charles Wood [two of the composition tutors at the
> RCM]. She has – as I say – in my opinion decided inven-
> tive powers but is of course at present like all young
> people going through a new phase every month. At
> present she has been badly bitten by Bartok [sic] and is
> of course anxious to study with him, but I rather doubt
> the wisdom of this. I feel possibly that Respighi or

Casella might be good for her – if they ever take pupils. On the other hand, neither Rome nor Buda-Pesth [sic] would I imagine be good from the point of view of general musical atmosphere and the hearing of plenty of good music etc. Also of course we must consider a place where we could find a nice family for her to live with and so on. Are Leipzig or Dresden any good nowadays? Prague has been suggested to me – what do you think of that? or I thought of sending her to Ravel but I doubt if he would take any pupils now. I should be most grateful for your advice.

Putting aside for a moment the perceived need for a 'nice family' for the nineteen-year-old girl, and the quiet suffocation of her desire to study with her favourite composer, Vaughan Williams was obviously keen for Maconchy to spread her wings, whether in Leipzig, Prague or Paris. Nothing came of the letter, however. Perhaps because of the young composer's youth and shyness, perhaps because of the family's lack of money to fund such travels, Maconchy remained in South Kensington, living with her mother and sisters at 188c Gloucester Terrace, Hyde Park, W2.

All was going well in London, however. Maconchy was awarded the Blumenthal Scholarship of 1927, which paid for her tuition fees and left about £90 to live on (about £5,500 in today's money), and then the following year, the head of the college, Hugh Allen, recommended the twenty-one-year-old composer's *Concertino for Piano and Orchestra* for performance by the BBC. The British Broadcasting Corporation, only founded some four years earlier, appreciated the work, describing it as quite 'jolly', but also noted that it had more in common with the 'strong water' of the Continent rather than 'the milk' of English tradition. The concertino was, however, never broadcast. It was not the BBC, but Maconchy, who withdrew the piece, an early sign of the composer's perfectionism, even at the expense of having her music performed and heard. The episode revealed two clearly visable fault-lines that would run through Maconchy's career: the tendency of others to be concerned themselves with her Englishness or lack of it, and the tendency of the composer herself towards the most stringent self-criticism. As her RCM report from midsummer 1927 says: 'Most satisfactory results. Still rather inclined to dwell on difficulties that she alone creates!'

By the autumn of 1928, Maconchy was entering her sixth year at the college. She and her female colleagues might have spoken in later years of the lack of 'prejudice' at the RCM, but the events of this year suggest that sexism was alive and well in the corridors of South Kensington. Encouraged by Vaughan Williams, Maconchy had put herself forward for the most prestigious of college prizes, the Mendelssohn Scholarship. Later, she remembered, wryly, that the judges were mostly 'aged about ninety', but things appeared to have gone well. A day after the competition, she was congratulated by the head of the college, Hugh Allen, on her success. Maconchy told him that he was wrong, the scholarship had gone to someone else, which bemused Allen. They must have changed their minds once he had left the room. But he soon recovered. No matter: 'if we'd given it to you, you'd have only got married and never written another note!'

Denied the Mendelssohn, Maconchy was, in a gesture of conciliation if not guilt, awarded the Octavia Scholarship, set up to enable recipients to benefit from travelling and studying abroad. In the spring of 1930, she at last packed her bags. Vaughan Williams was sorry to see her go, but gave his student high praise, and envisioned a glorious future for the young composer: 'Very sorry to lose her – but I can teach her no more – she will work for her own salvation & will go far.'

Maconchy's primary destination was Prague. The city was everything she had hoped it would be, and more. She found it to be 'a small . . . independent sort of place' where everybody 'was very much working on their own'. It was a perfect match for the independent composer, who discovered the music of Janáček (as great an influence as Bartók according to some commentators) and had lessons with the composer/conductor Karel Boleslav Jirák and the pianist/composer Erwin Schulhoff. Prague, unlike its neighbour and erstwhile imperial capital Vienna, described by Vaughan Williams as the best city for the music of the *past*, was hungry for new music. Maconchy gave it to them. The time had not yet come when a Czech Jewish Communist such as Schulhoff would fear for his life. In 1930, he was the guiding force behind, and the soloist in, the premier of Maconchy's *Piano Concerto* (a revised version of the withdrawn concertino) which took place on 19 March 1930 at the Smetana Hall in Prague. It was a very fine way to celebrate the composer's twenty-third birthday.

Wagner-loving Grace Williams, working happily in Vienna ('almost next door' as she wrote to a friend) came over to hear the performance. She reports:

> Arrived in time for the second rehearsal. Betty was quite happy after the first rehearsal, and at the end of the second things were going terribly well . . . but as the concert drew near we developed the usual fear that something would go wrong in the middle and spoil it . . . But the concert performance was even better than the rehearsal.

Her friend's *Piano Concerto* was a triumphant European debut, a fact even Maconchy herself appreciated, asking someone to make a translation of one of the glowing Czech reviews. The note survives in scribbled pencil in the archives of St Hilda's College, Oxford:

The piano concerto by the young Irish composer, E.V. Maconchy, was the best. In spite of the natural impulses due to her youth, it shows a remarkable creative genius both in the animation and sincerity of the first and third movements and in the individual temper and fine building up of the slow movement.

Already in 1930, Maconchy had established a distinct musical voice, characterized by driving rhythms and, most notably, the way in which she derived the entire harmonic and melodic material from the initial three notes. Both of these qualities were reminiscent of, not merely imitative of, Bartók.

Fired up by her success in Prague, Elizabeth Maconchy (as she told it later, in her typically deadpan way) did 'the only thing then open to a young composer – sent a score to Sir Henry Wood'. Sir Henry was, of course, the conductor behind the successful Promenade Concerts held in the Queen's Hall: the score was Maconchy's *The Land*, her compelling orchestral response to, rather than setting of, Vita Sackville-West's poetry. The work is one of the composer's most accessible, its long weaving contrapuntal lines magically opening up time and space, according to one critic. It also demonstrates that Vaughan Williams had not entirely failed to leave his mark upon his student.

Not only did Wood accept *The Land*, but it proved to be one of the sensations of the entire 1930 Prom season, with the work making headlines ('Girl Composer Triumphs'), and Maconchy even compared to Beethoven for her 'expression of emotion'. Maconchy's sex was, of course, a consideration, but she was seen to transcend or, if one is being generous, redefine what it was to be 'feminine': 'Modern it is, of course, in the plain meaning of that word; the method direct, terse, economical; the harmony at times acid and biting – never luxurious or sentimental or (in the pre-war sense) feminine.'

With premiers in Prague and at the Proms, could life get any better for the young composer? It seems it could. One William LeFanu had carefully engineered a meeting with Elizabeth Maconchy at a party a couple of years earlier. By 1929, he had gained the post of Librarian of the Royal College of Surgeons that would give him the financial and professional security to take a wife. On 25 August 1930 *The Times* noted the marriage, two days earlier, of 'Mr. W.R. Le Fanu [sic] and Miss E.V. Maconchy' (Billy and Betty to their friends and family) at the Santry Parish Church, Co. Dublin. The bride, *The Times* informs its readers, wore 'an ankle-length gown of flowered cream silk poplin, and a veil of old Honiton lace, which was held in place by a wreath of orange-blossom'. The bridesmaids, including Betty's sister Sheila, wore 'ankle-length gowns of pale yellow chiffon, with amber-coloured wreaths in their hair, and carried bouquets of amber-coloured chrysanthemums'. *The Times* does not record how the gentlemen were dressed, but does inform its readers that the honeymoon 'is being spent in Connemara'.

Connemara had to wait until September, however, because Maconchy needed to be back in London a few days after her marriage for the rehearsals of *The Land* with the BBC Symphony Orchestra at the Queen's Hall. The newlyweds spent a couple of days at Hunter's Hotel in County Wicklow, then travelled straight on to London, where William LeFanu had already prepared the flat in which they were to live. It was a sign of the man. No musician, instead a 'quietly distinguished' leader in the world of medical librarians, William was wholeheartedly supportive of his composer wife. At the Queen's Hall rehearsal, none other than Gustav Holst approached LeFanu, put his hand on his shoulder (he had to reach up, remembered William), and said: 'Keep her at it.' Elizabeth Maconchy's husband had a rather different, not to say less patriarchal view, both of his own role in the matter, and his wife's agency, saying, years later, remembering the moment: 'She's kept at it of her own accord, I think.'

The relationship between Elizabeth Maconchy and William LeFanu would prove to be a very different one to that of Clara and Robert Schumann, so often seen as the romantic template for a musical woman. Robert may have had a beautiful vision of a collaborative professional relationship that would continue through an erotically charged, loving marriage, but that vision could not, and did not, survive the grim reality of his wife's relentless childbearing, his own mental illness, her ability to earn more money than he did, the practical challenge of having two composers (and two pianos) in one house, not to mention the fact that Clara walked more quickly than he did. Clara, for her part, did not even need to be told to stop composing, as Alma Mahler famously would be by her husband Gustav, who informed her that the 'role of composer, the worker's role, falls to me, yours is that of a loving companion and understanding partner'. Frau Schumann simply silenced herself.

There was to be no silencing of Maconchy, at least not by marriage. When, in future years, she wryly quoted Hugh Allen's words regarding her failure to win the Mendelssohn scholarship ('if we'd given it to you, you'd have only got married and never written another note!') she provided her own gentle, pointed, riposte: 'I did get married but I did continue to write many notes.'

Marriage did not stop Maconchy, but she was coming of age as a composer in what were extremely hard times. By the end of 1930, there were 2.5 million unemployed in Britain. To earn one's living as a composer is hard at the best of times. After the crash of 1929 it was almost impossible. No wonder that when, shortly before taking up his place at the RCM in July 1930, the young Benjamin Britten was asked about his career choice and replied that he wanted to be a composer, the response was 'Yes, but what else?'

The musical establishment hardly made it easy for the new generation of British composers coming through, with Vaughan Williams expressing his exasperation at the fact that, despite the existence of four orchestral series in London, young British composers did not have 'the right of entry even for ten minutes, into a single one'. Meanwhile, the BBC's musical programming was spearheaded by Edward Clark, a former pupil of, and avid enthusiast for, Schoenberg, which might explain why the first two seasons of contemporary music concerts did not contain a single work by a British composer.

The lack of a career infrastructure and performance opportunities for all young composers was exacerbated for women by good old-fashioned sexism in the classical music industry. Even after the triumphs of 1930, Maconchy recalled that no one 'suggested a commission, or a grant, or even a chatty interview on the radio, let alone another performance. The publishers weren't interested. They were all men, of course, and tended to think of women composers being capable of only the odd song or two.' They would have 'liked some pretty little thing – I don't mean a pretty little person – not steady, serious music'. Maconchy singled out Lesley Boosey, of Boosey and Hawkes, as particularly hostile. One of Boosey's readers 'was frightfully keen to publish some songs and a string quartet' of hers, but 'all Boosey would say was that he couldn't take anything except little songs from a woman'. Later, using her typical understatement that masks but does not completely hide her bitterness, she would say 'that really was a very difficult thing to get over'.

Faced with the intransigence of the music industry, a remarkable group of women got together in 1931 and changed the face of music in London, at least for a few years. One was Iris Lemare, that rare thing: a female conductor. The other two were the violinist Anne Macnaghten and the composer Elisabeth Lutyens. Together they launched a series of concerts to showcase new music by young composers, alongside works from eras under-represented in the concert halls of London at the time. The Macnaghten-Lemare Concerts were to prove a lifeline for Elizabeth Maconchy through the 1930s.

The women's venue was the small, cheap Ballet Club theatre in Notting Hill, once a Ragged School, but bought in 1927 by Marie Rambert's husband as performing and rehearsal space. Their methods were collaborative and informal, with no committee, no hierarchy, just the drive to create a platform for their own work, whether as performer, conductor or composer: 'honestly', remembered one of the organizers, 'it wasn't altruistic, it suited each other's ends'. Anne Macnaghten, however, who shouldered much of the organizational responsibility, was eloquent about the driving vision, her words relevant to the world of music, past, present and future. As she said, 'the great thing is to have lots of music going on all the time, lots of things being performed'. Committees always sought:

> To set themselves up as judges, arbitrators, as to what is good and what is bad. The thing is to play music, and it will settle itself sooner or later. As long as there's plenty of opportunity to get new works performed, no harm will be done; what is awful is if somebody is really doing something very good but nobody knows about it.

As the *Musical Times* reported: 'there is nothing quite like these concerts in London. The concert givers get to grips with the real thing in a most delightful, unconventional way, and after an evening spent with them one feels that music is gloriously alive.'

Some of the critics, however, found it hard to see past the phenomenon of women composing, performing and conducting. Although the organizers insisted that the concerts were not a 'deliberate feminist gesture' and that they 'just happened', they were perceived by others as a 'decidedly feminist' business, and, in the case of Maconchy, once again her music was seen to challenge gender categorizations with her 'almost aggressive virility' pointedly contrasted with the 'gentle, melancholy and reflective little songs' produced by the single male composer on one particular programme. Not all were happy at this redefinition in the art of the possible for women, complaining that 'No lipstick, silk stocking or saucily tilted hat adorns the music.' Instead, 'all is grim, intense, and cerebral'. The 'ladies' involved were 'formidably clever, or tried to be'.

To be labelled as 'cerebral' was, of course, far from being a compliment, at least for a woman. It suggested not only that Maconchy had far more in common with the intellectual continental composers than her own British, let alone English, tradition, but, worse even, that she was assuming a masculine intellectuality that she could not possibly possess. It seems that Maddalena Casulana's message from over 350 years earlier was still not getting through. Reviewers believed that women did not, and could not, possess in equal measure the 'high intellectual gifts' of men. The irony for Maconchy was that her 'cerebral' qualities, which are certainly present in her music, were, according to her advocates and to the composer herself, always harnessed to those traditionally 'feminine' traits of feeling and emotion. Her fellow composer and friend, Richard Rodney Bennett, for example, described Maconchy as 'intellectually passionate, passionately intellectual', whilst Maconchy claimed that 'for me, the best music is an impassioned argument. I can find no satisfaction in the coldly reasoned discourse.' All the 'rigid self-discipline' she demanded from a composer 'must always be directed to the fullest expression of the underlying emotion and never to its exclusion'.

Perhaps it was the combination of these qualities that prompted the hard-working Anne Macnaghten to say that when she met Maconchy she thought: 'here is a composer who makes it all worthwhile'. Maconchy would be the most performed composer in the Macnaghten-Lemare series, with eleven works to Benjamin Britten's eight, but the series was not merely a platform for the composer but an impetus for her move into the genre that she would make her own, the string quartet.* Maconchy's *First Quartet* of 1933, 'strong young music of great energy', with its characteristic 'driving Bartókian rhythms' was inspired by Macnaghten's request for new music for her own all-woman quartet. Put simply, in those early years of the 1930s, at the Ballet Club, Notting Hill, Maconchy's music was indeed 'gloriously alive'.

The composer herself was, however, struggling. She faced a threat far greater than that posed by sexism, whether from the benign Hugh Allen or the prejudiced Lesley Boosey. In 1932, at the age of just twenty-five, Betty Maconchy contracted tuberculosis, the disease that had killed her father ten years earlier, and that she was told would now kill her. Her one chance for survival would be to move to Switzerland. Maconchy's response? She wanted to 'die here'.

Desperate times called for desperate measures. Billy and Betty moved to the village of Seal Chart, in Kent, away from the foul air of London. There they resolutely, some would say naively, set up home in a three-sided wooden hut (complete with piano), always open to the elements, although in a concession to the English climate the hut was mounted on a turntable so that it could be turned away from the prevailing wind, rain, sleet or snow. William LeFanu nursed his wife assiduously through a series of debilitating

---

* The sixteen-year-old Benjamin Britten had one of his first public performances in Notting Hill.

episodes. He wrote to Grace Williams on 23 August 1932: 'Betty was going to write to you herself but a week ago she had another attack of haemorrhage and she has been flat on her back for a week.' What he doesn't say is that night after night he had to place ice on Betty's chest to stop the haemorrhaging.

Whether it was the three-sided hut, the ice, the care of her husband, or the composer's sheer willpower, Betty Maconchy did not die. Three years of severe illness left her weakened, with one lung completely ravaged. And yet, even under these most testing of conditions, Maconchy continued to compose and to be performed. She was sustained by the loyalty and practical help of those friends who remained in London, the city itself now denied to her. Elisabeth Lutyens remembered, fondly, that in putting on the Macnaghten-Lemare concerts 'we were a family, all helping in comradeship with the necessary part-copying, arranging and playing as and when we could'. This 'comradeship' would come to Maconchy's aid in the autumn of 1933, when she was suffering from a renewed and severe flare-up of TB and found herself, unsurprisingly, unable to copy out the parts for a performance of her two motets for double chorus scheduled for 11 December. The composer turned to a copyist, which proved to be a mistake, as becomes clear in her exasperated letter to Grace Williams: 'The FOOL who was to have done the second choir parts has been completely useless – said when he saw the thing last Monday that he'd be able to do them quite easily – then took four days to do ONE and left a note to say he couldn't do any more!!!' Into the breach stepped Grace, the composer Dorothy Gow (another RCM friend) and the young Benjamin Britten, who together copied out the parts themselves between them.

Four years after the onset of TB, Maconchy returned again to quartet writing. Her *Second Quartet*, written in 1936, was, unsurprisingly given the experiences of the previous years, a 'more inward, more searching' work, according to the composer herself; music that is 'haunting, at times haunted', according to one critic. A photograph of Maconchy from the year before, taken in Prague shows the composer looking away from the camera, thoughtful, searching, preoccupied but not unhappy. All these qualities are present in her quartet, premiered at a Macnaghten-Lemare concert on 1 February 1937, then performed in Paris later in the year. The musicologist, Rhiannon Mathias, explains the significance of the work's form and, in particular, demonstrates that the intense lento opening movement was the composer's 'first attempt at creating a monothematic movement':

> [The movement's] powerful and compelling argument grows from the quiet viola melody heard in the opening bars. Characteristically, this expressive melody is built from close intervals of tones and semitones, and these intervals are used, as in the music of Bartók, as essential building blocks for the movement. Although the movement can be said to be based around the tonal centre of G, the music is contrapuntal in concept and as such does not follow a formal structure based on key, a feature underlined by the absence of key signatures.

Mathias argues that while the following three movements are 'closely related, each having their thematic origin in the first movement, the only tangible sense of tonal resolution comes in the finale; even then, the music is "C-centred" rather than being definitively in the key of either C major or C minor'. What is more, although the *Second Quartet* has 'a recognizably pastoral quality', it is of a 'dark and disturbed kind, far removed from the Englishness of Butterworth or even Vaughan Williams'. What had been evident in the 1920s, still held true in the 1930s. Maconchy would find her own distinct path, despite or because of the teaching she had received from 'Uncle Ralph'.

The composer would, over the course of her career, return again and again to the quartet. Her thirteen works in the genre were, according to Maconchy, her 'best and most deeply-felt works', and, from the start, they were something she 'enjoyed doing tremendously', the composing never losing 'the sense of excitement and exploration that goes with writing a string quartet'. In their creation, and their content, the quartets exemplify the combination of passion and intellect that is the hallmark of both the woman and her work.

Maconchy loved the quartet form because it represented a debate, a dialectic between four balanced, individual, impassioned voices. Here, and throughout her music, counterpoint is absolutely vital to the composer. For her, it meant more than making 'melodic lines coalesce vertically to create a new harmonic interest'. It meant creating what she called a 'counterpoint of rhythm'. By 'the free movement of several rhythms simultaneously we can hope for more rhythmic development than by any amount of experiment' with a single rhythm. Always, however, the counterpoint had a purpose. She understood a string quartet as 'four characters engaged in statement and comment, passionate argument, digression, restatement, perhaps final agreement – the solution of the problem'. There are echoes here of Maconchy's working relationship with the musicians who played her music, a relationship that entailed rehearsals becoming an intense dialogue between the composer and performer, a 'musical intimacy', all in the pursuit of the perfect realization of her score.

Passion, interplay, intimacy: but at the same time Maconchy was 'selfish and solitary' (her own words), unable to 'imagine working with others'. This was perhaps the secret of her professional survival. If there was a composer who could still maintain her 'rigid self-discipline' when forcibly isolated from the musical world whilst she battled with TB, then it was Elizabeth Maconchy. And if there was a composer who could continue a steady rise to musical prominence under these conditions, it was Elizabeth Maconchy.

Through the 1930s, Maconchy wrote three quartets (and began her fourth); was broadcast by the BBC; won prizes; and was widely performed at home and abroad. Krakow, Budapest, Brussels, Paris, Warsaw, Düsseldorf and Lausanne, to name but some of the cities where she was performed, all heard her music. Maconchy found time to support the Republican cause in the Spanish Civil War and to be active in the Left Book Club, established in 1936 – both further indications, if they were needed, of her republican, socialist politics. She even gained a publisher. Rhiannon Mathias records that:

> [A] carefully worded paragraph in the 'Notes and News' section of *The Musical Times* (May 1939) informed readers that Maconchy had decided 'to work in close collaboration with a publisher', and had 'appointed Mr. Max Hinrischen [founder of Hinrischen Edition Ltd.] as her business representative.' Fittingly, one of the first of her pieces to be issued in print by Hinrischen Edition was her formidably bullish *Third String Quartet* (1938).

Grace Williams was unstinting in her praise for this particular work, which consists of one movement, and lasts about ten minutes. The quartet was the:

> Real stuff of music, & making a lovely sound, it is your most mature work (Dorrie [Gow] agrees with me, too) & is really first-rate quartet writing ... It is grand when a

modern work gives one the same sort of wholesome complete feeling that one gets from listening to Mozart or any of the others. But oh what a rare experience!

Back in 1933, *The Times* had written that Maconchy had already reached the enviable position in which 'she can be sure that anything she may say will be listened to with attention'. By 1938, if Williams was coupling Maconchy with Mozart then others were hailing her as the future of British music: 'Pride of place goes to a girl', wrote one journalist in a survey of young composers.

She was hardly a girl. When she signed her contract with Hinrischen in May 1939 she was a married woman of thirty-two, only three years younger than Mozart at his death. And she was four months pregnant. The summer of 1939 was, however, not exactly a time for optimism, whether personal or national. Already, her friends in Prague were lost to her with Czechoslovakia falling to Nazi Germany in March. Now, on 3 September 1939, Britain declared itself at war. The composer, in her eighth month of pregnancy, was already in neutral Ireland, staying with relatives.* Elizabeth Anna LeFanu was born in Dublin's maternity hospital on 24 October 1939. In the spring of 1940, the decision was made to return to Seal Chart in Kent.

By September 1940, Maconchy is reeling from the personal and professional impact of living in a nation at war:

---

* Ireland in 1939 was nominally a Dominion of the British Empire and a member of the Commonwealth, although it had been declared a 'sovereign, independent, democratic' state in 1921. Britain's dominions were not required to follow their leader into war, and Ireland chose not to, fearing an invasion from the United Kingdom as much as from Nazi Germany.

Domestic jobs, & gardening . . . & 1st Aid lectures & practices keep me quite busy, & I get some work done too. I
was to have had my 3rd quartet played at the National
Gallery concert to-day – but the viola of the [Blech] quartet was called up for his training as a pilot in the RAF 2
days ago, which was rather sad – but I hope they will do it
later on. – I had a preliminary rehearsal of my 'Dialogue'
with the orchestra (at Queen's Hall) early in August. The
pianist Clifford Curzon is excellent – couldn't be better –
and he likes the work very much. The orchestra read it
pretty badly – but I think when it has had 2 proper rehearsals it will be allright [sic]. It's on Sept 26th – none of the
Proms are being broadcast, as you know, which is a pity.

Maconchy still clings to the idea that the show might go on, that
her professional life might continue, through these years of conflict.
She was not alone. As the programme to the cancelled concert
noted laconically: 'In case of an Air Raid Warning the audience will
proceed downstairs where adequate protection is available.'

Then, three days later, came the Blitz. At 5.30pm on 7 September,
some 348 German bombers escorted by 617 fighters pounded
London for thirty hellish minutes. There was a second round of
incendiary bombs maybe two hours later, lasting into the next day.
Nazi Germany's aim was to destroy British morale ahead of a land
invasion. The cancellation of a performance of Maconchy's
Dialogue, which had been rehearsed back in August, was just one
very small casualty of war. The premiere of Elisabeth Lutyens's
Three Pieces for Orchestra, on the first night of the Blitz, revealed the
stark reality that proceeding downstairs to 'adequate protection'
might not quite be enough. The composer, together with Sir Henry
Wood, the performers and the few audience members who had
been brave enough to venture out, were forced to spend the night

in the old Queen's Hall. 'The next day we learnt that the docks had been hit', Lutyens recalled. 'Whether it was the performance of my work or the German bombers, the Proms temporarily ceased.' Lutyens's very English irony was little defence against German bombs.

Down in Kent, LeFanu and Maconchy made a huge bonfire of all their letters and documents. They feared, and with good reason, that they lay in the path of the ascendant invaders, and wished to leave nothing that would make their friends, family or colleagues vulnerable to the Nazis. Given their commitment to the socialist causes of the 1930s, they had good reason to fear for themselves, but, meanwhile, there was urgent business to be done, because William LeFanu was tasked with the evacuation, from London to Shropshire, of the library of the Royal College of Surgeons. It was achieved, and only just in time: the building would be destroyed by the bombs only three weeks later. By the start of 1941, father, mother and baby Anna were based at Downton Castle, Shropshire, with LeFanu also working as an air raid warden, a member of the Home Guard and organizing the supply of periodicals to army and navy hospitals.

Maconchy could have been forgiven for focusing all her energies on survival, and her young daughter. There was no electricity, and simply keeping the paraffin or oil lamps filled, or the log fire supplied with wood, were arduous daily tasks. As for all families in 1941, food was scarce and rationing strict, so growing (and more importantly, preserving) one's own fruit and vegetables became a necessity.

It would take more than war, however, to silence Elizabeth Maconchy. In the dark days of 1942, her *Dialogue* was finally performed (at the Albert Hall, the new home of the Proms after the bombing of the Queen's Hall), and the composer made the arduous wartime journey to London to be present. That same year, she began her *Fourth Quartet*, her 'masterpiece' according to some. Rarely flamboyant in expression, the development of the musical material, particularly in some of the more chromatic passages, has what has been called a diamond-edged precision about it, with not a note straying out of place. Its motivic structure is a maze of inversion and retrograde patterns, and is established at the outset – the viola entry (bars four to six), for example, is an inversion of the first bar of the cello theme. Interestingly, while this is by no means twelve-note music, the use of integrative motivic cells suggests a thorough working knowledge of the method. Maconchy was, indeed, exploring twelve-note technique at around this time but, like Britten and Tippett, stopped short of embracing the method as a whole.

Maconchy understood very well that she was 'already an economical composer', and she did not need the discipline of twelve-note technique to make her even more so. When the work was performed by the Blech Quartet in June 1943, and broadcast by the BBC to Europe, the composer wrote, tellingly, to her sister Sheila that 'they made it sound "grimmer" than it need'; 'I wanted much more gaiety in the 2nd and 4th movements – it was all too careful and painstaking and they didn't let themselves go.' Gaiety, it seems, was hard to conjure in the summer of 1943.[*]

The *Fourth Quartet* was hailed by critics for its 'eloquence charged with a characteristic astringency', the composer for her ability to express 'a compact argument' with 'impassioned conviction'. As had been the case some ten years earlier, Maconchy was, flatteringly, allowed into the English canon, taking her place in the 'tradition of English chamber music to which Purcell belongs'. But now the comparison worked towards harnessing both composers

---

[*] Harry Blech was at the time in the RAF, and played in the air force band at Uxbridge.

to the imperative of national, in this case defined as *English*, survival. Something very similar had happened to Boulanger and her music during the Great War, nationalism trumping sexism at a time of crisis.

The war effort needed heroes, needed inspirational stories, and the dogged continuation of musical life in London through the years of Nazi bombs loomed large in the national consciousness. 'It takes more than a war to destroy an English tradition', the *Times* critic wrote in May 1943, before adding that 'music in the metropolis has the same function to perform for the national well-being as the hub has for the wheel'. Both Britten's *First Quartet* and Maconchy's *Fourth Quartet* were held up as evidence that British composers continued to work in the face of adversity.

A small composition from 1943 shows Maconchy responding directly to the war. 'The Voice of the City', for women's chorus and piano, marks if not honours the Battle of Stalingrad, often seen as a crucial turning point in the struggle by the Allies to overcome Nazi Germany. Astonishingly, the text Maconchy set was a poem written by a fourteen-year-old Welsh schoolgirl, Jacqueline Morris from Hengoed. Her class had been given the task of writing an essay entitled 'The Voice of the City'. Morris's head teacher was so impressed with the essay's passion that she asked the girl to turn it into a poem. The poem is three parts lament, one part rallying cry for the future, Stalingrad's future. It is powerful, emotive and simplistic: one suspects that Stalin himself might have approved of it as a patriotic text, and it was certainly an appropriate text to set for Maconchy's sponsor, the Workers' Music Association, an organization close to the composer's socialist heart. If the rigid self-discipline of one composer could win the fight against Nazi Germany, then Britain had nothing to fear.

On a personal level, the war years took their toll upon Elizabeth Maconchy. First her sister, Sheila, was diagnosed with TB. Unlike

Betty, she decided to head to Switzerland in order to combat the disease, so left England shortly before the outbreak of war. Violet Maconchy followed Sheila in 1940, escaping the Blitz only to die in Switzerland just a few months after her arrival. Sheila lived on only until 28 May 1945. In addition to the loss of both her mother and sister, Maconchy knew, perhaps more than most, what was happening to her friends and colleagues in central Europe. Just one example is enough. Erwin Schulhoff, communist and Jew, supporter of Maconchy, performer of her *Piano Concerto* back in 1930, died of tuberculosis in a concentration camp in 1942. It was a gentler end than that faced by many others. Maconchy and LeFanu did what they could, providing the necessary sponsorship for the daughter of the music critic, Jan Lowenbach, a friend from Prague. The young woman, known as Mimo, was able to make the journey to England, and lived with the couple and baby Anna for about a year before crossing to America to join her parents, who had found shelter there.

On a professional level, the war, which made it hard for any composer to be heard, made life particularly hard for the uncompromising Maconchy. Vaughan Williams wrote, sympathetic to the composer's frustration, wise as to her lack of 'popular' appeal, and offering practical support:

> I do feel it very hard that you do not get your stuff done –
> Have you anything new you could send in to the proms? If
> so let me know at once & I will write to [Sir Henry
> Wood] . . . I fear we must confess that you are not popular
> – I know though theoretically that is a very noble aspira-
> tion practically, it is galling. But dearest Betty, you are still
> young – I was about 30 before I ever heard a song of mine
> done in public . . . so push on and one day perhaps the key
> will turn in the lock.

Maconchy, now in her mid-thirties, was, however, finding it hard to create something new, to 'push on'. She had experienced what she called 'moments of silence' before. She knew she was neither a popular, nor indeed a comfortable, composer. But whilst in previous years, a friend like Grace Williams could help her keep her nerve, stay strong ('You mustn't bother your head any more, my girl, about writing safe scores. It doesn't become you'), this time the moment of silence did not feel temporary. Grace became seriously concerned and, like Vaughan Williams, attempted to help her friend, in this case with the BBC:

> A word about Betty . . . For the last few months her letters have shown that she is terribly depressed about composing. She has never shown any signs of losing heart before – but now she does sound very down-hearted and writes things like 'I think that perhaps I am finished as a composer' which isn't a bit like her, but hardly to be wondered at when you consider how consistent the neglect of her music has been ever since war began. A composer just can't carry on indefinitely without contact with players and performances. You know what I think about her things and I know I'm right and others will hear them with my ears some day – but don't let it be too late.

At Broadcasting House, moves towards a performance were made, but again events took over, this time the Doodlebug bombing of London in June 1944.

The ending of the war should have provided a respite, but did not. Although a return to Seal Chart was impossible, because the cottage had been almost completely destroyed by bombing, step by step, LeFanu and Maconchy rebuilt their lives. They moved to Wickham Bishops in Essex, where, happily, Nicola, a sister for Anna, already seven and a half, was born in April 1947, and then made another move, to Boreham, only six miles away, and to the house, Shottesbrook, where the family would remain for many years. The birth of a second child returned Maconchy to a life where, as she put it, 'you have to learn to compose between feeds'. Once breast feeding was no longer necessary, it was possible to work at night. Nicola LeFanu remembers falling asleep to the sound of her mother composing, whilst Maconchy herself spoke later of 'falling asleep in the small hours, my head on the keyboard.'* She combined mother-hood with composition by taking characteristically practical, common-sense steps: 'I always made sure there was someone to push the children in the pram for an hour or two. The rest of my writing I did when they were asleep.' Alongside caring for her children, she was also committed to making a home for them at Shottesbrook, which included creating a flower garden to complement their father's orchard of rare fruit trees. Maconchy was always quick to acknowledge William LeFanu's contribution, recognizing that everything would have been that much harder if she hadn't married a man sympathetic to her work. Things would also have been much harder if that man had not been able to support his composer wife financially, a fact Maconchy also acknowledged with her usual directness. The final element to the successful combination of family and professional responsibilities for a woman composer who works from home was a wall, or, more precisely, the two thick walls that divided LeFanu's study from Maconchy's piano. It was a domestic pattern that worked for both husband and wife.

* 'My earliest memories are of hearing my mother playing the piano when I was in bed going to sleep at night when I was very tiny. I think of it as a sort of romantic memory but it's really the opposite; she was a professional composer and at that stage the only time she had to write music was when her children were in bed.'

For all the practical solutions, for all the commitment, Maconchy was only too conscious of the impact upon a female composer of, if not the bearing of children, then the very serious business of *raising* children. When discussing composition, Maconchy would always insist that there was no difference in the capacity of the sexes, no difference between the music of men and women, but she did acknowledge the different roles in society taken by men and women when it comes to raising children:

> It is not impossible to write music if one has children
> – though difficult enough: but rearing them comes just
> at the time when one ought to be making a career, and
> it is almost impossible to combine the two, if one takes
> one's children seriously . . . Unfortunately, the experi-
> ence and stimulus of performance are an essential part
> of the growth and development of a composer – it is
> not only a matter of 'getting known'. This, and not infe-
> rior capacity, accounts I believe for the relatively small
> number of women composers who have so far estab-
> lished themselves. I think myself that it is a mistake to
> divide composers into men and women – as if the
> music they write is necessarily different . . . Can any
> honest and intelligent listener who does not know
> already tell which it is?

For Maconchy, it seems, occupation of the twin roles of composer and mother involved a kind of rigid compartmentalization. Her prize-winning *Fifth Quartet* was written, for example, in Dublin in 1948 at a time when Anna LeFanu, aged eight, was in hospital with appendicitis, and, back in London, Nicola, aged two, had been admitted to Great Ormond Street Hospital. Nicola suggested later that her mother's ability to produce a prize-winning quartet during these months demonstrated once and for all that 'adverse circumstances may have no direct bearing on works of art'. Maconchy's self-discipline ensured that they did not.

To some of her friends, Maconchy remained a conundrum. They could not square the domestic Betty (maker of jam, bottler of fruit and breast-feeder) with the fierce, uncompromising composer of avant-garde music. Anne Macnaghten, sounding both bemused and amused, described Maconchy as 'like a tiger inside . . . between nursery rhymes and washing nappies'.

What place did this tiger mother, as committed to her children and her fruit bottling as she was to her quartets, have in the brave new postwar musical world? At first sight, it was a significant place, because Maconchy continued to compose and to be performed. The *Fifth Quartet* was premiered in April 1949 at a London Contemporary Music Centre concert, the work demonstrating a kinship with that of the composer Grace Williams, yet another indication of the enduring importance of the friendship, personally and musically:

> It is fascinating to note this slow movement's musical kinship with Williams's own *Sea Sketches* for string orchestra (1944), a piece which Maconchy admired. The chords used at the beginning of the quartet's slow movement, for example, are the same chords heard in the strings at the opening of the *Sea Sketches*, although the effects achieved are quite different. This intriguing correspondence suggests that the deep friendship enjoyed by these two composers could find expression, perhaps most intimately, in purely musical terms.

Another quartet followed in 1950, and was premiered in 1951 at the Festival of Britain. Then, in 1954, Maconchy accepted an invitation to join the committee of the Composers' Guild of Great Britain and, five years later, was elected as chair. Working for her fellow professionals, as she did in many and various ways, including sitting on the music panel of the BBC or the Arts Council, was Maconchy's way of giving back to her industry, and also reflected and channelled her socialist belief in public solutions to individual problems. Always fired by the desire to get new music performed, she was later to become the first woman to hold the presidency of the Society for the Promotion of New Music, and Maconchy would, eventually, become a Dame of the British Empire in recognition of her tireless attempts to improve conditions for her colleagues and for her profession.

In other ways, the future Dame Elizabeth Maconchy appeared, on the surface at least, well and truly part of the British establishment. When, following the death of King George VI in February 1952, the London County Council launched a competition for a Coronation Overture for the new queen 'as part of London's contribution to British Music in the Coronation Year', Maconchy's majestic *Proud Thames* won. The work was premiered at a special gala concert at the Royal Festival Hall on 14 October 1953. The critics were, however, divided. One, perhaps predictably, lamented the lack of a 'decent tune'; another, far more positive, thought the only problem was that the work was too short.

And yet just as had happened after the Proms' performance of *The Land* in 1930, Maconchy's brief moment of apparent celebrity was not sustained. One can cast around for reasons. Did Maconchy fail to join the ranks of Benjamin Britten or William Walton in the nation's musical consciousness because of a sense that she was not really an *English* composer? After all, her music (or most of it) placed her in the camp of 'European toughness' rather than 'English lyricism'.* After all, she described herself as Irish, despite spending most of her life living and working in England's cities and villages, or, as expressed in a concert programme from the 1930s, 'Elizabeth Maconchy is of Irish parentage, but is English by residence and training'. In the pre-war era, Maconchy could be described as, at one and the same time, and without contradiction, Irish, British and English, and then, during the Second World War, she was fully harnessed to the cause of British/English patriotism, despite her avowed socialist republicanism. Now, however, full independence for Ireland in 1948 meant that this daughter of Dublin was a stranger in her own land, a woman with a Protestant, Unionist heritage and an English upbringing. No matter that she was a Republican, relishing her childhood memories of finding signs of secret camps and hidden ammunition as she and her friends played in the nearby woods, of having a relative whose car was stolen and used to assist Éamon de Valera on an escape mission. At the same time, however, was she perhaps also a stranger in her adopted home of England?

Or was it simply the effect of straightforward prejudice against a female composer? Elisabeth Lutyens was sure there was a double standard regarding the music of men and women: 'If Britten wrote a bad score, they'd say, "He's had a bad day." If I'd written one it was because I was a woman.' From time to time, Maconchy herself criticised the establishment, at least with regard to their limited expectations of women composers. As has been seen, she found it

---

* Maconchy is more indebted to 'Bartók and Hindemith than to Vaughan Williams or Britten' in the words of one recent music guide. Maconchy's contemporary, Elisabeth Lutyens, certainly believed that her own loyalty to Schoenberg's twelve-tone technique did her no favours. As she observed, 'to adopt a technique, like the 12-tone, associated with a German, Schoenberg (albeit that, earlier, I had thought I had "discovered" it myself, from my study of Purcell), was "mittel-European", un-English and iconoclastic. I was soon made to feel like a Communist before the Committee for Un-American Activities.'

hard to accept that Lesley Boosey thought women could only compose a few songs, whilst in 1949 she wrote to Grace Williams, asking 'Why oh! why haven't they given you a commission? (Possibly their "advisers" think anything so large as an opera unsuitable for women??)' Maconchy's daughter, Nicola LeFanu, believes that prejudice, whilst not as overt in the postwar period as it had been, remained the real challenge for her mother in these years. She remembers sensing her mother's lurking depression:

> My own first memories date from these years. On the one hand I remember her as the most positive and energetic person imaginable, devoting herself to creating a country life for us by day; at night we could hear the sound of the piano as she settled down to work into the small hours. On the other hand I can remember as a young child looking at her face in repose and saying 'Why do you look so sad?'

In the three years after the war she worked on a symphony, which she withdrew after its first performance. Her letters to Grace Williams reveal the extent of her self-criticism and her dissatisfaction with herself and the symphony. These were not easy years for her; she felt isolated, living in the country with no extended family to help her with two young children. It was very different from the international success she had had before the war. Nor were the postwar years easy for any other woman, a phenomenon noted by a number of historians.

As LeFanu notes, Maconchy, always a hard taskmaster, not least when it came to her own music, was at this time almost silenced by self-criticism. Others had previously noted that 'Elizabeth Maconchy is severe with herself and pursues her ideas relentlessly.' She could also be severe, at least in private, about her fellow composers if they failed to match her own rigorous standards.

Maconchy, for example, wrote to Grace Williams about the music of Elisabeth Lutyens, whose talent she admired ('she's got something up her sleeve') but whose self-discipline was sadly lacking: 'but oh it's so carelessly done: that sort of harum-scarum attitude towards composing shouldn't be allowed'. For Maconchy, writing music 'like all creative art, is the impassioned pursuit of an idea'. The great thing, she argued, was 'for the composer to keep his head and allow nothing to distract him'. She is not, at least consciously, referring to events such as her daughters' hospitalization, but the compositional 'temptations to stop by the way and to be side-tracked by felicities of sound and colour'. These temptations must be resisted: 'everything extraneous to the pursuit of this central idea must be rigorously excluded – scrapped'. Elsewhere, when writing about Vaughan Williams, Maconchy suggested that 'composers may be divided into Wrestlers and Speedwriters'. Vaughan Williams 'was always a Wrestler'. So was Beethoven. And so was Elizabeth Maconchy. These qualities go a long way to explain her sense of wonder at those composers, men like Mozart or Schubert, for whom, as she put it eloquently, music ran down their pen onto the paper. Scrapping, self-criticism, dissatisfaction: these had all driven Maconchy to 'push on', but now they threatened to paralyse her. The tiger was turning upon herself.

Maconchy's way out was a surprise, possibly even to her. She wrote a one-act erotic comic opera, based on an eighteenth-century libertine novel, with an 'irreverent, high-voltage score', packed with 'original tunes and rhythmic dynamism'. It was a witty and fearless work, both musically and morally.* *The Sofa*, gasped one critic,

---

* Mathias helpfully summarizes the plot. Dominic, a louche young prince, hosts a ball at his Parisian palace and is caught with capricious Monique in flagrante delicto on a sofa by his overbearing grandmother. In a fit of fury, grandmamma casts a spell on him, transforming him into a sofa, and informs

represented 'the only attempt I have ever seen to present the act of copulation on the public stage'. A member of the audience in 1959 noted that 'for a moment, one's eyes hardly dare accept their own testimony. There was raucous laughter, much indiscreet giggling and one felt the shudder of the superstitious; indeed I gather that some people that night were startled out of their lives, others indeed mortally shocked.' Unabashed in its treatment of the sexual act, the performance of the work in a semi-public form probably saved it from the censor's cut. Or maybe it was that Maconchy was simply 'too amiable and innocent' a composer for the subject, full of 'Irish whimsy' rather than 'Gallic satire', in the words of one critic. Once again, the composer's gender and nationality, rather than her music, occupy centre stage.

The writing of a libertine work seems to have prompted Maconchy into offering witty nods and winks to the operatic canon, whether Offenbach, Strauss or even Mozart's 'Queen of the Night'. Perhaps she was sending a message to the musical establishment: see, I can do what they do, it is simply that I have chosen not to do so. Perhaps she was just having fun. *The Sofa* appeared to get Maconchy out of the rut she was in during the mid-1950s. She is 'at her most relaxed and good-humoured' in her 1960 *Reflections*, and returns in a more serious, sustained way to her dialogue with

---

him that only someone successfully making love to him can break the spell and return him to human form. As the party progresses, various scenarios occur. Three party girls sit on the sofa (Dominic) and are eventually approached by three young men. Two of the couples leave to dance, but Lucille remains on the sofa with her admirer: 'so far so good', comments the upholstered Dominic, a line apparently contributed by Vaughan Williams himself. Instead of attempting to seduce her, however, the young man merely proposes to her, much to Dominic's exasperation. The couple leave and Monique now flirts with Edward, an old flame, on the sofa. Monique's seduction breaks the spell and she is shocked by the mysterious and, from her point of view, ill-timed, reappearance of the real Dominic.

Mozart, begun in *The Sofa*, but now continued in the creation of companion pieces to his *Clarinet Quintet* and *Sinfonia Concertante*. The composer was developing her skills as a writer for voice, whether the three John Donne settings for Peter Pears, in 1959 and 1965, or two further one-act operas. Maconchy would write with passion about this:

> In searching for words to set every composer stumbles upon a magic moment of recognition: this is it, this is what I've been looking for – a sort of love at first sight reaction. It may not in fact be one's first sight of the poem but suddenly there's an instinctive sense of possession. The poem becomes as it were part of oneself. That for me in any case is how the writing of song starts, or a choral work or any setting of words. This initial impulse starts the piece going, and the sense of complete identification with the words continues to grow as the work takes shape and persists to the end.

As the years passed, and Maconchy continued to work with the intensity implicit in every word here, her work (in the words of her daughter) always 'in a continuous state of regeneration', she also began to embrace an increased expressive freedom. This is nowhere more evident than in her fascination with 'free writing' whereby the performers are instructed to 'all sing, choosing from the phrases at will, unsynchronised'. Maconchy had used something akin to this in one of her one-act operas, *The Departure*, in the late 1950s, and she turned to it again in her *Eighth Quartet* of 1967, most strikingly in the work's slow movement in which, as musicologist Rhiannon Mathias explains, 'sections of long, braided melodic lines for all four instruments are played *tempo libero, senza misura*' (free time, without measure). Alongside the exploration of new compositional techniques, Maconchy remained true to her trade-mark ability to derive all of the musical material in a piece from a small number of core ideas, but now she developed these building blocks with even more skill, rigour and passion. The *Tenth Quartet* of 1972, a work of labyrinthine structure, uses, again in the words of Mathias, 'an alchemical-like process of motivic and thematic transformation', by which a series of quiet chords and an unassuming viola fragment, heard at the very beginning, 'transmute into the lyrical whole'.

In 1981, now in her mid-seventies, Maconchy chose to set the work of the Irish writer J.M. Synge, his prose versions of a number of Petrarch's sonnets, and the resulting *My Dark Heart* makes compelling listening, dealing as it does 'in intimate, half-articulated thoughts and desires'. Petrarch's poetry is at one and the same time tragic (his beloved Laura is dead), celebratory (of spring when 'the air and the waters and the earth itself are full of love') and, according to Maconchy's own programme notes, despairing yet anticipatory: 'the poet is in despair to be still living himself. Then his mood changes, "I am going after her – may she be there to meet me", and the words end in serene anticipation.' It has been said that *My Dark Heart* shows that Maconchy has 'moved a long way from the business-like, no-nonsense mood of her early style', but its expressive freedom neither denies nor outdistances her earlier self.

That Maconchy's 'earlier self' is somewhere present in *My Dark Heart* is only fitting, since the work was a commission from the RCM for their centenary celebrations, nearly sixty years after the college had set the teenage composer on her path in life. In the early 1980s Maconchy seems to be preoccupied with echoes and connections, with beginnings and endings. Two years after writing *My Dark Heart*, she took the work's closing chords and used them as the building blocks for the entirety of her *Music for Strings*, a commission for the 1983 Prom season. Two of the institutions that had launched Maconchy in her career as a composer now honoured her. Was it a coincidence, or just one final wry gesture from the composer, that made Maconchy decide to spring a surprise on the Albert Hall audience? So sudden and unexpected is the ending of her *Music for Strings* that it left the promenaders unsure of when to applaud.

Anne Macnaghten said of her friend Elizabeth Maconchy that she was 'incapable of writing half-heartedly'. Maconchy did not live half-heartedly either. This wholehearted, passionate, driven, intellectual composer created disturbing, exciting, often vehement music. Complex counterpoints of melody and rhythm, and rigorous structures, contain but never completely contain lyricism, wit and fire. The tiger might have bottled fruit, changed nappies and devoted herself to committee work, but she remained a tiger.

The process of composition was rarely easy. Maconchy began, each time, with a fragment or idea that came into her head 'of its own accord'. Then she worked outward, keeping the 'feel of the form' in her head. That form, she argued, 'must proceed from the nature of the musical ideas themselves – one cannot simply pour music into a ready-made mould'. Above all, 'the composer must try to evolve a form that is the inevitable outcome of his own musical ideas and provides for their fullest expression'.

Maconchy's life might have been easier, and her work more celebrated, had she been willing to pour her music 'into a ready-made mould'. But, as Vaughan Williams knew she would back in 1929 as he sent her into the world, Elizabeth Maconchy had to, and did, work out her own salvation. There could be no other way.

ENDNOTE

How to be a great composer? Genius is essential, of course. So too is a sustained education in composition. Usually the great composer needs a professional position, whether court musician, conservatoire professor or *kapellmeister*, and the authority, income and opportunities provided by that position. A great composer needs access to the places where music is performed and circulated, whether cathedral, court, printing house or opera house. And most, if not all, require wives, mistresses and muses to support, stimulate and inspire their great achievements. There is, of course, a simpler answer: be born a man.

And yet while many, perhaps all, of the composers in this book are great composers, they do not stand alone amongst their sex. And note they are great despite the fact that for centuries the idea of genius has remained a male preserve; they are great despite working in cultures that systematically denied almost all women access to advanced education in composition; they are great even though they could not, by virtue of their sex, take up a professional position, control their own money, publish their own music, enter certain public spaces; they are great despite having their music reduced to simplistic formulas about male and female music ('all the graces of her sex in her melodies, and all the vigour of ours in her knowledge of counterpoint', they wrote of Louise Farrenc); and they are great despite having to operate in the shadow of the courtesan, forced to enact proper, virtuous femininity, or pay the price.

Many, perhaps all, of the composers in this book were enabled to become great composers because an individual recognized a girl's latent ability, and then ensured that she received the advanced education and public (or semi-private) platform necessary to make her a composer, an opportunity that was denied to most women in her society. The motives of individuals such as Giulio Caccini, Giulio Strozzi, Metastasio, Friedrick Wieck, Raïssa Boulanger and Ralph Vaughan Williams might be very different, but the result is the same: a highly trained female composer.

What of the 'wife, mistress, and muse'? Let's hear it for the magnificent husbands. Wilhelm Hensel and William LeFanu, most obviously, Giovanni Battista Signorini and Marin La Guerre, quite probably, to name but four, are unsung heroes, every one, quietly challenging their respective society's assumptions about creative women and their partners, assumptions that endure to this day. Other supportive, perhaps even inspirational, figures remain shadowy, because of the nature of the records: in what ways did Antonia von Martines, Marianna's sister, support her composition? Was Miki Piré a muse to Lili Boulanger? These individuals matter, terribly. So does luck. Simply to survive childbirth is a statistical break for the mothers in this book.

But something else is needed for a great female composer to flourish. It was Virginia Woolf who wrote, famously and contentiously, that 'a woman must have money and a room of her own if she is to write fiction'. But for a composing woman, even more is needed, as expressed by one present-day musician and musicologist, Suzanne Cusick: 'because music is fundamentally about movement, sociability and change, women musicians do not so much need rooms of our own, within which we can retreat from the world, as we need ways of being in the world that allow us to engage with the often immobilizing and silencing effects of gender norms'. The female composer needs to be working in a community that not only values her art, but enables it to be heard beyond the traditional spaces for women's music, such as the nunnery or the home. From the Medici princesses and the court of the Sun King in the early and late seventeenth century, through to the world of the Paris Conservatoire or London's RCM in the early twentieth century, this book shows that particular communities enabled individual female composers to be heard in traditionally masculine spaces, from palace to concert hall.

We have come a long way. There is so much to celebrate, for example, in the life and work of Elizabeth Maconchy. A documentary about the composer, filmed in 1984, shows an articulate, if physically frail, woman still actively engaged in composition: 'age and illness have forced Elizabeth Maconchy to slow down a little', the voice-over tells the viewer, 'but the score she is currently working on is always to be seen, open at the piano, the notes inscribed in a clear, firm hand. More resting, more gardening, less time in London. But composing is still her way of life.' In the documentary, Maconchy is honest about the periods of depression, the 'moments of silence' that had afflicted her over the years, but her commitment remains unshakeable: 'I cannot imagine life without being engaged in composition.'

Dame Elizabeth Maconchy may not have been able to imagine it in 1984, but when the moment came to stop, she recognized it for what it was. The 'ideas weren't coming any more'; she could have gone on writing 'on technique', but where was the satisfaction in that? Her final years were silent ones, as her body finally succumbed to the damage done by TB all those years before. She died on 11 November 1994 in a nursing home in Norwich. Five months later, Billy LeFanu was buried beside his wife. Whereas so many of the composers in this book were silenced, whether by circumstance, illness, or the ideas held about women and music by their society, their family or, most painfully, the composer herself, only Maconchy chose when to stop composing, and that at the end of a long and rich career.

In so many ways, Maconchy ticks (almost) all the boxes for a 'great composer' which I list. She received a superb education in composition. She had access, sometimes after a struggle, to the institutions that would enable her music to be heard whether it be the Proms, the BBC or publishing houses, and Dame Elizabeth would be decorated precisely for her contributions to the classical music profession. She composed large-scale works for large-scale forces. She had the support of a devoted husband. She was admired and loved by her colleagues, and kept them strong. As the composer Jeremy Dale Robertson wrote in the programme for Maconchy's seventieth birthday concert:

> Betty's self is in her music, and I love in her what I love in her music: ardour; warmth; energy; gentle humour; youth – (futile and clumsy to try to list all the things that draw so many to her). But I cannot forget her practical wisdom, and grace; and a certain obstinacy and courage which have put spirit into a lot of us when we were low.

And there is absolutely no doubt of her talent, indeed, whisper it, her genius.

On a more mundane level, Maconchy did everything that her predecessor, the American composer Amy Beach, suggested needed to be done to create a world in which the public would 'regard writers of music' and estimate 'the actual value of their works without reference to their nativity, their colour, or their sex'. Get your work out there, advised Beach, compose 'solid practical work that can be printed, played, or sung', and eventually the world will forget that you are a woman and simply hear your music. Maconchy herself wanted to be called 'a composer', insisting on the absurdity of the term 'woman composer' and reminding us, if we needed reminding, that if you listen to an unknown piece of music, it is impossible to tell the sex of its creator.

And yet, every generation, the same cry is heard. Thirty years ago, we were told that Maconchy had written 'one of the finest quartet cycles of the century', that their neglect is 'a national scandal', and were told that their 'time will come'. In the new millennium, Maconchy is still being called 'our finest lost composer'. Why? Because, despite the desire of women composers to take their sex out of the equation, music does not exist in abstraction from the circumstances in which it is created, performed, received and heard. This is why I disagree with those, such as the conductor Christian Thiellemann, who, in making a weary defence of his favourite composer Wagner, insists that music cannot be politicized. Thiellemann argues that you 'cannot win over D major or C major for a certain political cause. That's the good thing about it.' Of course, on one level, that is correct because the chord of C major is the same whether written down by a woman or a man, and Maconchy is a composer, not a woman composer. But the questions remain. If the chord of C major is the same regardless of the sex of the person who wrote it, why are there so few women composers? If the chord of C major is the same whether in a quartet by Maconchy or in a quartet by Shostakovich, why are there as many performances of the latter in the space of one week (I just counted seven on Bachtrack) as there are of the former over the last five years? The answer is simple and runs like a seam through this book. Women, traditionally, have not been permitted access to the education and materials necessary to place that chord of C major on a score. If they do receive enough education, and are permitted sufficient access to materials, then that chord of C major is only permitted to appear in genres suitable to their sex, rather than the genres most valued by their society. If and when that chord is placed on the score, the sex of its author becomes part of the response to the chord, despite the pleas of composers such as Beach and Maconchy. Thiellemann's favoured Wagner, who chose to be an anti-Semite, had the opportunity to write the chord, when countless women, who, after all, did not choose to be women, did not. Wagner's music was then performed, in public, and continues to be performed and recorded every week of the year. Whether loved or hated, Wagner's music is heard, when the music of countless women is not. Yes, the chord of C major is not, in itself, political, but who is allowed to use it, and how they are allowed to use it, and where we can hear it when they have used it, is.

Words, however, can take one only so far. I was reminded of this when I heard the sheer excitement in the voice of the composer Judith Weir, the first female Master of the Queen's Music, speaking on BBC Radio Three's *Composer of the Week* in 2015. Weir was describing the way in which she rushed from venue to venue, from rehearsal to rehearsal, during the London Barbican's celebration of her work a few years earlier. Even for the composer, perhaps most of all for the composer, music exists most fully in ever-changing performance, and in the hearing. As Maconchy said, to write about a piece of music is as if one sought to paint a smell. Take, for example, the final phrases of that composer's late work *My Dark Heart*, which, for Maconchy herself, conveys 'serene anticipation'; for her daughter, the phrases are 'haunting'; whilst for musicologist Rhiannon Mathias the mood is 'sombre'. As ever, the only way truly to engage with *My Dark Heart*, and all the other works written about in this book, is to listen to the music itself, and experience your own response. I believe you will find much that is not currently, but could be gloriously, part of our musical heritage.

A HIGHLY PERSONAL PLAYLIST

Fanny Hensel – *Das Jahr*

This solo piano work is perfection from its haunting opening bars, with Hensel taking the listener on a profound, almost cathartic, emotional journey through the months of the year. You can listen to individual movements (such as the joyous month of March) but the work deserves to be heard in its entirety.

Francesca Caccini – *Lasciatime qui solo*, *Dolce Maria* and *Rendi alle mie speranze*

There are endless debates about what constitutes authentic performance for music from this period, but it is hard to spoil music of this quality. I have chosen three songs that show Caccini's ability to convey both despair and reverence, not to mention her exquisite formal control of the music's shape and texture. Heard live, these songs have a striking emotional and musical freedom to them, making the comparison to jazz not quite as far-fetched as it might seem.

Marianna von Martines – *Overture in C*

The bad news is that it is still hard to find recordings of Martines's music, but the good news is that the one recording I have is superb, with the rich, pure voice of Nuria Rial accompanied by the musicians of La Floridiana and directed by Nicoleta Paraschivescu. Thanks to them, I can turn to Martines's joyous *Overture in C* whenever I feel a bit flat. It never fails to make me smile.

Barbara Strozzi – *Che si può fare*

For a song that will get into your head and stay there for ever (but in a good way) seek out *Che si può fare*. If you want more, then listen to Strozzi's *Begli occhi* (not to be confused with '*Voi pur begl' occhi*' mentioned in the main text), informed by the useful guide at http://www.wwnorton.com/college/music/listeninglab/shared/listening_guides/strozzi_begli_occhi.pdf.

Elizabeth Maconchy – *String Quartet No. 5*

Maconchy's own favourite, *String Quartet No. 5* epitomizes her capacity to be 'intellectually passionate and passionately intellectual', providing food for the heart and mind in equal measure. The slow movement is particularly powerful. (An easier way into Maconchy's music is her lush orchestral work *The Land*, from 1930, which, for all its pastoral qualities, nevertheless has an eerie quality that gets under my skin in ways I don't quite understand.)

Lili Boulanger –*Du fond de l'abîme* (Psalm 130)

This major work reminds me of the best kind of film music. Boulanger forces the listener to strain to hear the suspenseful opening notes and then never lets us go. The ending, with its modal harmonies, is often described as despairing or ominous, the work as a whole viewed as Boulanger's requiem for herself. I hear the ending as enigmatic in tone, even peaceful. (For an insight into some of Boulanger's musical techniques, see http://www. musikmph.de/musical_scores/vorworte/1001.html.)

Élisabeth Jacquet de la Guerre – *Sonata No. 1 in D minor for violin and basso continuo*

From its exquisite, heartbreaking, slow opening bars, this sonata moves effortlessly between moods, always full of life and emotionally charged for all its formal control. This was avant-garde music for its time and in some performances it still has an edge to it.

Clara Schumann – *Three Fugues on Themes of J.S. Bach*

It is hard not to enjoy anything written by Schumann, and it is therefore hard for me to pick a stand-out work. If pushed, I would choose these short piano works, because they show the composer at her most ambitious, but also her most austere. Easier to find, and perhaps more representative of Schumann as a composer, is her accomplished *Piano Trio*.

Discography

Shannon Mercer sings Caccini on *O Viva Rosa*, Analekta, 2010.

Michel Angers and Peggy Bélanger perform Strozzi in *Passioni, Vizi & Virtù*, Stradivarius, 2010.

Ensemble La Rêveuse play Jacquet de la Guerre's *Sonata No. 1*, Mirare, 2010.

Nicholetta Paraschivescu directs La Floridiana in Martines on *Il Primo Amore*, Deutsche Harmonia Mundi, 2012.

Lauma Skride plays *The Year* by Fanny Mendelssohn-Hensel, Sony, 2007.

Jozef de Beenhouwer performs Schumann's *Preludes and Fugues* in his *Complete Piano Works*, COP, 2001. Radio 3's 'Building a Library' recommends the recording of the *Piano Trio* by Antje Weithaas (violin), Tanja Tetzlaff (cello) and Gunilla Sussmann (piano), Avi Music, 2013.

Yan Pascal Tortelier directs Ann Murray, mezzo-soprano, Neil MacKenzie, tenor, the City of Birmingham Symphony Chorus and the BBC Philharmonic in Boulanger's Psalm 130, Chandos, 1999.

The Bingham Quartet play Maconchy's *String Quartet No. 5*, Unicorn Kanchana, 1999 (only available on CD). *The Land* can be found at www.lorelt.co.uk.

GLOSSARY

A Cappella Unaccompanied singing.

Allegro Fast.

Alto The female voice (also known as *contralto*) with the lowest register. Can also refer to a male voice that, for a man, sings in a very high register.

Aria Any closed lyrical piece, usually for solo voice, with or without instrumental accompaniment. An aria can be an independent piece, or part of a much larger work, such as an opera or *cantata*.

Arpeggio The spread notes of a *chord*, played one after the other from the bottom upwards, or from the top downwards. Arpeggiations are patterns of arpeggios, often used as an accompaniment to a melody.

Baritone Male voice between *bass* and *tenor*.

Bass The lowest male voice. In instrumental music, a *basso continuo* (through bass) is an instrumental bass line that runs throughout a piece, over which the continuo player improvises ('realizes') an accompaniment of chords. A walking bass is a type of bass line which moves continuously and with purposeful regularity. A ground bass occurs when the bass part is repeated throughout the piece.

Cantata A work for one or more voices with instrumental accompaniment. In the early seventeenth century, it was a fairly small-scale form, with a succession of contrasting sections, usually for solo voice, and usually on secular subjects. The scale of the accompaniment to the voice or voices expanded over the years, and religious subjects became more popular. The form almost completely died out by the end of the eighteenth century.

Character piece A piece designed to convey, without the use of extra-musical materials such as a text, a specific atmosphere, mood or scene, and thus to arouse the listener's emotions. Characteristic of Romantic piano music.

Chorale The congregational hymn of the German Protestant church service.

Chord A group of typically three or more notes played at the same time, and used as the basis of harmony.

Chromaticism The use of a scale that divides the octave into twelve equal intervals of a semitone (as can be found on a piano).

Clavichord A small keyboard instrument.

Concerto This has come to mean a work for a solo (or, occasionally, more than one) instrument accompanied by an orchestra. Before 1700 the term was applied to pieces in a variety of forms, involving both voices and instruments, and could also be found as a synonym for 'ensemble' or 'orchestra'.

Continuo See *Bass/Basso Continuo*.

Contralto See *Alto*.

Cornet Wind instrument of the trumpet family.

Counterpoint Derived from the expression *punctus contra punctum* ('point against point' or 'note against note'), the combination of simultaneous parts or voices. Each line is significant in itself, but the whole results in a coherent texture.

Diatonic scale A set of seven-pitch intervals of unequal size, adding up to an octave, which can be repeated indefinitely in other octaves: for example, the white notes on the piano, played from C to C. The diatonic scale became the basis of Western art music. Two *modes* of the diatonic scale, the Ionian (with its final on C) and the Aeolian (on A), have survived as the modern major and (natural) minor *scales* respectively.

Dissonance The effect created by intervals that induce for the listener tension and the desire for resolution (into consonant intervals). Beliefs about what constitutes consonance and dissonance have changed over time.

Dulcimer An instrument whose strings, normally in multiple courses of two to four to each note, are struck by light beaters (or 'hammers'): also known as a *salterio*.

Dynamics Alterations in the volume within a piece of music.

Etude The French word for a study: a piece principally designed to improve a player's ability in a particular area of technique.

Forte Loud: also *fortissimo* (very loud) and *mezzo-forte* (quite loud).

Fugue A contrapuntal (see *counterpoint*) composition for a particular number of parts or voices. The voices enter successively, in imitation of each other, the first entering with a short melody or phrase known as 'the subject'.

Harmony An ambiguous term that can simply refer in a general way to (pleasing) combinations of notes, but is also used to describe chordal support to a melody, and thus in contrast with counterpoint, in which each part is significant.

Harpsichord A keyboard musical instrument. The sound is produced by the plucking of a string when a key is pressed.

Improvisation The creation of a musical work, or the final form of a musical work, as it is being performed. The work may be composed from scratch during performance, or be an elaboration upon an existing framework.

Intervals The distance between two notes, whether these notes are played together or separately.

Key The major or minor scale to which a passage or work most closely adheres. The principal key will often begin or end a movement, and even if there are large parts of a composition that deviate from the principal key these parts are regarded as ultimately dependent upon it. The concept of a principal key developed during the seventeenth century, and is fundamental to *tonality*.

Le nuove musiche Italian for 'The New Music': specifically the title of a work by Giulio Caccini, but sometimes used now to describe developments in vocal music in the early seventeenth century (see *monody*).

Legato Smoothly.

Lento Slowly.

Libretto The text of a dramatic musical work, such as an opera.

Lieder Literally the German word for 'songs', but now usually associated with a distinctive and dramatic type of German solo vocal composition in the late eighteenth and early nineteenth century.

Lute Plucked string instrument with a large half-pear body, frets and a pegbox turned back at a right angle from the neck.

Melisma A group of notes sung to one syllable of text.

Meter The arrangement of a piece of music's rhythms in a repetitive pattern of strong and weak beats.

Modes A range of scales (that is, ways of dividing up an octave) that dominated European music for about a thousand years prior to 1500, and continued to influence composers until c. 1600. Two of the many modes available to a composer became the standard major and minor scales upon which Western art music is based. The others were generally discarded, although occasionally explored by later composers, in particular in the twentieth century.

Modulation The movement from one key to another. An *enharmonic modulation* is one in which the actual note names change in the new key, although the sound remains the same: for example, E flat becomes D sharp in the new key.

Monody A modern term for the solo song with continuo accompaniment, which developed in Florence in the first half of the seventeenth century, championed by Giulio Caccini, and involved a new, direct style of singing. The monodic vocal line could not only follow more closely the meaning and rhythm of the text, but also allowed for more virtuoso, embellished singing than was possible in *polyphonic* (multi-voice) song.

Monothematic Describes a musical composition that is constructed around a single theme.

Moteta A piece of religious, polyphonic vocal music: important in early music, and expanding in the seventeenth century to include secular settings and orchestral or continuo accompaniment.

Motifs A short musical idea – melodic, harmonic, rhythmic – or any combination of these three. If a work has a *motivic structure*, then it is generated from, and built around, this short idea.

Motor rhythms Insistently regular rhythmic repetition.

Movement A self-contained section within a larger piece of music.

Nocturne A Romantic piano piece of a slow and dreamy nature in which a graceful, highly embellished melody in the right hand is accompanied by a broken-chord pattern in the left.

Octave The distance between two notes that sound similar, because the higher note's frequency (its pattern of sound waves) is double the speed of the lower note. The essential pattern of the two notes is the same. In the diatonic scale, the interval is of eight notes, counting bottom and top notes. Notes an octave apart have the same letter-names.

Opus The word used for the numbering of a composer's work, shortened to Op.

Oratorio A musical setting of a religious libretto for solo singers, choir and orchestra, in dramatic form but usually performed without scenery or costumes in a concert hall or church.

Ornament A decorative note that embellishes a melody, such as a *grace note* (an extra added note) or a *trill* (swiftly alternating the written note with the one about it).

Part-song A secular vocal work, for three or more voices.

Passacaglia ('passacailles') A slow dance in triple time.

Passage work Section of a work that allows the performer to display a particular technique at a virtuoso level.

Piano Quietly (also *pianissimo*, very quietly).

Piano Trio A work written for piano with two other instruments, usually the violin and cello. Also the work's performers.

Pianoforte The full name of the piano, meaning soft-loud, drawing attention to this keyboard instrument's ability to vary dynamics because of the use of hammers and dampers to strike the strings, in contrast to the earlier plucked-string harpsichord.

Plainchant A single, unaccompanied melodic line (chant) used in the Western church (also known as plainsong).

Prelude In earlier music, usually used to describe an opening piece in a larger work. In the late eighteenth and nineteenth centuries, a prelude could be a standalone, quasi-improvisatory work, often using a small number of motifs to organize the piece.

Presto Very fast (and *prestissimo*, very, very fast).

Prima Donna Literally, Italian for 'the first lady': refers to the leading female singer in an opera company.

Recitative A narrative song that describes some action, thought or emotion, and which follows the natural rhythms of the words, and resembles sung ordinary speech, in contrast to an *aria*, which might repeat phrases or extend single words for musical and dramatic effect.

Register The range of musical notes that a voice or instrument can reach.

Requiem A musical setting of parts or all of the Mass said for someone who has died.

Romance A term usually applied to a simple lyric composition, for voice(s) or instrument(s), and suggesting a personal, tender quality to the music.

Romanesca A particular form of ground *bass*, based around the interval of a fourth.

Scherzo Derived from the Italian word for joke, typically the third movement in a four-movement piece (often linked to a trio), then, later, in the nineteenth century, a lively standalone piece with three beats to the bar.

Score The written form of a musical composition.

Serpent A bass cornet (which would later evolve into the tuba).

Sinfonia A term used from the sixteenth century onwards to designate pieces in various forms for a variety of performers, but usually an instrumental ensemble. In the eighteenth century, a sinfonia was the term used for an orchestral piece that served as an introduction to an opera, suite or *cantata*, that is, an early form of overture.

Sonata Now refers to an instrumental composition for piano or another instrument (with piano accompaniment), usually comprising several movements. However, in the sixteenth and seventeenth centuries, the term referred to a piece that was played, not sung.

Soprano The highest female voice. A *mezzo-soprano* will have a slightly lower range.

Strophe A short section of a piece of music that is repeated (such as a verse in a hymn).

Syncopation A rhythm in which emphasis is given to the weak beats instead of the strong beats. For example, in a waltz, the listener expects the stress on the first beat of three in a bar. If that stress falls on the second or third beat, then the rhythm is syncopated.

Tempo The speed (or speeds, *tempi*) at which a piece of music is played.

Tenor The male voice with the highest register. A countertenor describes the highest form of tenor, which enters the alto register.

Theorbo A plucked string instrument of the lute family.

Timbrel Similar to a modern tambourine, a percussion instrument associated primarily with the Israelites.

Tonality The key centre of a piece. *Tonal* music is in a major or minor key. *Atonal* describes music unrelated to a tonic note (the first note in a diatonic scale, for example, A in the scale/key of A major). It therefore has no key centre.

Tremolando The rapid up-and-down movement of a bow on a stringed instrument creating an agitated, restless effect.

Trillo An ornament, the tremolo-like repetition of a single pitch (also called the 'Monteverdi trill'), used in the seventeenth century, and in contrast to the modern trill, which alternates between two notes.

Tutti When all the instruments play together (in contrast to a passage from a soloist or small group of players).

Twelve-note music Music in which all twelve notes of the chromatic scale have equal importance, that is, music that is not in any key or mode and thus may be described as *atonal*.

Viol A bowed string instrument of the lute family. It is usually played held downwards on the lap or between the legs, therefore *viola da gamba* ('leg viol').

Word painting Composing music with a text to reflect the literal or figurative meaning of a word or phrase. A common example is a falling line for '*descendit de caelis*' ('He came down from heaven').

FURTHER READING

Caccini

For all things Caccini, see the eminently readable work of the scholar Suzanne Cusick, *Francesca Caccini at the Medici Court: Music and the Circulation of Power*, Chicago, University of Chicago Press, 2009.

Strozzi

There is, astonishingly, no full-length biography of Barbara Strozzi, but a fascinating insight into one researcher's work in the Venetian archives can be found in Beth L. Glixon's two articles 'New Light on the Life and Career of Barbara Strozzi', *Music Quarterly*, 1997, and 'More on the Life and Death of Barbara Strozzi', *Music Quarterly*, 1999.

Jacquet de la Guerre

The only biography is in French, Catherine Cessac's *Élisabeth Jacquet de La Guerre – Une femme compositeur sous le règne de Louis XIV*, Paris, Actes Sud, 1995.

Martines

Irving Godt was a great champion of Martines, but did not live to see his *Marianna Martines: A Woman Composer in the Vienna of Mozart and Haydn* published. The work was finished by his friend, John A. Rice, and, like Cusick's work on Caccini, is both scholarly and accessible. Woodridge, Boydell & Brewer, 2010.

Hensel

I warmly recommend the work of eminent Mendelssohn scholar R. Larry Todd. His *Fanny Hensel: The Other Mendelssohn*, Oxford University Press, 2009, is packed with information and analysis. Further insights can be gained from Sebastien Hensel's family memoir originally published in 1881, now available online: https://archive. org/details/mendelssohnfamil01hens; and http://www.fannyhensel. de/ – a website (with English translation in parts) devoted to Hensel and her works.

Schumann

It is fairly easy to get hold of a biography of Clara Schumann. I would recommend the short, but illuminating, account of her life by Monica Steegmann, *Clara Schumann*, Haus Publishing, 2004. There is also plenty about Schumann online (see for example http://www.geneva.edu/~dksmith/clara/schumann); whilst for something a little different try Janice Galloway's compelling *Clara: A Novel*, Vintage, 2003.

Boulanger

The biographies that do exist for Boulanger have tended to court controversy. For the least contentious analysis of the music, and some information about Lili's life, see Caroline Potter's *Nadia and Lili Boulanger*, Ashgate, 2006. Academic articles (in French) about the Boulanger sisters can be found in *Nadia Boulanger et Lili Boulanger: Témoignages et études*, edited by Alexandra Laederich, Symétrie, 2007. The Nadia and Lili Boulanger International Centre (www.cnlb.fr) is an important focus for current interest in the composer and her sister.

Maconchy

There is no full-length biography of Maconchy, but she is one of the composers featured in Rhiannon Mathias's study, *Lutyens, Maconchy, Williams and Twentieth-Century British Music: A Blest Trio of Sirens*, Ashgate, 2012, which contains plenty of analysis of Maconchy's music. For more about the composer herself, see an intriguing documentary, *Elizabeth Maconchy*, made in 1985, and available on DVD from MJW Productions. The scholars Jenny Doctor and Sophie Fuller are currently working on an edition of the Maconchy/Williams correspondence, which, when published, promises to be fascinating.

WORKS CONSULTED

Ambrosini, F. 2000. Toward a Social History of Women in Venice: From the Renaissance to the Enlightenment. In Martin, J.J. and Romano, D. eds. *Venice Reconsidered: The History and Civilization of an Italian City-State, 1297–1797*. Baltimore, MD, USA: Johns Hopkins University Press, pp. 420–53

Anderson, M. 1991. Elizabeth Maconchy: String Quartets Nos 5–8 and String Quartets Nos 9–13. *Tempo*, 176, p. 46

Bar-Shany, M. 2006. The Roman Holiday of Fanny Mendelssohn Hensel. *Min-Ad: Israel Studies in Musicology Online*, 5:1

Block, A.F. 1998. *Amy Beach, Passionate Victorian: The Life and Work of an American Composer, 1867–1944*. Oxford, Oxford University Press

Blunnie, A. 2010. *Passion and Intellect in the Music of Elizabeth Maconchy DBE (1907-1994)*. Masters thesis, Maynooth, National University of Ireland

Borchard, B. and Bartsch, C. Leipziger Straße Drei: Sites for Music. *Nineteenth-century Music Review*, 4:2, pp. 119–38

Bronzini, Cristofano. 8 vols. Florence. 1622–32

Cabrini, M. 2012. The Composer's Eye: Focalizing Judith in the Cantatas by Jacquet de La Guerre and Brossard. *Eighteenth Century Music*, 9, pp. 9–45

Caccini, F. 2010. *La Liberazione di Ruggiero dall'isola d'Alcina*, trans. Anne Graf and Selene Mills. Arbroath, Prima la musica

Calcagno, M. 2003. Signifying Nothing: On the Aesthetics of Pure Voice in Early Venetian Opera. *The Journal of Musicology*, 20:4, pp. 461–97

Calvi, G. 1989. *Histories of a Plague Year: The Social and the Imaginary in Baroque Florence*, trans. Dario Biocca and Bryant T. Ragan. Berkeley, University of California Press

Cardamone, D.G. 2002. Isabella Medici-Orsini: A Portrait of Self-Affirmation. In: T.M. Borderging, ed. *Gender, Sexuality and Early Music*. London, Routledge

Carter, S. and Kite-Powell, J.T. eds. 2012. *A Performer's Guide to Seventeenth-Century Music*, 2nd ed., Bloomington, IN, Indiana University Press

Carter, T. and Goldthwaite, R.A. 2013. *Orpheus in the Marketplace: Jacopo Peri and the Economy of Late Renaissance Florence.* Cambridge, MA, USA: Harvard University Press

Cessac, C. 1995. *Élisabeth Jacquet de La Guerre – Une femme compositeur sous le règne de Louis XIV.* Paris, Actes Sud

Cessac, C. 2000. Notes to CD of *Le Sommeil d'Ulisse.* Isabelle Desrochers, Les Voix Humaines, Christine Payeux. Alpha Productions

Citron, M. 1993. *Gender and the Musical Canon.* Champaign, IL, University of Illinois Press

Conway, D. 2007. *Jewry in Music: Entry to the Profession from the Enlightenment to Richard Wagner.* Cambridge, Cambridge University Press

Crum, M. and Ward Jones, P. 1980–89. *Catalogue of the Mendelssohn Papers in the Bodleian Library.* Oxford, Bodleian Library

Cusick, S. 2009. *Francesca Caccini at the Medici Court: Music and the Circulation of Power.* Chicago, University of Chicago Press

Cyr, M. 2014. *Style and Performance for Bowed String Instruments in French Baroque Music.* Farnham, Ashgate

D'Accone, F.A. 2007. *Music and Musicians in 16th-century Florence.* Aldershot, Ashgate Variorum

Dopp, B.J. 1994. Numerology and Cryptography in the Music of Lili Boulanger: The Hidden Program in 'Clairieres dans le ciel'. *The Musical Quarterly*, 78, pp. 556–83

Fauser, A. 1997. Lili Boulanger's 'La Princesse Maleine': A Composer and Her Heroine as Literary Icons. *Journal of the Royal Musical Association*, 122, pp. 68–108

Fauser, A. 1998. 'La Guerre en dentelles': Women and the 'Prix de Rome' in French Cultural Politics. *Journal of the American Musicological Society*, 51: 1, pp. 83-129

Feldman, M. and Gordon, B. eds. 2006. *Cross-Cultural Perspectives.* Oxford, Oxford University Press

Ferris, D. 2003. Public Performance and Private Understanding: Clara Wieck's Concerts in Berlin. *Journal of the American Musicological Society*, 56:2, pp. 351–408

Franco, Veronica. 1999. *Poems and Selected Letters.* Trans. Ann Rosalind Jones and Margaret F. Rosenthal. Chicago, IL, USA: University of Chicago Press

Fuller, S. 2013. 'Putting the BBC and T. Beecham to Shame': The Macnaghten–Lemare Concerts, 1931–7. *Journal of the Royal Musical Association*, 138:2, pp. 377–414

Gillett, P. 2000. *Musical Women in England 1870–1914: 'Encroaching on all Man's Privileges'.* London, Palgrave Macmillan

Gjerdingen, R.O. 2007. *Music in the Galant Styles.* Oxford, Oxford University Press

Glixon, B.L. 1997. New Light on the Life and Career of Barbara Strozzi. Music Quarterly, 81:2, pp. 134–41

Glixon, B.L. 1999. More on the Life and Death of Barbara Strozzi. *Music Quarterly*, 83:1, pp. 311–35

Godt, I. 2010. *Marianna Martines: A Woman Composer in the Vienna of Mozart and Haydn*, ed. John A. Rice. Woodbridge, Boydell & Brewer

Gordon, B. 2004. *Monteverdi's Unruly Women: The Power of Song in Early-Modern Italy*. Cambridge, Cambridge University Press

Haine, W.S. 2000. *History of France*. Westport, CT, USA: Greenwood Press

Hanning, B.R. 2006. 'Love's New Voice: Italian Monodic Song'. In: Stauffer, G.B., ed. 2002. *The World of Baroque Music: New Perspectives*. Bloomington, Indiana University Press

Harness, K. 2002. Chaste Warriors and Virgin Martyrs in Florentine Musical Spectacle. In: T.M. Borderging, ed. 2002. *Gender, Sexuality and Early Music*. London, Routledge

Harness, K. 2005. *Music, Art and Female Patronage in Early-Modern Florence*. Chicago, University of Chicago Press

Head, M. 2004. Cultural Meanings for Women Composers: Charlotte ('Minna') Brandes and the Beautiful Dead in the German Enlightenment. *Journal of the American Musicological Society*, 57:2, pp. 231–84

Head, M. 2013. *Sovereign Feminine: Music and Gender in Eighteenth-Century Germany*. Oxford, Oxford University Press

Heller, W. 2006. Usurping the Place of the Muses: Barbara Strozzi and the Female Composer in Seventeenth-Century Italy. In: Stauffer, G.B., ed. 2006. *The World of Baroque Music: New Perspectives*. Bloomington, Indiana University Press

Hensel, F. 1987. *The Letters of Fanny Hensel to Felix Mendelssohn*. Citron, M.C., ed. New York, Pendragon Press

Hensel, F. 2002. *Tagebücher*. Klein, H.G. and Elvers, R. eds. Wiesbaden, Breitkopf & Härtel

Holland-Barry, A.B. 2012. *Lili Boulanger (1893–1918) and World War I France: Mobilizing Motherhood and the Good Suffering*. Madison, Wisconsin, University of Wisconsin-Madison thesis

Howell, James. 1651. S.P.Q.V: A survay of the signorie of Venice: of her admired policy, and method of goverment, &c. With a cohortation to all Christian princes to resent her dangerous condition at present. London

Iitti, S. 2006. *The Feminine in German Song.* Oxford, Peter Lang Publishing

Keller, J.M. 2011. *Chamber Music: A Listener's Guide,* Oxford, Oxford University Press

Kendrick, R.L. 2002. Intent and Intertextuality in Barbara Strozzi's Sacred Music, *Recercare,* 14, pp. 65–98

Laederich, A., ed. 2007. *Nadia Boulanger et Lili Boulanger: Témoignages et études.* Lyon, Symétrie, Lyon

LaMay, T. 2012. Composing from the Throat: Madalena Casulana's *Primo Libro de madrigali,* 1568. In: LaMay, T., ed. 2012. *Musical Voices of Early Modern Women: Many-Headed Melodies.* Aldershot, Ashgate

LeFanu, N. 1994. Elizabeth Maconchy. *Contemporary Music Review,* 11, pp. 201–04

LeFanu, N. 2004. Interview. In: Elizabeth Haddon, ed. *Making Music in Britain: Interviews with those Behind the Notes.* Aldershot, Ashgate

Lerner, N. and Straus, J. eds. 2006. *Sounding Off: Theorizing Disability in Music.* New York, Routledge

Macnaghten, A. 1955. Elizabeth Maconchy. *Musical Times,* 96, pp. 298–302

Maconchy, E. 1965. The Image of Greatness. *Composer,* 15, pp. 10–12

Maconchy, E. 1971–72. A Composer Speaks. *Composer,* 42, pp. 25–29

Martin, J.J. and Romano, D. eds. 2000. *Venice Reconsidered: The History and Civilization of an Italian City-State, 1297–1797.* Baltimore, MD, USA: Johns Hopkins University Press

Martin, M. 1996. *Essential Agréments: Art, Dance, and Civility in Seventeenth-Century French Harpsichord Music.* PhD thesis. University of California

Mathias, Rhiannon. 2012. *Lutyens, Maconchy, Williams and Twentieth-Century British Music: A Blest Trio of Sirens*. Aldershot, Ashgate

McPhee, P. 2004. *Social History of France, 1789–1914*. Gordonsville, VA, Palgrave Macmillan

Middleton, J. 2012. Theatrical Productions. In: Carter, S. and Kite-Powell, J.T. eds. *A Performer's Guide to Seventeenth-Century Music*. Bloomington, Indiana University Press

Monson, C.A. 2005. *Nuns Behaving Badly: Tales of Music, Magic, Art, and Arson in the Convents of Italy*. Chicago, University of Chicago Press

Morrow, M.S. 1989. *Concert Life in Haydn's Vienna: Aspects of a Developing Musical and Social Institution*. New York, Pendragon Press

Muir, E. 2007. *Culture Wars of the Late Renaissance: Skeptics, Libertines, and Opera*. Cambridge, MA, USA: Harvard University Press

Novak, J. 2011. Biographical Fiction to Historiographic Meta-fiction: Rewriting Clara Schumann. *Brno Studies in English*, 37:2, pp. 145–58

Olleson, Philip. 2012. *Journals and Letters of Susan Burney: Music and Society in Late Eighteenth-Century England*. Farnham, Surrey, Ashgate Publishing Group

Perry, B., ed. 2007. *The Cambridge Companion to Schumann*. Cambridge, Cambridge University Press

Potter, C. 2006. *Nadia and Lili Boulanger*. Abingdon, Ashgate

Potter, C. 2012. Marche Gaie: A Rediscovered Work by Lili Boulanger. *Notes*, 68, pp. 715–28

Przbyszewska-Jarminska, B. 2007. Notes for CD recording, *La Liberazione di Ruggiero*, performed by Musicae Antiquae Collegium Varsoviense, Pro Musica Camerata

Reich, N.B. 2001. *Clara Schumann: The Artist and the Woman*, London, Cornell University Press

Ribiero, A. 2002. *Dress in Eighteenth-Century Europe: 1715–1789*, London, Yale University Press

Rickards, G. 1990. Elizabeth Maconchy: String Quartets Nos 1–4. *Tempo*, 172, p. 40 and p. 43

Robertson, R. 2007. The Complexities of Caroline Pichler: Conflicting Role Models, Patriotic Commitment, and The Swedes in Prague (1827). *Women in German Yearbook*, 23, pp. 34–48

Rosand, E. 1978. Barbara Strozzi, 'virtuosissima cantatrice'. *Journal of the American Musicological Society*, 31, pp. 241–81

Rosand, E. 1990. *Opera in Seventeenth-Century Venice: The Creation of a Genre*. Berkeley, University of California Press

Rose, Adrian. 2008. A Newly Discovered Source of Vocal Chamber Music by Elisabeth-Claude Jacquet de la Guerre and René Drouard de Bousset. *Early Music*, 36:2, pp. 245–64

Rosenthal, M.F. 2006. Cutting a Good Figure: The Fashions of the Venetian Courtesans in the Illustrated Albums of Early Modern Travellers. In Feldman, M. and Gordon, B. eds. 2006. *The Courtesan's Arts: Cross-Cultural Perspectives*. Oxford, Oxford University Press, pp. 52–74

Sanford, S. 2012. National Singing Styles. In: Carter, S. and Kite-Powell, J.T. eds. *A Performer's Guide to Seventeenth-Century Music*. Bloomington, Indiana University Press

Schleifer, M.F. and Glickman, S. 1996–2006. *Women Composers: Music Through the Ages*. New York, G.K. Hall

Schumann C. and Schumann R. 1994. *Marriage Diaries of Robert and Clara Schumann: From their Wedding Day Through the Russia Trip*. ed. Gerd Nauhaus; trans. Peter Ostwald. London: Robson

Siegel, E.J. 2012. *'What a Delicious, What a Malicious Imputation!' Gender and Politics in the Reception of Elizabeth Maconchy's 'The Sofa'*. Thesis. University of California Riverside

Spycket, J. 2004. *A la recherche de Lili Boulanger: essai biographique*. Paris, Fayard

Steegmann, M. 2004. *Clara Schumann*. London, Haus Publishing

Stras, L. 2012. The *Ricreationi per monache* of Suor Annalena Aldobrandini. *Renaissance Studies*, 26, pp. 34–59

Taruskin, R. 2009. *Music in the Early Twentieth Century: The Oxford History of Western Music*. Oxford, Oxford University Press

Vircondelet, A., ed. 2006. *Venice.* 3 vols. Paris, Flammarion

Von Glahn, D. 2013. Music, *Nature, Place: Music and the Skillful Listener: American Women Compose the Natural World.* Bloomington, IN, USA, Indiana University Press

Ward Jones, P., ed. 1997. *The Mendelssohns on Honeymoon: The 1837 Diary of Felix and Cécile Mendelssohn Bartholdy, Together with Letters to their Families*. Oxford, Clarendon Press

Weissweiler, Eva, ed. 1995–2002. *The Complete Correspondence of Clara and Robert Schumann*. Vols 1–3. Transl. Hildegard Fritsch, Ronald L. Crawford and Harold P. Fry. New York, Peter Lang

Wiesner-Hanks, M.E., ed. 2008. *Women and Gender in Early Modern Europe*. Cambridge, Cambridge University Press

Williams, B. 2007. Biography and Symbol: Uncovering the Structure of a Creative Life in Fanny Hensel's Lieder. *Nineteenth-Century Music Review*, 4:2, pp. 49–65

Williams, M. (Director). 1985. *Elizabeth Maconchy*, Film Documentary. MJW Productions Ltd

Wolfe, H. 2009. Women's Handwriting. In: Knoppers, L.L. *The Cambridge Companion to Early Modern Women's Writing*, Cambridge, Cambridge University Press, pp. 21–39

Wollenburg, S., ed. 2007. Fanny Hensel (née Mendelssohn Bartholdy) and her Circle: Proceedings of the Bicentenary Conference, Oxford, July 2005. *Nineteenth-Century Music Review*, 4:2

Websites

http://www.fannyhensel.de/
http://www.geneva.edu/~dksmith/clara/schumann
http://www.metmuseum.org/toah/hd/vien/hd_vien.htm
http://portlandartmuseum.us/mwebimages/tours/venice/
venice_tour/index.html
http://www.theguardian.com/music/2011/mar/13/
london-oriana-choir-women-composers

General guides to music and to female composers

Fuller, S. 1995. *The Pandora Guide to Women Composers: Britain and the United States 1629–Present*. London, Pandora

Sadie, J.A. and Samuel, R. 1994. *New Grove Dictionary of Women Composers*. London, Macmillan

Schleifer, M.F. and Glickman, S. 1996–2006. *Women Composers: Music Through the Ages*. New York, G.K. Hall

http://www.oxfordmusiconline.com, which includes the invaluable *Grove Music Online, Oxford Companion to Music* and *Oxford Dictionary of Music*

ACKNOWLEDGEMENTS

A generation and more of music scholars have transformed our understanding of female composers, and made it possible for this book to be written. I am particularly grateful to Suzanne Cusick, Sophie Fuller, Beth Glixon, Anya Holland-Barry, Julia Lajta-Novak, Buford Norman, Caroline Potter and Fiorella Sassanelli for taking the time to share their expert knowledge. Others, from beyond the music world, including Jonathan Gibson, Clare Morgan and Rosamund Bartlett, have been equally generous. Hearing the performances of, and in many cases, talking with practising musicians and composers has been the most exciting part of writing this book: my warm thanks to Din Ghani, the Albany Trio, C.N. Lester, Nicolette Moonen and, especially, the composer Nicola LeFanu who has provided a unique insight into her mother's life and work. It goes without saying that whilst I have drawn heavily throughout this book on the work of others, any errors are entirely my own.

My research has taken me to some very special places, from the Villa Medici in Rome to the Schumannhaus in Leipzig. Many visits were made all the more special by knowledgeable guides, amongst them Denis Demoulin, Directeur des Affaires Culturelles at Les Maisonnettes in Gargenville, and the charming woman at the Mendelssohn-Remise in Berlin, whose fluent English saved me much embarrassment. I thank the Gesellschaft der Musikfreunde, Vienna, and the Bibliotheque Nationale, Paris, for the opportunity to consult their collections. Closer to home, Elizabeth Boardman (then archivist at St Hilda's College, Oxford) made the task of looking through the Maconchy archive a pleasure, whilst the librarians at the Music Faculty Library at Oxford answered all my questions with patience, and, what is more, opened up new vistas through their expert advice. Zappi's Bike Café provided another home from home: thanks to Dan and the team for the coffee and bara brith (served at the same time). And, still in Oxford, words cannot express my appreciation of the skill and kindness of Mr Rana Sayeed, Dr Colin Forfar and all the staff of the Heart Centre at the John Radcliffe Hospital, where the first draft of this book was actually completed. Together, they ensured the survival of its dedicatee. My last and best thanks go to my friends and my family, however far flung you may be. Again and again you demonstrate your belief in me and my work and, even more importantly, you make me smile.

The continuing and glorious adventures of my daughters, Becca and Elise Roberts, inspire me to seek out the words to tell the stories of remarkable women. Keep going, my lovelies – the world is all before you! This book is, however, dedicated to Roger Harvey, without whom . . .

INDEX

INDEX

INDEX

INDEX

INDEX

twelve-note technique 310, 318

Urban VIII, Pope 30, 31

Vallière, Louise de la 108

Vaughan Williams, Ralph 290–1, 292–3, 294, 299, 312, 326

Venice 18, 53–5, 57–8, 77, 80–1
and courtesans 68, 75–6
and music 83, 84–5

Venier, Domenico 58

Versailles 93–4, 95, 96–7, 99–100

Viardot, Pauline 244

Victoria, Queen 200

Vidal, Paul 244, 248, 256

Vidman brothers 54

Vidman, Giovanni Paolo 59, 60, 61–2, 64, 79, 80

Vienna 127, 129, 133–4, 146, 155–6, 215
and music 140–5, 148

Villa Medici (Rome) 249, 261, 262, 263–5, 266, 271

Villa Poggio Imperiale (Florence) 11, 12, 31–3, 36

violins 113, 232

Vivaldi, Antonio 83

Wagner, Richard 208, 329, 330

Walton, William 317

Weir, Judith 330

Well-Tempered Clavier (Bach) 159

Widor, Charles 249–50

widowhood 42–3, 44–5

Wieck, Clara, see Schumann, Clara

Wieck, Friedrick 205–7, 208–9, 211–12, 220, 222, 326

Williams, Grace 291–2, 295, 303, 306–7, 313, 316, 319–20

Wladislaw Sigismund Vasa, Crown-Prince of Poland 11, 31, 34–5, 42

women 4–5, 123, 172–3, 318–19, 325–6, 329–30
and composing 8–9
and dress 150
and First World War 277
and instruments 231–3
and merit 19
and music 154–5, 175, 201–3, 299–301, 326–7
and politics 35–7
and Prix de Rome 248–9, 250, 259–60
and sexuality 1–2, 37–9, 66–8
see also concubinage; courtesans; motherhood

Wood, Sir Henry 296, 308

Workers' Music Association 311

Ysaÿe, Eugène 246

Zelter, Carl Friedrich 160–1, 162–3